Mentoring and Induction Programs That Support New Principals

*With admiration, respect, and love for Betty Allen, who modeled how
a keen mind, a big heart, and a feisty style operate synergistically to achieve
results, and for Marlyn Miller, who insisted on equity for all students and their families
as she mentored them through the system with dignity, caring, and a sense of belonging.*

MENTORING AND INDUCTION PROGRAMS THAT SUPPORT NEW PRINCIPALS

SUSAN VILLANI

FOREWORD BY ROLAND S. BARTH

CORWIN PRESS
A SAGE Publications Company
Thousand Oaks, California

For information:

Corwin Press
A Sage Publications Company
2455 Teller Road
Thousand Oaks, California 91320
www.corwinpress.com

Sage Publications Ltd.
1 Oliver's Yard
55 City Road
London, EC1Y 1SP
United Kingdom

Sage Publications India Pvt. Ltd.
B-42, Panchsheel Enclave
Post Box 4109
New Delhi 110 017 India

Printed in the United States of America

Library of Congress Cataloging-in-Publication Data

Villani, Susan.
Mentoring and induction programs that support new principals/Susan Villani.
    p. cm.
Includes bibliographical references and index.
ISBN 0–7619–3145–7 (cloth)—ISBN 0–7619–3146–5 (pbk.)
    1. First year school principals—United States. 2. Mentoring in education—United States. 3. School principals—Training of—United States. I. Title.
LB2831.92.V556 2006
371.2′012—dc22   2005002541

This book is printed on acid-free paper.

05   06   07   08   09   10   9   8   7   6   5   4   3   2   1

Acquisitions Editor:	Elizabeth Brenkus
Editorial Assistant:	Candice L. Ling
Production Editor:	Beth A. Bernstein
Copy Editor:	Barbara Coster
Typesetter:	C&M Digitals (P) Ltd.
Proofreader:	Teresa Herlinger
Indexer:	Rick Hurd
Cover Illustrator:	John T. Ward (Cover Copyright © 2005)
Cover Designer:	Anthony Paular

Contents

Preface

Singing to the choir or preaching to the congregation is an activity that elicits a lot of nods, yet the message is not new to the people who are listening. If you are reading this book, you are aware of the important roles principals play in their school communities. Yet, how well are new principals prepared and supported? Those of us who have been school principals probably carry many strong memories of our first year. How many of us had a mentor we could trust to support, teach, and encourage us during the difficult times? Perhaps it's that yearning that fuels my passion for providing new principals with strong mentoring and induction.

This book is written for people interested in developing a mentoring or induction program as well as for those who want to enhance their existing program. Part I discusses the state of the principalship and what new principals need to be successful. While you might be familiar with some of this information, you may find the ideas, facts, and examples useful as you share your concerns with others who have given less thought to the potential crisis in educational leadership that we are facing. Part II is a compilation of mentoring and induction programs throughout the United States, all presented in the same format for easy comparison. Part III invites you to think about next steps.

This book is organized as follows:

PART I. THE PRINCIPALSHIP: THE ROLE, THE PEOPLE, AND THE SUPPORTS

Chapter 1, "Making the Case for Mentoring," describes and discusses the needs of new principals, the importance of the principalship, and the need for new principals at all levels of public schools. Factors contributing to the growing need for new principals are explored, with examples from throughout the United States. The types of situations and issues new principals face are also considered, making it abundantly clear how important it is for new principals to have mentoring support as they enter school communities.

Chapter 2, "Mentoring and Induction Program Components and Considerations," suggests that mentoring and induction programs are essential to support new principals. The Standards for School Leadership, jointly prepared by the Interstate School Leaders Licensure Consortium (ISLLC) and the Council of Chief State School Officers (CCSSO), are described as achievable and measurable standards for administrators. These standards are the foundation for many of the programs included in Part II. Stage theory is presented to assist you in supporting principals at their differing developmental stages. The key components of mentoring programs are discussed, providing a way for you to think about what kind of induction or mentoring program would be useful in your context. Consideration of the need for an equitable climate in which new principals may learn and grow is emphasized.

Two different induction programs are described: one in which there is a large team of support for the new principals, and the other in which there are leadership training modules to engage principals in solving real school problems.

PART II. MODELS OF MENTORING AND INDUCTION FOR NEW PRINCIPALS

This part is organized by chapters based on the contexts in which organization(s) and/or program providers offer support to new principals. There are resources that list some common features of programs. You may find it useful to look at Resources C1–C6 before you read Part II to help you select models that are of the most interest to you.

Chapter 3, "District and Regional Models," features programs that are offered to new principals in their own school districts or regions.

Chapter 4, "State Models," features programs that are offered to new principals statewide (or regionwide).

Chapter 5, "Professional Association Models," features programs offered by administrator associations, both at the national and state levels.

Chapter 6, "University Models," features programs that are exclusively offered through a university.

Chapter 7, "Collaborative Models," features programs that are collaborations of several institutions.

PART III. NOW WHAT?

Chapter 8, "Planning or Enhancing Your Program," poses clarifying questions about the beliefs and values of those people within the context of your organization. They will help you identify the program components most useful for the new principals you will support. The State Action for Education Leadership Project is described, and a call is made for redefining school leadership.

ACKNOWLEDGMENTS

Heartfelt thanks and deep appreciation to Henry Damon for thought-provoking conversations about administrator induction, for accommodating my writing schedule even when it was at cross-purposes with meals together, recreation, and vacations, and for helpful "just in time" review and discussion of my writing; Jerry Villani and Barbara Stillman for their belief in the timely completion of this book despite occasional evidence to the contrary; Su. Henry for insightful questions and meticulous attention to overall organization as well as nuance; Rose Feinberg and Larry Jacobson for editing suggestions on initial chapters and information on best practices and current research; Kathleen Sciarappa and Linda Hartzer for generously sharing their research; Betsy Warren, for "just in time" conversations about coaching and induction; Gray Manford for immediate responses to requests for information; Katie Latham and Kuong Ly for research assistance; Mary Benkert, Bob Garvin, and Tony Phillips for strategies and therapies to deal with the sometimes painful consequences of hours and hours of working at a computer; my family and dear friends for their support and understanding of my absences to research and write; Lenore Hersey, who mentored me when I was a board member and then president of the North East Coalition of Educational Leaders (NECEL) and she was the executive director; Roberta Sherman, Joanne Benton, and Susi Ware for mentoring as I joined their school communities; Penelopes Kiritsi, Yiannis and Thodores Mantheakis, and Michalis Tsichlakis for insight and affirmation; educators throughout the country who responded promptly and carefully to my requests for information about their programs; Lizzie Brenkus for enthusiastic collaboration and commitment to the quality of this book; Robb Clouse for continued encouragement and interest in my work; Barbara Coster and Corwin peer reviewers, whose suggestions led me to write with greater clarity; Beth Bernstein, for keeping the project on course; and John Ward, whose painting was made for the cover.

Corwin Press gratefully acknowledges the contributions of the following individuals:

Tom Chenoweth
Professor
Graduate School of Education
Portland State University
Portland, OR

Arthur Foresta
Director
Principal Mentoring Program
New Visions for Public Schools
New York, NY

David Lepard
Author and Educational Consultant
Vienna, VA

Donald Poplau
Principal
Mankato East High School
Mankato, MN

Hal Portner
Educational Consultant
Florence, MA

Erin Rivers
Principal
De La Salle Middle School
Kansas City, MO

Bess Scott
Principal
Goodrich Middle School
Lincoln, NE

Foreword

Roland S. Barth

When the superintendent and the school board have appointed the new principal you can almost hear the sigh of relief. The decision has been made and the problem solved.

Well, for them maybe. But not for the beginning principal! One parent–teacher selection committee drew up the following list of characteristics of their sought after new principal. It conveys a sense of the incredible—and impossible—expectations that the beginning school leader must now confront:

Ability to see another's point of view

Trust in teachers' judgments

Supportive

Relaxed and flexible

Knowledgeable about curriculum areas

Experienced in school administration

Decisive

Strength in one's convictions

Self-confident

Ability to distinguish the important from the unimportant

Sense of security

Ability to set goals

Ability to provide guidance for teacher growth

Ability to promote staff communication

Personal warmth

Understanding of human differences

Ability to deal with pressure groups

Offers strong leadership

Add to these the expectations from the central office, the state department of education . . . and No Child Left Behind. And then add the myriad duties the principal will soon be responsible for. Among them:

The safe passage of students from their homes to school

Ensuring that the sidewalks are plowed of snow

The physical condition of the plant

The security of its occupants

Health education

Sex education

Moral education

Teaching children to evacuate school buses

Teaching them to ride their bikes safely

Lunch programs and then breakfast programs

Students' achievement of high standards at each grade level

Children with special needs

Those who are gifted and for those who are neither

Administering tests and ensuring that all children score above average

None of these responsibilities is backbreaking in itself, but taken collectively they present an enormous burden few are capable of assuming let alone sustaining.

Small wonder that many experienced principals are dropping out. And small wonder that the line forming to replace them is getting shorter and shorter. And that so many beginning principals flounder or wash out. I know. I have never felt as vulnerable, so much at risk, so clueless, and as innocent as I did that first year as principal . . . after which I was fired! And things in the principal's office are much tougher now than then.

One would suppose that fellow principals would come to the aid of their new brethren. Alas, there seems to be a taboo in our profession against both disclosing our problems to others and giving assistance to others who have problems. Too often one is, as one school leader put it, "forbidden not to know." And competition with others leads to a situation where "the worse you look the better I look; the better you look, the worse I look."

This leaves the beginning principal to suffer under impossible expectations with little help from within the schoolhouse or without.

Susan Villani also served as principal for many years. It is her belief that novice principals need not rely solely upon the school of hard knocks to educate them. The good news is that in this volume her heart and her head go out to those who are taking on this critical work. This is her gift to her colleagues . . . and her legacy to the profession.

And a valuable and generous gift it is. I see in these pages an astonishing resource for those in universities, school systems, and state departments of education who would assist beginning principals. This is a book about making wise and pervasive use of one of the most powerful means possible for promoting the learning of the novice leader . . . alignment with a mentor who has "successfully been there and done that."

I also see here a "self-help" book. For the names, locations, and detailed descriptions of scores of principal mentoring programs is now available for any practitioner to see and make use of as well.

Mentoring is a very difficult and sophisticated art form to perform well. To be done successfully, many conditions must be in place for mentor and the mentored alike. It's all here.

The purpose of school and of schooling is to promote profound levels of human learning. I believe the real gift that effective mentoring can provide is only in part providing a resource system for the new kid on the block. The more enduring gift mentoring gives the new principal is an immediate opportunity, to reveal him- or herself to the school community as an insatiable learner. The *head learner!* To the extent principals, through their mentoring activities, will make their learning known and visible to students, teachers, and parents they will model and exemplify the most important business of the schoolhouse . . . learning. And they will thereby telegraph the message that "learning is for important people." There is no more powerful and more desperately needed message they can convey.

The first year on the job will always be tough. So will the second and third. But thanks to Susan Villani's words you are about to read I am confident that the next generation of principals will never have to "go it alone."

About the Cover

John Ward is an art teacher in the Saranac Lake Schools. I met him in Malone, New York, when I was presenting and facilitating two days of mentor training and he was one of the mentors. Serendipitously, during a break I mentioned that I was writing this book. John said he'd like to do the cover and suggested his Web site for examples of his work. That's where I found that John is also an internationally acclaimed artist. As an illustrator of high repute, I wondered if he was serious about his offer to make the cover. Indeed he was, and John's offer is a striking example of the mutuality of mentoring. Furthermore, John generously suggested a contract that made it possible.

The cover of the book was actually John's idea. Based on what he learned and knew about mentoring, John found an image for the cover that is both aesthetically attractive and symbolic of mentoring. I believe that just as fruit ripens at different times, new administrators are at many stages of career development. The variation of hues in the blueberries depicts the growth of new principals. With support from mentors and other colleagues, they have the promise of maturing in the role and becoming vibrant.

About the Author

 **Dr. Susan Villani** is an educator who cares deeply about the growth of adults and children. As a teacher, principal, and college professor, she collaborated with students, staff, and families to create safe learning environments that honor all the members and promote their achievement and self-actualization. Her commitment to the inclusion of all students and the richness of the diverse cultural identities of every member of a school community was a major theme in her work when she was a principal and an elementary school teacher, as well as when she taught graduate students.

Mentoring aspiring and new administrators is an aspect of her work that began when she wrote her doctoral dissertation on mentoring and when she was President of the North East Coalition of Educational Leaders (NECEL) in 1981–1983. She worked with educators throughout New England to promote women and other minorities in educational leadership and also directed a resume assessment service. This work and her own experiences as a principal enhanced her dedication to provide strong support for new principals.

She is currently a Senior Program/Research Associate at Learning Innovations at WestEd. She works with school systems, departments of education, and educational organizations to design and implement mentoring programs for new teachers and to support the wisdom and learning of experienced faculty. She seeks to empower administrators to work with teacher leaders and other staff to promote their teaching and leadership capacities.

She is the author of *Are You Sure You're the Principal?* and *Mentoring Programs for New Teachers.*

Dr. Villani takes inspiration from the turtle: You have to stick your neck out to make progress.

PART I

The Principalship:
The Role, The People,
and The Supports

Making the
Case for Mentoring

This chapter discusses the importance of the principalship, the needs of all new principals, and the number of new principals needed at all levels of public schools. Factors contributing to the growing need for new principals are explored, with examples from throughout the United States. The types of situations and issues new principals face are also considered, making it abundantly clear how challenging it is for new principals to enter school communities and be effective leaders.

THE IMPORTANCE OF THE PRINCIPALSHIP

Many educators and parents believe that the principal is the key to an excellent school. According to a recent report, "Virtually all superintendents (99%) believe that behind every great school there's a great principal" (Public Agenda, 2001, p. 21). Many parents believe that the principal determines school quality, thinking "As goes the principal, so goes the school."

There is significant research about the importance of the principalship and the impact school leaders have on student achievement and the wellness of the school community. In her research on highly effective principals, McEwan (2003) comments, "Policymakers have discovered that teachers, tests, and textbooks can't produce results without highly effective principals to facilitate, model, and lead" (p. xxi). Many fine educators have left the classroom, drawn by the challenges and possibilities of being a principal. They know that being a principal is a unique opportunity to impact the lives of students, teachers, parents, and even whole communities.

When new principals are appointed, members of the school community may experience a variety of emotions, including curiosity, relief, apprehension, frustration, and/or excitement. Students may worry about possible changes in discipline policies, for example. Teachers may fear a loss of autonomy with a new principal. Parents may be concerned about their access to the new administrator. Other district principals may be wary of a newcomer who could garner the community's attention, while others are relieved to have the attention off themselves. Central office administrators may be counting on the new principal to implement districtwide initiatives and carry their vision to the community at large. Will this person be someone who is able to meet the multiple challenges of the principalship?

How do newly appointed principals feel? With the initial elation about their appointment, they may be hopeful, eager, and possibly impatient to get started. They may also be nervous and uncertain. As they begin their new positions, how prepared are they for the diversity of demands they will encounter? For example, before the opening of school, they might have to deal with

- Sudden staff resignation(s)
- Building construction that is still not finished the week before the opening of school
- New student enrollment, including some students with significant requirements, as outlined in their individual educational plans (IEPs)
- No pencils and other necessary supplies
- Computer glitches in the schedule

Within the first month of school they might face

- Teachers demanding that a specialist be reprimanded and transferred because of inappropriate teaching methodologies with young children
- The former interim principal filing a reverse sex discrimination suit against the school board, claiming that the only reason the new principal was hired was because she was female
- Teachers acknowledging that the custodian doesn't do routine cleaning and maintenance in their classrooms, but they are afraid to complain because in their experience, if they do, their favorite belongings are likely to disappear from their classrooms

- Parents demanding that their child be transferred to another classroom because the teacher is humiliating the child in class
- The fire department trying to schedule time to do fire safety awareness assemblies for the students, but a number of teachers objecting because they don't think the students' time is well spent
- Several teachers reporting to the principal that a teaching colleague is unstable and shouldn't be in front of students
- Bees' nests in the playground equipment
- Parents complaining to the superintendent after the principal spoke to their child after the child was referred by a bus driver for misbehavior
- Teachers complaining that a cafeteria worker is identifying children who receive free lunch as they get their lunch in the school cafeteria
- A teacher asking for an air-quality test because she suspects her classroom is literally making her sick

Are these situations exaggerated? They are not. I can verify every one of them, based on personal experience. Struggling to find equitable solutions to these issues is a challenge to experienced principals, let alone principals who are new to a school community. Too many principals have dealt with these issues in a vacuum, only to later find that their solutions did not solve the problem and antagonized people will remember their dissatisfaction for years to come. The facility with which new principals become respected and trusted educational leaders is crucial, since the entire school community is impacted by their effectiveness. In fact, there is research suggesting that the extent to which principals are socialized in their position in the first year is often an indicator of their future socialization in the school community (Parkay, Currie, Gaylon & Rhodes, 1992).

The principal is the appointed leader of the school community. How many principals, whether they are new to the role and/or new to the school, experience moments of doubt about their ability to be an instructional leader as well as the manager of operations, staff developer, arbiter of justice, chief financial officer, and role model? How many experienced principals wish that more resources had been available to them when they assumed their first principalship? It is imperative that new principals have appropriate support through comprehensive induction and mentoring programs so that they can enter schools confident in their ability to foster a strong learning community and be sensitive to the culture they are joining.

NEEDED: PRINCIPALS AT ALL LEVELS, IN ALL COMMUNITIES

During the next decade, a substantial number of new principals will need to be hired. A number of factors are contributing to the growing need for principals. While some are demographic, the majority relate to the nature and expectations of the principalship.

There is the potential for a crisis in school leadership. Projected retirements and resignations predict an extremely high rate of turnover for school leaders in the coming years. Consider that

> Sixty-six percent of respondents to a National Association of Elementary School Principals (NAESP) survey in 2002 indicated that they will retire in the next 6–10 years (NAESP, 2004).

- Sixty-six percent of respondents to a National Association of Elementary School Principals (NAESP) survey in 2002 indicated that they will retire in the next 6–10 years (NAESP, 2004).
- The U.S. Department of Labor projects that 40 percent of the country's 93,200 principals are nearing retirement (Malone, 2001).

- The Maryland State Department of Education expected that 45 percent of the state's principalships would be vacant during the 2003–2004 hiring season (Maryland Task Force on the Principalship, 2000).
- In Minnesota, about 75 percent of current principals will retire or leave the profession by 2010 (Institute of Educational Leadership, 2000).

SHORTAGE OF APPLICANTS FOR THE PRINCIPALSHIP

Fewer educators are applying for principalships. How serious is the problem?

Eighty-six percent of the superintendents interviewed in 1998 discussed the difficulty in filling principalship openings in their districts (Institute of Educational Leadership, 2000).

- Eighty-six percent of the superintendents interviewed in 1998 discussed the difficulty in filling principalship openings in their districts (Institute of Educational Leadership, 2000).
- Less than 50 percent of Connecticut educators who are certified as administrators currently work as administrators; the median number of applicants for principalships in Connecticut dropped from 60 to 30 (Committee on the Future of School Leadership in Connecticut, 2000).
- Fifty percent of surveyed superintendents indicated a shortage of qualified principal candidates during the previous year—at all levels (elementary, middle, and high school) and in all types of communities (rural, suburban, and urban) (Educational Research Service [ERS], 2000).

There are many reasons cited by principals and superintendents for the shortage of applicants for the principalship. Some of these reasons follow.

Insufficient Compensation

Principals may actually earn less than veteran teachers who are paid at the top of their career ladder. The executive director of the NAESP said, "They trade their 180–190-day work year for 210–240 days per year; they take on enormous responsibilities and headaches; they lose their job security (most principals do not belong to unions); and they may earn just a little more or even less on a day-to-day basis than they do now. It's a no-brainer" (Ferrandino, Tirozzi, 2000). In addition, the amount of money allocated for these positions reflects the decreased value placed on these roles by society at large compared to many other professions. This often demoralizes current principals and dissuades prospective principals from taking the job.

Job Stress

The number of tasks required daily of a principal is understandably a source of great stress. Principals make a strikingly large number of decisions each day, often with little time for full fact-finding and/or reflection. New principals can find it especially difficult to move to the next task without feeling they are shortchanging time given to the previous one. This is particularly the case when they are doing something for the first time or for the first time in a new context. New principals often need strategies to help them handle many tasks and issues simultaneously.

Elementary principals often have the additional stress of being the sole administrator in the school, in contrast to middle and high school principals who often have several layers of administration, including department heads and assistant principal(s). As a result, everyone feels that they need to speak with the elementary school principal. When principals try to share responsibilities with other school personnel, they may be perceived as avoiding some of their work. New principals often need to learn how to share leadership and build the capacity of teacher leaders and other members of the school community.

Secondary principals are responsible for schools that are typically larger, with many challenges, including facility, budget, and human resource development and evaluation. Principals may feel torn if other building administrators do not share their vision for the school. For example, tenured department chairs are part of an embedded administrative structure that principals inherit when they assume the principalship.

Excessive Demands on Time

The number of hours principals work is increasing dramatically. The position often requires 60–80 hours of work per week, including many evening meetings and events. Worse yet, many principals feel that no matter how many school functions they attend, it is never enough. The Kentucky Association of School Administrators and the Appalachian Education Laboratory (KASA-AEL) found that the top inservice request of new principals was for time management.

In the early years of my first principalship, I took a time management seminar. One suggestion was to block out time for specific tasks in your appointment calendar. When people come and start speaking with you without an appointment, the recommendation was to look at the schedule, look up at the person, and remark, "It says that at 10:00 I am working on the budget. Are you budget?" This would not be well received in most schools. People want their principal to be available when they need help to talk over a concern. Balancing the many role responsibilities with the professional and interpersonal needs of staff and community is challenging. Therefore, principals may need mentors who can help them work toward such a balance.

Principals leaving the profession often say that they want a life outside the principalship. In addition to principals being superb educational leaders, communities want principals who are concerned about their own families and friends, who have interests and hobbies outside of their work, and who take good care of themselves physically. Yet the more that is heaped on the shoulders of principals, the less likely they are able to do all of these things and still feel satisfied that they are meeting their responsibilities as principals. How unfortunate that peoples' expanding expectations of principals may be driving away some of the individuals that schools most need to attract and retain and may be contributing to the shrinking pool of candidates. These expectations include the following:

Conflicting Demands

Principals work to satisfy the needs of all the constituencies in their school community: students, teachers, support staff, parents, central administration, and community affiliations. At times, satisfying everyone is clearly impossible, as needs may be mutually exclusive. For example, some constituents

- Believe that competition between students in the school is the key to motivation, while others believe children should not be stressed by the achievements of others and should be more focused on their own learning
- Believe that teachers' salaries should be commensurate with other professions and should receive primary consideration in the school budget, while others believe the amount dedicated to teacher salaries must accommodate adequate funding for arts, technology, athletics, and other educational concerns

- Advocate for increased taxes to reduce class sizes, while others advocate for focusing on affordable tax limits
- Want community-sponsored programs and services provided during the school day, while others want students to have protected class time for core academics.

Principals often find there isn't a way to honor the wishes, or perhaps demands, of some without alienating others. I once had an angry parent complaining to me about the increase in her water bill. I listened, trying to understand the connection with our school. Finally, I asked why she was telling me this information. "Well, you're a town employee, and the town did this, and I want someone to fix it."

5) Societal Changes

In order for students to be ready to focus on instruction and learning, they need to be

- Present to take advantage of what their school offers
- Safe, both physically and psychologically, inside and outside of school
- Clothed and fed
- Physically and emotionally healthy
- Trusting that their school is a good place to learn
- Able to study after school so that they may prepare for the next day

Unfortunately, these conditions do not occur for all children because of issues at home or in the community. In response to societal factors that interfere with students arriving at school ready to learn, principals and schools often devote significant amounts of time, money, and effort to students' basic needs so that they will be available to learn. Principals operate programs for beforeschool and after-school care, breakfast, health care, adult literacy, and English language learning. I know of a principal who drove daily to a student's home to pick him up in the morning because he was school phobic. Another principal had a washing machine installed near the nurse's office so that students who were homeless could have clean clothes. After doing any number of these activities, plus attending sports and musical events after school and in the evening, it takes an exceptional principal to have the stamina to focus on instructional leadership all day, every day.

6) Accountability Pressures

Accountability has become a major focus of state and federal legislation over the past decade. While it is a very important issue for education, many faculty and administrators are concerned that the legislation and testing requirements are counterproductive. They question the methods prescribed to assess student learning and/or the content that students are required to learn. Debates throughout the country and within districts are time consuming, as is the systemic change that is often necessary to improve student learning. Even when principals are in total agreement with these goals and procedures, these requirements take a significant amount of time and resources that may not be readily available.

Accountability and testing have become major factors that stress principals, particularly since the passage of the No Child Left Behind (NCLB) legislation. Principals in every state are responsible for extensive testing schedules and demands related to tasks ranging from the mundane packing and distribution of tests to the complex issues related to reporting and documentation. In some districts, principals have been reassigned or fired when school scores have not improved, regardless of the population challenges or special needs of students. Many principals with whom I've spoken have cited mandatory state testing as one of the major stresses they face.

Another consequence of NCLB is the negative impact on districts' abilities to recruit effective principals for schools that haven't been meeting average yearly progress (AYP) goals. NCLB may have the unintended consequence of driving away talented leaders. Therefore, new principals need mentors who will help them through the procedural as well as curricular aspects of the testing, as well as the emotional and public relations aspects of communicating testing results.

New principals often face overwhelming, stressful, even bleak situations. While it is difficult to obtain attrition rates of new principals, consider these:

- After five years in the district, one-third of all principals hired had left that district (Denver Board of Education, 2002).
- Administrators with less than one year of experience have attrition rates of 23 percent (Illinois State Board of Education, 2001).

New principals must learn to focus on issues that are within their span of control or influence, learn to recognize conditions beyond their control, and try not to be discouraged. Mentoring and induction programs provide significant support for new principals as they tackle the challenges that await them. Mentoring and induction programs for new teachers have strengthened teacher performance and retention; mentoring and induction programs for principals have enormous potential for the same outcome.

> New principals must learn to focus on issues that are within their span of control or influence, learn to recognize conditions beyond their control, and try not to be discouraged. Mentoring and induction programs provide significant support for new principals as they tackle the challenges that await them.

REWARDS AND CHALLENGES OF THE PRINCIPALSHIP

Rewards

Why do educators become principals? They may want to

- Make a difference
- Impact a larger number of people
- Establish a safe environment
- Support teachers
- Ensure that all students learn and achieve
- Build or strengthen a professional learning community
- Work with many constituencies toward a common goal
- Make the decisions rather than be told them
- Find a better way

There are many examples of principals achieving and even surpassing their visions, turning a school around, uniting a community, and/or empowering a faculty. These principals manage to share with the school community their passion for student achievement and teachers' lifelong learning.

For example, a principal who was concerned about every student's proficiency in state-assessed learning goals worked with teachers at each grade level to set quarterly benchmarks for learning, create weekly tests to assess student achievement, and track student progress. He and the staff then instituted a half hour each day for small group remediation or enrichment (any student not attaining proficiency would receive remedial support, and the rest would receive enrichment). Every faculty member worked with a group of eight students or less, thereby ensuring individualized attention and student progress. This staffing arrangement was possible because everyone agreed to a 10-minute reduction of preparation time. This school leader had inspired the faculty to see the possibilities and collaborate to achieve them.

Another principal was determined to provide her students with an appropriate learning environment. She and parents painted over graffiti as many Saturdays as it took to keep the school free of defacement. Through this symbolic act, she forged alliances within the community that strengthened the school's voice in the district's policymaking and budget support.

Some of the very factors that make the principalship challenging also provide some of the rewards. Principals are leaders of complex organizations. To be an effective principal is to have a wide range of skills and knowledge.

Challenges

New principals may unexpectedly encounter experiences for which they are unprepared, regardless of their teaching experience and administrative leadership preparation. Principals need readily available support if they are to acquire the tools and insights needed to help them cope with the following:

Isolation

Principals are often unprepared for the isolation that comes from being an educational administrator. For some staff, the fact that the principal writes evaluations and is "the boss" creates a distance that may be new for principals accustomed to having close relationships with colleagues. As an evaluator, it is difficult for a principal to be personal friends with staff members; it could be perceived as creating inequitable relationships. In many schools, teachers are "we" and the principal and district administrators are "they."

Principals are often isolated from other administrators in the system. New principals need to spend a lot of time in their buildings, and as a result, they don't have much time to meet with other new administrators who are facing the same issues or experienced principals who work in the district and could share information about the culture and history of the school system.

The more overwhelmed new principals may feel, the less likely they are to take time away from work to take the "balcony view" of their work and context. Not surprisingly, the perspective and experience of mentors can be invaluable at this crucial time in a new principal's career.

Fear of Being Seen as Incompetent

Principals were often master teachers who were well respected and often loved in their school communities. A teacher who is accustomed to feeling confident and highly capable may suddenly feel uncertain, ineffective, or overwhelmed in a new role as principal. As well, principals may sometimes feel misunderstood or misjudged by people who are attributing motivations and intentions to the principals' behavior and decisions. Therefore, new principals need help seeking answers for questions and asking for help from staff or others without feeling or being perceived as incompetent.

Difficulty Setting Priorities

Principals are concerned about the welfare and growth of both children and adults in the school; therefore, a variety of things need attention. For example, principals might need to balance and/or choose between (a) parents' wishes for immediate access to the principal, (b) teachers' wishes for the principal to be in their classrooms for more frequent and lengthy visits, (c) lunch supervisors wanting principals in the cafeteria during lunch periods, and (d) central office administrators wanting principals to do extensive committee work to implement systemwide initiatives. New principals are not in a good position to prioritize tasks because they have no way of knowing what is urgent, what or whom can wait, or what will need someone else's attention. New principals often need help determining what is essential to do and when to exercise selective neglect.

The Constraints of Confidentiality

Administrators must honor confidentiality with many people in the school community. While others may speak, sometimes at great length, about negative interactions with the principal or about perceived or poorly made decisions, the principal is not typically at liberty to share the professional or personal circumstances behind her or his decisions, particularly when related to personnel and student behavior. Principals must maintain confidentiality for both ethical and legal reasons. For example, a few situations I've experienced include the following:

- Angry teachers who couldn't understand why I tolerated a teacher's late arrival to school or occasional departure during the school day (I couldn't reveal that the teacher was fighting cancer and dealing with chemotherapy treatments)
- Teachers who worried that a new colleague was incompetent and falsely believed that I wasn't doing anything about it
- Parents, angry about the behavior of their child's classmate, demanded that I immediately remove the classmate from the classroom (it was not appropriate for me to discuss that classmate's educational and psychological challenges nor the specific support and remediation that the teacher was providing in consultation with doctors and other service providers)

Principals, like anyone else, may be inclined to justify decisions and actions that may be misunderstood. However, they often don't have the option to do so, and the court of public opinion may unfairly judge them without benefit of full disclosure of information. A critical skill for principals is to know when to maintain information as confidential. New principals need mentors who can help them work through difficult situations involving confidentiality.

Technical and Logistical Problems

Running schools smoothly requires attention to a lot of details. Principals need to anticipate and address logistical issues before they become problems. Often what might seem like a management issue has larger implications for the practice of the teachers and staff. Becoming a principal could include having to address the following situations:

- Resetting the hall bells in accordance with daylight savings time changes
- Dealing with an outbreak of head lice and the nurse's recommendation to remove all pillows and stuffed furniture from the entire school
- Understanding how to read and utilize a spreadsheet for budget preparation and tracking
- Developing a master schedule
- Working out a complex testing situation so that it has a minimal impact on instruction

Classroom teachers who become new principals often don't have experience dealing with these problems and don't always know where to turn for support while everyone else is turning to them for solutions. New principals need mentors who can share their own experiences and help principals problem-solve or determine where to go for more information or assistance.

Legal and Moral Responsibilities

The principal is a leader in establishing a safe and accepting learning environment and a stable and moral school culture. Many issues have been added to the responsibilities of schools, including nutrition and health issues, drug education, societal issues such as multiple family structures, AIDS awareness, and computer literacy. For instance, a principal might have to address the following situations:

- Clarifying the rights and responsibilities of high school students cross-dressing and being provocative with football players in the locker room
- Providing a safe environment for a student with life-threatening allergies to peanuts
- Discontinuing the appearance of Santa Claus, who historically had been personified by the head of the school committee
- Balancing issues of free speech with student dress or student publications

Regardless of their personal beliefs, principals have the legal and moral responsibility to uphold the laws of our country and to protect the rights and feelings of students and their families who are in the minority. New principals need mentors who can direct them to find the legal information needed and can provide help in dealing with the delicate interpersonal aspects of difficult situations.

School Culture and History

What is school culture? Schools, like other institutions, have cultures that shape their operations. Although school culture is not written down anywhere, if you've unknowingly violated it, you will soon experience the negative emotions and behaviors your faux pas evokes.

A new principal's arrival is an opportunity for anyone who is dissatisfied with a school policy or practice to try to get it changed. Not knowing the history, a new principal may respond in ways that alienate others while trying to be responsive and demonstrate competence; new principals may inadvertently do something "wrong" or undo something that many people do not want changed. Unfortunately, these "mistakes" may haunt the new principal long after the specific situations are forgotten. As a result, it is imperative that new principals learn about the school and district cultures during the earliest stages of their work. New principals need mentors who will help them anticipate issues related to school or district cultures and help them find ways to resolve missteps the new principal may make. It may also be necessary to balance this walking-on-eggs hells strategy with the need to understand when it is necessary to break a few eggs as an ethical responsibility.

Heightened Visibility

For new principals, heightened visibility can be disconcerting, as everyone seems to be watching their every move. Each constituency in a school—faculty, students, staff, parents—have their own expectations of the "new" arrival. In addition to expectations about role responsibilities, a new principal may experience behavioral expectations that are culturally based. New principals who have a cultural identity that is in the minority in the school community may rightly feel that they are being watched even more closely (Gupton & Slick, 1996). There were times when I wondered, "What am I doing in a fishbowl if I'm a mammal?"

From my own experiences and those of others, principals need to share information with the staff and community. This is also an effective means of rumor control. Mentors can help new principals write introductory letters as part of their entry plan and can help new principals draw the line between public information and their personal lives.

Principals as Middle Managers

Teachers, students, and parents may think of the principal as the leader and ultimate decision maker of the school. Yet many principals feel bedraggled by trying to implement systemwide initiatives and directives and being responsive to faculty and staff-initiated school endeavors. Principals often wonder when they will be able to implement some of the initiatives they feel are important.

Clearly, the challenges are enormous and the stakes are very high. If that is the bad news, the good news is that the problems have not gone entirely unnoticed. Induction and mentoring programs designed to support new principals can be found throughout the United States, in urban, suburban, and rural districts. Some programs are coming from the top down through legislative actions, while others have been developed by one or two people in a district. They are generally new, vary enormously, and as yet, many of them have just begun to collect data about their effect on principal performance and retention, as well as school improvement and student achievement. More research is needed to better inform these important beginnings.

LEGISLATION LEADS THE WAY

As states begin to grapple with the increasing need for principals and the shortage of qualified applicants, new legislation is emerging to ensure careful attention to the induction of new principals. For once new principals are hired, it is imperative that they are supported in order to enhance their performance and increase the likelihood that they will want to remain in their positions.

Certification requirements for mentoring, or state requirements that school districts revise their evaluation and support of new principals, provide an external force for the establishment or revision of mentoring and/or induction in your district or state. There are significant variations in the ways states approach principal induction and mentoring. Some of these, from Hartzer and Galvin (2003), include the following:

- Mentoring training and a training manual (Kentucky)
- Face-to-face and online mentoring (Louisiana)
- Standards for induction programs (Massachusetts)
- Joint training for mentors and new principals at the beginning of the program (Mississippi)
- Performance assessment (New Jersey)
- The state Department of Education is required to give eligible beginning administrators in qualifying districts in need up to $3,000 per year to help with program costs (Oregon)
- One-week summer institute and three or more full-day follow-up sessions for training in essential leadership and management skills (South Carolina)
- A 30-day assessment process that requires principals to demonstrate the standards for the Principal Certificate (Texas)
- Development of a customized professional development program developed jointly by the principal, superintendent, university, and mentor (Tennessee)

An example of legislation addressing the need to support beginning administrators is the following excerpt from the State of Iowa, House File 2299, bill introduced: H.J. 319:

Section 1 *New Section.* 256F.1 LEGISLATIVE FINDINGS

1. The general assembly finds and declares that the purpose of school administration is to provide leadership for school improvement and student achievement. Large numbers of

new principals and superintendents are entering the field of administration just as many experienced administrators retire and expectations for student achievement rise. . . . Research indicates that administrators who have quality mentoring experiences remain in administration longer. Administrator mentoring is also likely to reduce the isolation felt by many new administrators in rural Iowa. Therefore, it is the intent of the general assembly to establish a school administrator mentoring and induction pilot program administrated by the department of education. . . .

2. The department shall adopt rules establishing a grant application process and award criteria. The criteria for a quality school administrator mentoring and induction pilot program shall include, but shall not be limited to, all of the following:

- An effective screening process for mentor applicants
- Coaching tied to the Iowa standards for school leaders developed by the school administrators of Iowa, with increasing school achievement as the cornerstone of the program
- Support networks for new administrators, augmented by use of technology to facilitate networking opportunities
- Systemic support offered through regional coordination by area education agencies with skill-building professional development opportunities
- Time for self-reflection and development of professional growth plans based upon research-validated administrator assessment instruments
- Multiple opportunities for formative assessment, leading to a culminating portfolio for summative evaluation
- Opportunities to observe experienced and successful administrators in the administrator's environs
- Practical assistance in the day-to-day managerial tasks for operating a school

More and more states are identifying the need to support new principals. These initiatives are intended to both enhance new principals' ability to promote high student achievement in their schools and increase the retention of new principals. Legislation is mandating ways to induct new administrators, emphasizing the roles of professional development, observation and networking with successful administrators, and mentoring. National and state reform efforts have also focused public attention on school performance.

As educational leaders, principals are under careful scrutiny by their many constituencies. Considering the potential rewards as well as the challenges principals face, it's clear that there need to be thoughtful and planned initiatives to induct new principals and retain them in the profession. Chapter 2 discusses the components of effective mentoring and induction programs and a variety of ways to support new principals.

Mentoring and Induction Program Components and Considerations

This chapter elaborates on how mentoring and induction programs support new principals. The Standards for School Leadership, jointly prepared by the Interstate School Leaders Licensure Consortium (ISLLC) and the Council of Chief State School Officers (CCSSO), are described as achievable and measurable standards for administrators. These standards help define the professional development that new principals need and are the foundation for many of the programs included in Part II of this book.

The key components of mentoring and induction programs are discussed, providing a way for you to think about what kind of induction or mentoring program would be useful in your context. Emphasis is given to the need for an equitable climate in which new principals may learn and grow.

Two different induction programs are described: one in which there is a large team of support for the new principals, and the other in which there are leadership training modules to engage principals in solving real school problems.

WHAT NEW PRINCIPALS GET AND WHAT THEY NEED

Barth, founder of the Principals' Center at Harvard, stated that a new principal often gets "a title, an office, responsibility, accountability, and obligations. Nothing more. . . . [School officials often say] 'You were hired for the school because, among hundreds of qualified applicants, we felt you could do the job. Now do it'" (Barth, 1980). While there are no longer hundreds of qualified applicants for most positions, Barth's observation about the expectation for new principals' performance still reflects a predominate attitude.

Principals, as well as teachers, learn a great deal in their first few years on the job, particularly when well supported through effective mentoring and induction. When asked "Which was the most valuable in preparing you for your current position?" fifty two percent of principals surveyed responded that it was the mentoring and guidance they received from colleagues; fourty four percent said it was previous on-the-job-experience (Public Agenda, 2001). Particularly for those with no previous administrative experience, mentoring is essential in preparing for new positions.

> When asked "Which was the most valuable in preparing you for your current position?" fifty two percent of principals surveyed responded that it was the mentoring and guidance they received from colleagues.

What new principals learn must be based upon best practice and current research. If not, new principals will form approaches and habits that will be difficult to unlearn or rethink. In addition, if principals make serious mistakes in their first year, they may suffer the fallout for many years to come. Therefore, programs designed for mentors should include best practice and current research. Sparks (2000), executive director of the National Staff Development Council, calls for state and district professional development efforts that are "standards-focused, sustained, intellectually rigorous, and embedded in the principal's work day."

PROFESSIONAL STANDARDS FOR SUCCESS—ISLLC STANDARDS

Principals need standards that articulate the professional knowledge, skills, dispositions, and performance they need to know and be able to do to be effective. States have tried to respond to this through certification or licensure, which is often the way that professions decide and then require the competencies necessary to successfully perform each role. Once these are articulated, the training and performance requirements of novices can be designed accordingly.

By 1988, nearly every state had principal certification requirements that included having a master's degree in educational administration or its equivalent (McCown, Arnold, Miles, & Hargadine,

2000, p. 15). However, this did not seem sufficient, as many questioned whether certification could guarantee high-quality administrators. In the 1990s, 24 states and the District of Columbia formed the ISLLC. The ISLLC worked with the CCSSO and developed a set of national standards for school leaders. Their goal was to strengthen the professional development of school leaders (Educational Testing Service, 1998). It was no longer considered sufficient to have principals working to emulate the practices and traits they admired in other principals and avoiding those they did not consider productive.

When McCarthy (2002, in Balch, Frampton, & Didelot, 2002) reviewed Indiana legislation and regulations, she identified the following themes regarding school leaders' effectiveness:

- School principals have far more responsibilities specified in laws and regulations than they did 15 years ago, and even policies that do not mention school leaders often impose school duties for which administrators are ultimately accountable. These duties are continually expanding without any reduction in responsibilities.

- Districts and building school leaders are being held more accountable for school improvement, with academic standards and assessment of student achievement driving the accountability system.

- There is a shift in emphasis from inputs to outcomes in standards-based licensure for educators and in accreditation of schools and leadership preparation programs.

- There is a shift in orientation pertaining to professional development in that these activities are viewed as an integral part of the school's ongoing efforts to satisfy academic standards and meet school improvement objectives.

The ISLLC standards are the joint efforts of the ISLLC and the CCSSO to indicate the expectations of successful school principals. These standards are achievable and measurable.

ISLLC Standards for School Leadership

Each of the standards reflects key aspects of the principalship and areas where mentoring can be crucial to a new administrator's success. Therefore, these standards should be considered when developing mentoring programs.

A school administrator is an educational leader who promotes the success of all students.

Standard 1: Facilitating the development, articulation, implementation, and stewardship of a vision of learning that is shared and supported by the school community

Standard 2: Advocating, nurturing, and sustaining a school culture and instructional program conducive to student learning and staff professional growth

Standard 3: Ensuring management of the organization, operations, and resources for a safe, efficient, and effective learning environment

Standard 4: Collaborating with families and community members, responding to the diverse community interests and needs, and mobilizing community resources

Standard 5: Acting with integrity and fairness and in an ethical manner

Standard 6: Understanding, responding to, and influencing the larger political, social, economic, legal, and cultural context

(For more information about ISLLC, see the Web site of the Council of Chief State School Officers, www.ccsso.org/projects/Interstate_School_ Leaders_Licensure_Consortium. Also see Resource E for an Educational Leader Self-Inventory [ELSI].)

A PROFESSIONAL SOCIALIZATION HIERARCHY FOR PRINCIPALS (STAGE THEORY)

The induction of new principals is best achieved when it addresses the needs of principals in their different developmental stages. "Professional socialization" is Van Maanen and Schein's (1979) term to describe the processes of becoming a member of a profession and developing an identity with that profession. Consider the following professional socialization hierarchy for principals articulated by Parkay et al. (1992, p. 56):

> The induction of new principals is best achieved when it addresses the needs of principals in their different developmental stages.

Stage 1: Survival

Individual experiences the "shock" of beginning leadership and has concern with "sorting it out." Personal concerns and professional insecurity are high. Tendency to overreact may be great.

Stage 2: Control

Primary concern is with setting priorities and "getting on top of" the situation. Behaviors are "legitimated" by positional power (power of the position of principal) rather than personal power.

Stage 3: Stability

Frustrations become routinized, and management-related tasks are handled effectively and efficiently. Difficulties related to facilitating change are accepted. Individual has achieved "veteran" status.

Stage 4: Educational Leadership

Primary focus is on curriculum and instruction. Confirmation comes from external sources (faculty, district personnel, professional, etc.). Behaviors are "legitimated" by personal power.

Stage 5: Professional Actualization

Confirmation comes from within. Focus is on attaining personal vision (i.e., creating a culture characterized by empowerment, growth, and authenticity).

IMPLICATIONS OF STAGE THEORY ON INDUCTION AND MENTORING

Certainly, the primary goal of a support program would be to help new principals move through Stages 1 and 2 as quickly as possible. Without mentoring or other induction support, principals may struggle with personal concerns and strive to lead by asserting their authority. The sooner they can move to a stage of stability, the more effective they will become. When new principals are in a survival or control stage, for example, mentoring will be somewhat different from when the new principals are in a stability stage. As the new principals become more competent and respected, the role of the mentors will be to help them stretch and expand their scope beyond the day-to-day management of their schools.

With these stages in mind, what are the implications for training and support? This question is addressed to mentors, coaches, supervising administrators, university faculty, and people working to support new principals through professional organizations, state departments of education, and the private sector. How can educators provide the necessary programs in support of new principals?

INDUCTION AND MENTORING

Induction is a multiyear process for individuals at the beginning of their careers or new to a role or setting and is designed to enhance professional effectiveness and foster continued growth during a time of intense learning. Some believe that the induction process should continue throughout a principal's career (Crow & Matthews, 1998). Many educators believe that mentoring is the key component of induction, especially for inexperienced principals. There are induction programs without mentoring, and some offer extensive skill building and support. The challenge in these programs is for new principals to have someone with whom they can share their concerns and to feel confident that this person has their best interests in mind and will keep their conversations confidential. There are also mentoring programs that are not part of a larger induction program. Their challenge is to address the growth needs of principals as they develop in their role.

Induction is a multidimensional process that orients new principals to a school and school system while strengthening their knowledge, skills, and dispositions to be an educational leader. The following are a variety of induction techniques:

> Induction is a multidimensional process that orients new principals to a school and school system while strengthening their knowledge, skills, and dispositions to be an educational leader.

- Graduate courses
- Assigned mentor
- Unofficial mentor
- Guidance by superintendents/assistant superintendent
- Network of experienced principals
- Network of beginning principals
- Support from the state principals' association
- Attendance at workshops/conferences
- Principal shadowing
- Visitations to other schools
- Readings
- Meetings with district administrators
- Administrator internships
- Previous experience as an assistant principal
- Orientation provided by the district
  (Sciarappa, 2004)

Mentoring is support from a more experienced colleague to help a beginner or someone new to a position or school system perform at a high level. Mentoring can powerfully enhance the learning of new principals. In order for this to happen, mentors need to be experienced and effective colleagues who are trained and continually coached to promote new principals' heightened job performance and self-reflection.

"Effective mentoring and coaching of school and district leaders depend on solid training and time set aside for the collegial work" (Abeille, Hurley, & Nesbitt, 2001, p. 39). Without such training, mentors may be little more than buddies. Buddies offer help as they think of it, may listen and help problem-solve, and may introduce and support the new principal in the community. However, buddies don't make a commitment to systemically support and challenge new principals to reflect on their practice. Buddies may be well-intentioned colleagues but have little idea how to coach a new principal. So while it's always good to have a buddy, that is insufficient support for someone beginning, or even continuing in, a principalship. A formal mentoring program is far more likely to meet the needs of new principals and the system in which they work.

Some mentor program coordinators, as well as some administrators who are prospective mentors, do not initially see the need for the training of mentors or coaches. They believe that administrators should already have the knowledge of education and the skills needed to be effective mentors. However, good administrators do not necessarily make good coaches. Training before mentoring begins and ongoing support of mentors often yield significant results: the mentors will be more effective in supporting new principals that will be professionally gratifying. In addition, the mentors will likely experience professional growth and satisfaction as a result of the acquisition of new skills and reflecting on their own practice. Therefore, it is crucial that mentoring programs incorporate strong training components for mentors or coaches.

Formal mentoring supports should continue for a minimum of one year, preferably longer, while induction and professional development supports should extend over several years. The fusion of an ongoing induction program with effective mentoring will help principals to more quickly align their practices with district goals and initiatives. It can also help provide the opportunity and an invitation to make contributions to district efforts earlier in a principal's career.

The following program design is based on a review of many induction and mentoring programs and current information about mentoring as well as my experience as a mentoring consultant and former principal. The components included are those others and I believe are essential for an effective program.

PROGRAM DESIGN: COMPONENTS FOR CONSIDERATION

Orientation and Entry

Orientation to the school system is an important first step in an effective induction program. This may be in the form of meetings with district or building-level administrators, entry events in the school with the students, or receptions with parents and the community. A bus tour of the district given by someone who knows the community may be invaluable as principals strive to become familiar with their students and families.

New principals need to recognize the importance that secretaries and custodians may have in their school community. These positions touch the lives of everyone in the school, and those in them often have an extensive knowledge of the people in the school and the institutional history. New principals may need help thinking about how to cultivate strong relationships with the secretary and custodian.

New principals should develop entry plans, and their mentors may be very helpful in designing this plan. The entry plan for a principal can be a major aspect of a new principal's success. An entry plan includes all aspects of "entering" the new position, from getting to know people in the school, district, and community to establishing procedures they will follow. Mentors can be major contributors to well-designed entry plans for new principals. Mentors can help new principals think about how to implement aspects of orientation, including scheduling meetings with people, writing letters to the staff and parent community, and prioritizing the use of time during the first few months. (For more information on entry planning, see Jentz & Wolford, 1981.)

A "journey process" is also useful for helping new principals learn the history of their school. This is done with the staff and is particularly helpful if facilitated by a mentor or someone other than the principal. During this process, the staff who have been at the school the longest begin telling the highlights, lowlights, and special events in the school's history. Little by little, the story unfolds, charted on paper that unfolds in the same fashion as the history. People may disagree on events as well as whether things were beneficial or detrimental to the school community. This will provide the new principal with the opportunity to listen and learn from the balcony. All too soon, the principal will be in the thick of the action.

A formal welcome by other administrators, including time allotted for them to share experiences and support, is another critical layer in the induction process and a first invitation for informal mentoring.

Incentives for Mentors

Mentors are often surprised by how much they learn while they are mentoring a new colleague. Actually, mentor training may be one of the most effective approaches to the professional development of veteran principals. The process of promoting reflection evokes self-reflection. Mentors think about their own practice as school leaders as they help a new principal think about leadership beliefs, core values, and ways to be effective with the multiple constituencies in their school communities. The hectic nature of school administration often makes it difficult for practitioners to find much-needed time for reflection. When mentors commit to the mentoring relationship, they are helping to prioritize time for the colleague to learn, and both the new principal and the mentor reap the rewards. Invariably, it is a journey of mutual self-discovery and sharing.

During this process, administrators gain satisfaction from contributing to the induction and support of new principals. Mentor training expands their capacity as coaches and as reflective practitioners in ways that reach far beyond a single mentoring relationship. Mentors may be recognized by their peers or given different career opportunities. Mentors typically report that they feel rejuvenated and excited about their work. These are then benefits to the district as well as the individuals.

Mentors should be compensated, whether they are full-time or retired principals. Mentoring requires skills and a disposition to serve the new principal's learning needs. It is also time consuming, especially when done well. Schools and school systems need to better understand the many advantages of mentorship and show their commitment by appropriately rewarding mentors. If coaches of school sports activities are compensated, surely coaches for school principals should be as well.

Money is not the only remuneration that may be used. Mentors' time and expertise may be recognized with additional vacation days, extra funding for attendance at a national conference, or other rewards suggested by the mentor.

Mentor Selection and Matching

Mentors should be experienced administrators who are interested in supporting the professional growth of beginning principals. Preferably the mentor is someone who doesn't have any evaluation responsibility related to the person being mentored, thus allowing the novice to be more candid about job uncertainties and insecurities, which leads the mentor to provide more relevant and individualized coaching.

Mentoring programs that are within districts often utilize principals in the district to mentor new principals. There are advantages and disadvantages to selecting district-based administrators. Mentor administrators from the district will be able to help the new principal with cultural issues and the nuts and bolts of working productively with district staff and the parents and broader community. Geographic proximity may also make it easier for new principals to work with them as needed. On the other hand, new principals may not feel comfortable sharing their doubts and needs for assistance with their new colleagues. They may feel the need to show building and district administrators that they were the right choice for the position. They may not know if there is a culture of sharing and learning together, and they might be wary of admitting to their own fears and perceived weaknesses. In most large urban districts, there is probably a large enough pool of administrators to offer more anonymity to mentorships.

Regional or statewide mentoring programs have the opportunity to draw mentors from a larger pool of school systems, thus taking into account the specific skills and experiences the mentors may offer to new principals. Retired principals are often asked to serve as mentors, either within their former district or beyond, because they are knowledgeable and also may have more time to devote to mentoring.

A combination of the district-based and regionally based mentoring is optimal. New principals will benefit from an administrator who knows the system for the much-needed information about "how we do things around here." Mentors from outside the district can be sounding boards and can give suggestions for issues the novice principal does not want to share with an in-district mentor.

Mentor Selection Criteria

A good mentor is

- Positively disposed to serve colleagues' growth
- Culturally competent and proficient
- Secure enough to value the different and evolving leadership styles of new principals
- Committed to promoting a new principal's reflection
- Generous and willing to share resources and ideas
- A lifelong learner
- An effective communicator

Thoughtful mentor selection and matching with new principals is crucial. Good administrators do not necessarily make good mentors. Mentors need to want to be mentors and need to be interested in the training they will participate in to enhance their coaching skills to promote reflection as well as to learn useful ways to share their craft wisdom and experience (see Resource H, "Craft Wisdom"). In addition, mentors need to be able to give feedback and advice, when requested, without being judgmental or critical. Mentors contribute to the development of new principals by doing cognitive and technical coaching. As new principals become more acclimated to the school and school system, they are increasingly able to take advantage of their mentor's coaching through deeper and broader levels of skill development and conceptualization. Optimally, mentors are able to build sufficient trust that they may pose questions that challenge new principals' thinking without them feeling judged.

Mentor Training

Mentors need to be effective cognitive coaches as well as technical coaches. *Technical coaching* is probably what administrators are more accustomed to doing. In this role, they share their wisdom with someone who is interested in their experience and ways of doing things. New principals want technical coaches when they need information or need new skills. Sometimes new principals need technical coaching because they don't yet know the depth of what they don't know. When expressly asked for advice, practices, or procedures that they have found useful, mentors should feel free to respond by sharing what they know and can do.

Cognitive coaching, on the other hand, is not about mentors telling new principals what to do and how to do it. Cognitive coaching involves promoting another's self-reflection by asking questions and sometimes by also collecting data the person wants collected. For example, a new principal may want coaching on how to work with the parents' association. Through cognitive coaching, the mentor might ask a series of questions about what the principal hopes to achieve with the group, how the new principal plans to participate in the next meeting, and if there are things the principal might do in advance of the meeting. If the new principal requests it, the mentor might come to the next parents' association meeting to observe the principal. If the new principal has asked the mentor to pay particular attention to a certain aspect of the principal's participation in the meeting, the mentor will collect that information and do so in a way that the principal has said it will be most useful.

After the meeting, or at another time soon thereafter, the mentor and new principal would have a reflecting conference. The mentor's role would be to ask questions and sometimes combine the data collected with questions. The idea is for the mentor to help the principal think about her or his performance; the mentor is not going to judge the principal. Judging, even if it is positive, doesn't promote learning. If the mentor says the principal did well, that will probably end the discussion and any chance for reflection. Whereas if the mentor asked what went well, why did the new principal think so, is there anything she or he might do differently in the future and why, the principal has a lot to think about.

Asking good questions and promoting another's thinking is actually a lot harder than sharing lessons learned and war stories. Cognitive coaching promotes self-reflection, and ultimately new principals will be able to ask themselves the same questions. Mentors who do cognitive coaching are trying to promote independence with collaboration and collegiality. (For more information about cognitive coaching, see Costa & Garmston, 2002.)

Mentors' Responsibilities

Mentors and new principals should meet regularly at scheduled times as well as communicate on the phone and/or through e-mail, as needed. Regular meetings are opportunities for the mentor to share specific content useful to the new principal as well as listen and help problem-solve current issues. In addition, the mentor should call frequently to check in. It's often these impromptu phone calls that elicit a concern about a current problem or situation where mentors can be most helpful.

If the mentor works in the same school system as the new principal, the mentor should share information about district and school culture and history. If the mentor does not work in the same school system, the mentor should encourage the new principal to seek out this information from another administrator in her or his school system.

Mentors should promote new principals' reflection through cognitive coaching. Cognitive coaching is not advice-giving or "constructive feedback"; it is a process that helps people consider their own practice. Mentors should also be technical coaches to new principals when there is information or skills that the new principals don't know and want to learn from their mentor. Information from the mentor is received very differently if new principals have requested it. Regardless of the context, mentors and new principals should establish clear goals and ways of being in relationship early in the process.

Mentors should also help new principals develop individual professional development plans and support their efforts to achieve their stated goals. In addition to promoting reflection, mentors can provide valuable information. Mentors may promote beginning principals' thinking through a school improvement activity, thereby linking the needs of the school with the new principals' growth plans. Furthermore, mentors may help new principals document their growth through portfolios. The following are mentoring responsibilities (also see Resource F, "Expectations of Key Players"):

- Welcome and orient the new principal to the district
- Reduce the new principal's sense of isolation
- Socialize the new principal to the community and share school and district culture
- Help the new principal manage the highs and lows of the job
- Give technical information, teach skills, and/or help the new principal identify other resources for specific skill instruction
- Promote the new principal's self-reflection through cognitive coaching
- Problem-solve, commiserate, or just plain listen as needed and requested by the new principal
- Be an advocate for the new principal
- Share resources and ways to comply with state and federal mandates
- Help the new principal gain perspective and understand which issues are out of her or his control and what's worth fighting for

New Principals' Responsibilities

New principals and mentors should meet regularly at scheduled times as well as communicate on the phone and/or through e-mail as needed. Weekly meetings are preferable. New principals should understand that "nothing is obvious to the uninformed," and it is better to ask for information and assistance than to create unnecessary difficulties for themselves and others.

New principals work with their mentors in a cognitive coaching process that will facilitate them becoming more reflective about their practice. New principals should also use their mentors as technical coaches, asking for sources of content information and modeling of skills. They should also ask to observe their mentors or other administrators to develop a greater awareness of leadership behavior. Mentors may also be requested to shadow the beginning principals.

New principals should formulate professional development plans in collaboration with their mentors. The professional development plan should focus on what the principal needs to know and be able to do to be successful in her or his first year in the position. The plans should include steps and resources to meet their goals. New principals may also use journal or portfolio entries to document school improvement, as well as their own growth, as they identify continued challenges and next goals.

Other Principals' (Who Are Not Mentors) Responsibilities

Paul Young, NAESP president in 2003, urged, "Every effective, practicing principal should identify, encourage, and nurture at least five aspiring principals before retiring or leaving the principalship" (Young & Sheets, 2003). There are many ways that principals who are not mentors may share the responsibility for supporting new principals, and they must assume this responsibility as part of their professional commitment.

District Responsibilities

Clearly, districts must plan for strong orientation and induction programs and budget for mentor remuneration and training. Throughout the first years, districts should plan professional development sessions for districtwide initiatives as well as for issues that will make special demands on a new principal's skill development and/or leadership. Job-alike meetings with other principals in the district provide important supports for discussing curriculum and instruction initiatives as well as various operational issues. Furthermore, a support group of new administrators is useful when a number of new principals are being inducted into the district simultaneously. If possible, this group should be chaired by someone who doesn't have evaluative responsibilities for anyone in the group. Knowing they are not alone will greatly reduce the isolation that new principals report as their primary challenge.

(See Resource I, "Caveats for Mentor Program Leaders.")

A Fair Climate for Growth

Race and gender issues, as well as other ways in which people are different, can complicate the successful induction and mentoring of new principals. According to one study, "Ninety-six percent of the nation's public-school superintendents, over 80% of school-board presidents, and 60% of all principals are White males, whereas more than 73% of all teachers (and future leaders) are women" (Blackman & Fenwick, 2000). These data suggest a need for training supervisors and mentors regarding cultural awareness, bias, and fair treatment of new female principals and principals of color.

When principals are assigned to schools, principals of color are often treated differently than their White peers. The match between principals and the schools for which they are hired should be based on many things, including principals' educational background, credentials and prior experience, content knowledge, and their particular talents and interests. Yet, race and ethnicity can often largely determine new principal placement. Crow and Matthews (1998) found that "[n]ew African American principals were placed in schools with high Chapter I (Title I) populations, high student poverty, high staff absences, low student attendance, low teacher salaries, and few certified teachers.

These features affect the organizational climate, socialization sources, and expectations of new principals" (Crow and Matthews, 1998, p. 102). New principals in these situations especially need a mentor to help them navigate through particularly challenging assignments.

Principals who are in the racial or ethnic minority in their school or district are also frequently asked to represent their race or ethnicity when participating in discussions with colleagues. Colleagues may ask them, for example, what the Black parents will want regarding a particular issue or how to motivate the Hispanic students. These questions are very complicated, and it would be impossible for one person, because of racial background, to give a definitive answer. Similarly, if White principals are in the minority in their school district, it would be inappropriate to expect their focus to be only on White students and their families. New principals need mentors who can help them address erroneous assumptions in a diplomatic and effective way.

All principals, especially new ones, need effective supervision and evaluation and focused and frequent feedback for growth from their supervisors. Principals in a minority in their school context may face particular challenges concerning supervision and support. Before mentoring became popular in education, business and industry recognized the importance of mentoring. Pat Carmichael, senior vice president overseeing Chase (bank) branches in Queens and Long Island, New York, has mentored many employees during her 30-year career in banking. She advises minority employees to ask their bosses for tougher assignments and feedback. "What do I need to grow?" Carmichael says that bosses are often afraid to give constructive criticism to minority employees because they don't want to appear biased (Mehta, 2001). In education, we need to also build a culture of high expectations, coupled with honest and constructive feedback for all new administrators.

Gender issues can also pose challenges for new principals. Women have historically reported receiving feedback about their behavior in terms that are different from ones applied to men demonstrating the same behavior. Recognizable examples of this include the following:

"She's aggressive; he's assertive."

"She's indecisive; he takes time to consider the options."

"Everything has to be her way; he knows what he wants and goes after it."

All new principals will be compared with their predecessors. It is important that judgments about personal style are not based on gender stereotypes.

Only in the last 30 years have mentoring programs for administrators been discussed and studied. Previously, mentoring took place when novices found their own mentor. Women and people of color often did not have a mentor because the majority of school administrators were White males and the mentoring relationships formed were often "like producing like" (Samier, 2000). Special attention must be paid to appropriate mentor assignments, selection, and matching to ensure effective supports for all new principals. Given the challenges of mentoring relationships, particularly related to race and gender, the selection and training of mentors are key to a successful mentoring program.

To provide a fair climate for growth, cultural proficiency is a goal that every organization must achieve. According to Lindsey, Roberts, and CampbellJones (2005), cultural proficiency is "knowing how to learn and teach about different groups in ways that acknowledge and honor all people and the groups they represent" (p. 74). Their five principles of cultural proficiency are the following:

1. Culture is a predominant force in people's lives

2. The dominant culture serves people in varying degrees

3. People have both personal identities and group identities

4. Diversity within cultures is vast and significant

5. Each individual and each group has unique cultural values and needs

Educators should be vigilant about the range of cultural responses in their organizations, both institutionally and by individuals. (For more information on cultural proficiency and school leadership, see Lindsey et al., 2005.)

> Administrators must ensure that mentoring and induction programs are offered in a fair and equitable climate for everyone, majority and minority.

The negative impact on anyone in a school community or organization of responses that are anything less than culturally competent is a source of disempowerment and interferes with learning and growth. It is incumbent on all school leaders to be aware of these issues as they affect new principals as well as for new principals to be as aware of how these issues affect other members of the school community.

Administrators must provide the necessary training and establish a fair and equitable climate for everyone, majority and minority, to grow if mentoring and induction efforts for all new principals are to be successful.

PROGRAM EVALUATION

The program leader plays a critical role in overseeing and ensuring the evaluation of the mentoring program. Sometimes an outside evaluator is hired and perhaps asked to use a variety of methods to assess the program. Often the person in the system who is responsible for overseeing the program conducts the program evaluation. If there isn't one person responsible for the program, the planning group may conduct the evaluation.

Program assessment should begin with new principals assessing their needs and then providing ongoing feedback throughout the year(s). Multiple opportunities for new principals to give feedback about the usefulness of the program will enable program planners and supporters to make necessary adjustments or additions as the program progresses. In addition, mentors, principals, and other school personnel should have opportunities to give feedback because their insights are also crucial to improving and building support for the program. Feedback may be given in writing on survey instruments and session evaluations, in focus groups, and/or in interviews. A practical and easy-to-use guide for conducting local evaluation is *Collaborative Evaluation Led by Local Educators: A Practical, Print- and Web-Based Guide*, by A. Brackett with N. Hurley (2004), which can be retrieved at www.neirtec.org/evaluation.

The authors describe the stages of the Collaborative Evaluation Process, and there are how-to resources for each of the following stages so that a design team becomes capable of creating and implementing an evaluation they develop:

- Gathering Together and Planning
- Preparing to Collect Data
- Collecting Our Data
- Making Sense of Our Findings
- Making Improvements

What follows are two ways to think about induction. They may be useful constructs for considering ways to provide ongoing professional development in differing contexts.

TWO DIFFERENT WAYS TO THINK ABOUT INDUCTION

These are different approaches to the mentoring and induction of new principals. The following models suggest two ways you might think about mentoring/induction for new principals, one in which there is a large team of support for the new principal and the other in which there are leadership training modules to engage principals in solving real school problems.

A Three-Point Standards-Based Model: Elaine Wilmore

The following are excerpts from E. L. Wilmore's (2004, Chap. 2) *Principal Induction: A Standards-Based Model for Administrator Development*. This model ties the Educational Leadership Constituent Council (ELCC) standards, which are very similar to the ISLLC standards, with an administrative induction process. Wilmore describes The Induction Partnership Model as a three-point plan for new administrators, as well as others, to get support for achieving goals that they set.

Point 1: A Supportive Team

Mentoring should occur in a familiar and supportive manner; the sole purpose is to help someone else succeed on his or her own terms. The climate of the team must be conducive to providing a strongly supportive environment. The team is comprised of

- A *mentor* who is an experienced administrator, within or outside the same school or district as the mentee, and to whom he or she has regular access and who agrees to serve on the team
- A *district representative*, probably from the upper administrative level, who will incorporate the district's global perspective
- A *university or certifying agency representative*, who will help connect the theoretical concepts gained in the learning and certifying process to the reality of school leadership
- A *business school community representative*, who will bring grassroots views to ensure the teams stay grounded in community needs, concerns, and school improvement from a citizen's perspective
- *Family/friends* (p. 13)

The combination of people should be able to create a culture, climate, and vision for the group that centers on the mentee's growth and development for the purpose of improved student learning and organizational productivity. The mentee can select additional criteria to address specific things that he or she thinks will be helpful to the team process (p. 15).

Point 2: A Strategic Plan

A team facilitator or chair is selected for organization purposes and to keep the team focused. Each team discusses effective structures and processes, including the following:

- The team discusses the ELCC standards, which are very similar to the ISLLC standards, which provide the framework for the Induction Partnership Model.
- The mentee talks informally about joys, concerns, and frustrations with regard to his or her preparation for the principalship; the mentee also discusses what is taking place at school as well as current and anticipated challenges.
- The team holds an initial discussion, connecting the issues the mentee described to the appropriate standards.
- The team brainstorms ways the team can facilitate growth for the mentee and potential goals of the process.
- The team discusses the merits or potential drawbacks of various tools for [new] administrator development.
- The team designs a 360-degree feedback tool that directly targets potential mentee strengths and weaknesses.

- The team determines preliminary resources that will be needed.
- The team determines benchmarks for mentee success.
- The team develops cross-checks as a backbone of the model that hold each team member accountable for his or her input and responsibilities.
- The team creates an accountability system of ongoing, cyclical assessment, modification, and refinement to plans and projects for the purpose of continuous renewal and growth for all stakeholders.
- The team develops a preliminary time line of meetings that will meet each team member's schedule. This will vary from team to team, and there is no required number of meetings. This is an issue of quality versus quantity.
- The exact date, time, and location of the next meeting should be determined before the initial meeting is over (pp. 15–16).

Point 3: Team Implementation

Utilizing the perspectives of each stakeholder, a series of meetings are undertaken over an extended period of time. The process must be long term to ensure change, growth, and reflection for each stakeholder. Throughout the process, each stakeholder will support all other stakeholders, respect the diverse perspective of each member, and keep the focus on helping the mentee develop knowledge, skills, dispositions, and wisdom for the singular purpose of increasing PreK–12 student success. Every meeting should include time for assessment, critical thinking, accountability, and reflection on what is being done and how it can be improved.

The Southern Regional Education Board (SREB) Leadership Training Modules

The following excerpts from "SREB's Leadership Training Modules Engage Leaders in Solving Real School Problems" (2004) were retrieved from the SREB Web site at www.sreb.org.

Why Develop a New Leadership Curriculum?

Most states have adopted new standards for preparation and certification of principals. However, the traditional sources of training for school principals still are simply out of sync with the challenges faced by today's leaders. Everyone now agrees that instructional leadership should be at the center of the principal's role, yet most universities continue to require only one three-hour course in curriculum and instruction, and the offerings of many leadership academies continue to be daily specials— one-day workshops on new state or federal mandates, management, leadership style, building safety, etc. Thus aspiring principals are unable to lead change in school and classroom practices that improve achievement.

The framework for the Leadership Training Modules is the set of 13 critical success factors used by principals who are able to lead instructional improvement and raise student achievement. The modules make explicit the knowledge and skills principals must learn and apply as they put the critical success factors into practice. Each module provides specific activities that engage school leadership teams in solving real school problems.

Ideally, the SREB Leadership Training Modules will be integrated into new systemic state initiatives to improve school leadership. These systemic initiatives should arise from designated state agencies that have authority and responsibility for education leadership preparation, professional development, and licensure and evaluation. To be systemic, state initiatives would include, among other things, a support component for universities, academies, and districts as they take on the challenge of leadership program redesign. This support component would include training modules that align with state-adopted standards for leadership and provide clear direction for the redesign.

How the SREB Modules Are Structured

SREB's Leadership Training Modules are organized around key learning objectives. They follow the principles of adult learning theory and the standards for professional learning established by the National Staff Development Council. Each module includes activities that engage participants in

- Completing prework designed to create an anticipatory set
- Reading and discussing current research and literature on the topic
- Sharing prior knowledge and experiences
- Learning from case studies
- Reflecting on current beliefs and practices in their own schools
- Practicing strategies, tools, and processes
- Working in real-school-based teams to solve problems that impede student achievement
- Reinforcing new knowledge and skills by completing take-home assignments between workshop sessions
- Building portfolios to extend learning and track progress after the workshop

These instructional strategies are embedded in a module structure that begins with intensive content instruction, followed by school-based application, several more content-application cycles, and, finally, extended learning and follow-up at the school site. The on-site work is supported and coached by local staff who have participated in the training with the school teams.

Intensive sessions are one or two days in length, followed by a period of at least six to eight weeks during which participants apply new learning and try out new strategies in the school setting before returning for the next session.

During the intensive sessions, participants learn the rationale for the leadership practices addressed in the module, review supporting research, identify key elements specific to the topic, make initial applications of the key concepts in case studies and vignettes, apply key concepts to their own schools by completing self-evaluations and reflecting on current beliefs and practices in their own buildings, and make plans for how they will lead their own faculty and staff.

SREB Leadership Modules

- Using Data to Lead Change
- Prioritizing, Mapping, and Monitoring the Curriculum
- Leading Assessment and Instruction
- Meeting the Standards: Looking at Teacher Assignments and Student Work
- Creating a High-Performance Learning Culture
- Providing Focused and Sustained Professional Development
- Creating a Personalized Learning Environment
- Organizing the Learning Environment
- Building and Leading Effective Teams
- Communicating Effectively for Student Achievement
- Understanding Self and Others: Individual and Organizational Value Systems

- Advanced Data, System Thinking, and Problem Solving in Schools
- Giving Leadership to Literacy
- Giving Leadership to Numeracy

ORGANIZATION OF PART II

Since the purpose of this book is to offer a variety of programs for readers to consider, and readers are in organizations that have different resources, a broad spectrum of programs are included. You will need to determine what criteria are important to you as you decide which programs to consider.

Part II presents models of mentoring and induction that have been designed and implemented in different contexts and by different providers throughout the United States. They were selected as examples of programs that were created and developed by organizations with different resources and expertise to respond to the needs of newly appointed administrators in their district, region, state, or professional group.

Mentoring and induction programs require human and financial resources, so organizations need to see the value of such programs before they will support such endeavors. Many of the programs in this book are relatively new. Some have been developed by one or two people and implemented with very little money. As a result, some of the programs included have not had the benefit of summative program evaluation. Other programs are long-standing, have sufficient human and financial resources, and have more data about their efficacy. Judgments are not made by the author about the merits of one program versus another. Rather, they are included because they present different conceptions and designs of induction or mentoring that might help you expand your thinking about possibilities for your organization.

Models were also selected for their usefulness to readers in a variety of settings. It is more difficult for small and/or rural school districts to offer induction or mentoring programs, because they often don't have enough administrators to justify the expenditures. The program in Englewood, Colorado, is an example of an in-house mentoring program that is done in a small district with unique demographic factors. Regional models may be more applicable for districts that are too small to offer their own programs. Districts that are near colleges or universities may want to cultivate or enhance relationships with administrator preparation programs to support new principals. Two university programs are presented in Chapter 6, and there are also universities involved in some of the other models. Collaborations between different providers are presented to show how they share the responsibility for supporting new principals. The Arkansas Leadership Academy—Master Principal Program has brought together 44 partners in service of the needs of new principals.

The programs are grouped into different chapters based on the context of the group offering the mentoring or induction and the potential participants. Every program is described through a template, which is Resource B, and a summarizing chart, which is Resource A. Resources C1–C6 summarize specific aspects of the programs: state mandates and funding, mentoring ratio, duration of program, program cost, mentor remuneration, and unique features. You may find it helpful to scan the resources to determine which programs are of greatest interest.

The template was designed to gather and present the greatest amount of relevant information about each program in a consistent format. There may be some questions that don't apply to specific models by virtue of their design. You may readily compare models, because they share the same descriptive format. The ultimate goal is that you will consider the programs and then adopt, adapt, or create your own program based on your own specific needs and resources.

PART II

Models of Mentoring and Induction for New Principals

District and Regional Models

MODEL 3.1

Extra Support for Principals (ESP)
Principals Mentor Program
Albuquerque Public Schools
Albuquerque, NM

Carl J. Weingartner, Coordinator
Albuquerque Public Schools
10209 Santa Paula, NE, Albuquerque, NM 87111-3652
505-299-2918   Cwein87@aol.com

Urban/suburban/ rural school	All	Grade levels of school	Pre-K–12
Student population	83,000	Per pupil expenditure	$5,713
Mentoring is/is not mandated for ongoing certification/licensure	Mentoring is not mandated	Mentoring program is/is not funded by the state	Not funded
Unique feature of program	New principals have a strong voice in the selection of their mentors	Duration of program for new principals	One year
Mentors are Full-time principals from same district from another district Retired principals	Full-time principals from the same district; occasionally retired principals	Mentor selection criteria exist/do not exist Mentor matching process exists/does not exist	Mentor selection criteria do not exist Mentor matching process does exist
Mentors are trained/not trained for role Mentors receive/do not receive ongoing support	Mentors are oriented by the coordinator Mentors receive ongoing support	Mentors are/are not part of a team to support new principals	Mentors are part of a team
Coaching is/is not a component	Coaching is not a component	Daily/weekly/yearly expectations for mentors	Contact every other week
Mentors evaluate/do not evaluate the new principals	Mentors do not evaluate the new principals	Portfolio is required/ is not required	Portfolio is not required
Mentor remuneration	$1,000	Higher education affiliation	None
Cost of program	$30,000	Funding	District and business partnership
Years program in existence	10 years	Full-time/part-time program coordinator/program coordination is part of another role in system/organization/state	Part-time coordinator

Used with permission of Carl J. Weingartner, Coordinator, ESP.

STATE MANDATES

Is mentoring mandated for new principals?

No, mentoring is not mandated for new principals.

Is mentoring part of certification or licensure?

No, mentoring is not part of certification or licensure.

Is funding provided by the state to support the mandate?

No, the state doesn't fund mentoring for new principals.

HISTORY

Why was the program started?

It has been recognized for several years by the Albuquerque principals and upper administration that the principalship is becoming more stressful and demanding. District expectations, federal guidelines, a complex budgeting process, a lawsuit society, at-risk students, dysfunctional families, increased school violence, weapons on campus, and No Child Left Behind expectations make the principalship a challenging experience under the best of conditions. For the novice principal, this experience can be a difficult transition from the classroom or an assistant principalship.

The Albuquerque Public Schools (APS) and the Albuquerque Public Schools Principals Association (APSPA) are attempting to provide a support system of experienced peers and professional development for new principals. Through a great deal of time and effort on the part of a dedicated committee of administrators, a principals' mentor program was developed. Research and justification of need were used to convince the district of the importance of such a support system.

GOALS

What are the goals of the program?

The goals of Extra Support for Principals (ESP) are to

- Help principals into a positive leadership role
- Provide advocacy and consultation in support of effective school leadership
- Utilize the expertise and experience of practiced principals in a supportive relationship with new principals

PROGRAM DESIGN

Who designed the mentor program?

In 1995, a committee of principals at all levels, headed by Peter Espinosa, was successful in getting support from the district, both philosophically and financially. The organizing committee became the ESP Advisory Board. The advisory board selected the name of the program. The program became known as Extra Support for Principals. Roles and responsibilities were established, and the program was implemented.

When the money was allocated by the district, the advisory board requested that Carl Weingartner develop the program. (Carl, who is the coordinator of ESP, had mentored Peter informally when he came to the APS.) The program began its 10th year in 2004 and has supported 134 new principals over its first 9 years.

What are the components and recommended schedule of the program?

The components of the program are as follows:

- The principals' mentor program is a collaboration of the APSPA and the APS.
- New principals are assigned to the program based on the timing of their appointment.
- The ESP coordinator makes initial contact by phone to the new principal and meets for an hour to explain the program, answer questions, and discuss
  - Administrative style
  - Type of support expected or provided
  - Orientation training
  - Inservice training programs or possibilities
- In October, the ESP coordinator brings the mentors and mentees together for an orientation.

Are there any programs that complement the mentor program?

The superintendent has set up monthly content briefings with the new principals. These meetings pertain to topics of importance to the district. The ESP coordinator does the ones in December and March and provides lunch. The mentors come to these two, joining the new principals. These two meetings give mentors and new principals an opportunity to interact and meet with other new principals and mentors.

PROGRAM ADMINISTRATION

Who coordinates the program?

The executive director for human resources oversees ESP. The director of staff is the budget control agent of the principals' mentor program. The ESP Advisory Board makes recommendations to the executive director for human resources and the control agent for the ESP coordinator. The ESP coordinator keeps the ESP Advisory Board informed as to the happenings and progress of the principals' mentor program and works closely with the program control agent.

How is information communicated to shareholders?

Information is communicated through memos or monthly newsletters.

Who coordinates the integration of this program with other professional development opportunities or requirements in the school or district?

The ESP coordinator organizes the integration of this program with other professional development opportunities or requirements in the district.

PARTICIPATION IN THE PROGRAM

Who is served?

New principals are identified as those who have been assigned to the position of principal for the first time. ESP is offered to first-year principals, principals changing levels for the first time, and experienced principals hired from out of district.

Is the participation of new principals voluntary or mandatory?

Participation in the program is voluntary.

How long is the program?

The program lasts one year.

WHO PROVIDES THE MENTORING AND INDUCTION?

What are the criteria for being a mentor?

Mentors should be qualified, experienced principals from the level of the appointment, preferably with five years of experience. It is sometimes difficult to recruit mentors, even though APS is the 26th biggest district in the nation. There is a shortage of potential mentors because many of the administrators in the district have fewer than five years of experience. Many principals have moved from principalships to upper-level administration or have left the district.

Are mentors full-time principals or retired principals?

Active-level principals are given first consideration for a mentorship. However, retired principals are considered if they are recent retirees from the principalship. The ESP Advisory Board must approve exceptions to the selection process.

Are mentors from the same district as new principals?

Mentors are from the APS district.

How are mentors selected?

New principals are able to make recommendations for the selection of their mentors. The ESP coordinator reviews their requests, honoring the vast majority of them. The ESP Advisory Board and the superintendents are informed of the mentor–mentee assignments. The coordinator contacts and meets with the selected mentors to explain the program and responsibilities, create an awareness of the time commitment, discuss inservice training programs, and inform them of the compensation for their time and expertise.

How are matches made between mentors and new principals?

New principals make recommendations for the person they want to be their mentors. Mentors should be selected from the same level as the mentees (elementary–elementary, middle school–middle school, high school–high school).

If an ascending principal requests the departing principal, the ESP coordinator may recommend another choice so that the school community doesn't perceive that the former principal is still in a leadership role in the school. If new principals don't have a recommendation for their own mentors, the ESP coordinator gives them choices of mentors who would be appropriate for them at their level.

WHAT IS EXPECTED OF MENTORS?

What are the job responsibilities of mentors?

The job responsibilities of the ESP mentors are to

- Establish initial contact with their mentees to let them know they are there to provide support whenever they feel they need help
- Establish a routine for communicating on a regular basis. Communication is very important even though opportunities will vary depending on need and level of support. Mentors should contact their mentees, by phone, e-mail, or established meetings, at least every other week to see how they are doing
- Foster an environment that encourages intellectual freedom, creativity, experimentation, and risk taking
- Offer advice, support, share experiences and frustrations, and give mentees opportunities to vent their feelings

- Be available to see and/or talk about mentees' professional growth, daily work, or personal issues and conflicts in both formal and informal settings
- Attend scheduled meetings and inservice programs provided through the mentor program, if possible
- Communicate with the ESP coordinator as needed
- Participate in the end-of-the-year evaluations

Is the relationship between the mentor and the new principal confidential?

Yes, the relationship between the mentor and the new principal is confidential.

Are observation and coaching requirements of mentors?

Observation and coaching are not requirements of mentors because the advisory committee and coordinator believe that coaching is not designed to provide the level of trust, confidence, and freedom that mentoring does. They clarify that the mentor's objective is to provide a climate of trust that would permit the mentee to feel safe enough to risk new behaviors. They offer that although coaching is an excellent process used to provide growth and enrichment, it does not always provide the safe, confidential environment of a mentoring program because coaching may induce in mentees a feeling of pressure to achieve or exceed the coach's expectations. They acknowledge that in many cases a principal could use a mentor and a coach to develop into a master principal.

Do mentors formally evaluate new principals?

No, mentors do not evaluate new principals.

How much time are mentors expected to work with new principals (weekly, monthly, and for how long)?

Mentors are expected to contact their mentees at least every other week.

When do mentors meet with the new principals?

The meetings between the mentors and mentees are arranged at mutually convenient times.

WHAT SUPPORTS ARE AVAILABLE FOR MENTORS?

Are mentors remunerated?

Mentors are paid $1,000 for the year of the program.

Are mentors trained? If so, by whom?

The ESP coordinator meets with the mentors when they join the program to go over the handbook and encourage them to set up meeting times with their mentees. The coordinator trains one-on-one on an as-needed basis.

Is there professional development for mentors after the initial training? If so, who provides it?

The ESP coordinator offers a content briefing and luncheon inservice in December and March.

Do mentors meet regularly with other mentors? If so, how often and for how long?

Mentors may meet informally when they are in the same geographic area. Sometimes several pairs meet on a regular basis.

Is there any other ongoing support for mentors? If so, who provides it?

The ESP coordinator supports mentors throughout the year.

Are there any other resources available for mentors?

There are no other resources for mentors through the ESP program.

Are mentors supervised? If so, by whom and how frequently?

Mentors are not formally supervised. The ESP coordinator calls mentors periodically to see if they are meeting with their mentees on a regular basis.

WHAT IS EXPECTED OF NEW PRINCIPALS REGARDING THEIR PARTICIPATION IN THE MENTORING PROGRAM?

How often do new principals meet with their mentors and for how long?

New principals communicate with their mentors at least every other week in person or by phone or e-mail.

Are there other people with whom the new principal meets for mentoring and support?

New principals might meet with the ESP coordinator. New principals are also part of a cluster within the district, and there is a cluster leader who is their evaluator. New principals may go to the cluster leader for support regarding district issues.

Is formative assessment of new principals required? If so, when, how, and by whom?

No, formative assessment of principals by mentors is not required.

Are new principals required to prepare a portfolio?

No, new principals are not required to prepare a portfolio.

ARE ADDITIONAL SUPPORTS AVAILABLE FOR NEW PRINCIPALS?

Is any other professional development provided? If so, when and by whom?

There are also monthly content briefings with the superintendent.

Do new principals meet regularly with other new principals?

New principals meet at the monthly content briefings.

What resources are required for the mentoring program?

The ESP program costs $30,000. If there are more new principals, the human resource department may supplement that to cover the cost of additional mentor stipends. The costs of the program are as follows:

- Coordinator's salary: $12,000 (the committee sought a retired principal to be the coordinator)
- Mentors: $1,000 each
- Supplies, materials, and postage
- Room rentals for social gatherings
- Handbook
- Office service department in-kind service
- Luncheons, socials (the ESP coordinator has solicited funds from business partners to underwrite the cost of food)
- Congratulation rose, mug, and handbook for new principals
- Business partnership funded
- Appreciation rose to mentors, mug, and handbook

FUNDING

What are the funding sources?

The district allocates $30,000 and the ESP coordinator supplements with business partner funds. The ESP coordinator also approaches businesses that have an association with the school, including a photography company, the Educators Federal Credit Union, and a mutual fund that deals with educator annuities. Anytime the ESP coordinator does a publication, he gives recognition to the business partners.

Who requests the funding?

The ESP coordinator requests the funding from the businesses. The district allocation is under the human resources department.

EVALUATION OF THE PROGRAM

Is the program evaluated formatively? Summatively? Who does the evaluation?

The Research, Development, and Accountability department within the APS does the evaluation. They send a survey to the mentors and another one to the new principals. They tabulate the results and include any comments.

Who sees the results?

The superintendent and all the upper-level administrators see the results of the evaluation. The results are posted in the handbook, so everyone can see the evaluation of the previous year's program.

RECRUITMENT, HIRING, AND RETENTION OF NEW STAFF

How many new principals are recruited and hired each year?

On average, 15 new principals are hired. The lowest number was 9, the highest was 24. Though the program is voluntary, everyone who is hired has participated.

Are there any data that correlate the mentoring program with the retention of new principals?

Unofficially, the retention rate is approximately 80 percent. One hundred and forty principals have participated in ESP in its first 10 years. In those years, 10 or fewer principals have left the district. The turnover is typically when principals go to other districts or move to higher levels of administration within the district. Many administrators stay in the principalship for a few years and then move to upper administration.

Are there any data that correlate the mentoring program with the performance of the new principals?

No, there aren't any data that correlate the mentoring program with the performance of the new principals. Based on feedback from the new principals, some upper-level administrators have commented on the importance of the ESP program. The superintendent would like to tie the goals and objectives of the school district to the ESP program.

What are the indicators of program success?

The indicators of success are

- The small number of principals leaving the district
- The evaluations
- Individual feedback to administrators
- Anecdotal information such as the following:

My mentor has been and still is my rock during many interesting and challenging storms I have faced. . . . As a first-year principal, the support shown and shared was not only appreciated, but in my opinion it is crucial. It was reassuring to know that I was not the only one out there feeling like a minnow in a big pond.

—*Audie Brown Jr., Principal, Mountain View Elementary, APS*

I believe the ESP mentorship was a great help for me. It brought a sense of relief to know I had someone I could turn to and ask the "stupid" questions. There is no way to explain the difference between moving from assistant principal to principal. The pressure changes and suddenly you are expected to know everything. I just appreciated having a resource to turn to.

—*Scott Elder, Principal, McKinley Middle School, APS*

One of the powerful things about the ESP model of mentoring is the relationship that develops between the two individuals. I still work and collaborate with a principal that I mentored three years ago. Now she is teaching this old dog new tricks.

—*Nancy Lacher, Principal, Seven Bar Elementary School, APS*

I am still convinced that the best form of professional development is to learn from one's peers. Having a mentor can be a very valuable asset to a new person trying to learn the ropes.

—*Michael Bachicha, Principal, Sandia High School, APS*

The ESP program is unique in that it not only blends a much needed understanding of the ins and outs of the district's procedures and policies a new principal must understand, but it goes further and has the insight and compassion to provide a lift to the human spirit and soul of the new principal as he or she goes about the almost impossible task of leading a modern-day school.

—*George Jackson, Principal, Petroglyph Elementary School, APS*

Piaget tells us that it is impossible to go back to the point in your life when you didn't know something. For first-year principals, there is so much that you don't know, no matter what your training program may have been, that sometimes it is hard to know what you DO know. Mentoring of first-year principals helps remind you what you DO know and what you NEED to know and how to do both. What a gift!

—*Letha Oman, Principal, McCollum Elementary School, APS*

MODEL 3.2

New Administrator Induction Program
Bridgeport, CT

Linda Hartzer, Program Administrator
Bridgeport Public Schools Administrative Offices
948 Main Street, Bridgeport, CT 06604
203-847-8943   lhartzer@bridgeportedu.net

Urban/suburban/rural school	Urban	**Grade levels of school**	Pre-K–12
Student population	23,000	**Per pupil expenditure**	$8,617
Mentoring is/is not mandated for ongoing certification/ licensure	Mentoring is not mandated	**Mentoring program is/is not funded by the state**	Mentoring is not funded
Unique feature of program	New administrators participate in a regional network of collegial support; includes all positions in administration; includes expanded definition of "new"	**Duration of program for new principals**	Two years
Mentors are **Full-time principals** **from same district** **from another district** **Retired principals**	A program facilitator mentors new principals: Mentors of other administrative positions are typically full-time administrators in the same district; occasionally retired principals are utilized	**Mentor selection criteria exist/do not exist** **Mentor matching process exists/does not exist**	District selects its own mentors Mentor matching process does exist
Mentors are trained/ not trained for role **Mentors receive/do not receive ongoing support**	Mentors are trained Mentors receive ongoing support	**Mentors are/are not part of a team to support new principals**	Mentors are part of a team to support new principals
Coaching is/is not a component	Coaching is encouraged, not required	**Daily/weekly/yearly expectations for mentors**	Mentors meet monthly with new administrators
Mentors evaluate/do not evaluate the new principals	Mentors do not evaluate	**Portfolio is required/is not required**	Portfolio is not required
Mentor remuneration	District mentors are not remunerated; outside mentors are remunerated	**Higher education affiliation**	None
Cost of program	Cost of part-time facilitator/principal mentor plus $4,000 budget for books, materials, resources, conferences, and meetings (budget depends on the number of new administrators)	**Funding**	Grant and district
Years program in existence	Seven years	**Full-time/part-time program coordinator/program coordination is part of another role in system/ organization/state**	Part-time director

STATE MANDATES

Is mentoring mandated for new principals?

No, mentoring is recommended but not mandated for principals.

Is mentoring part of certification or licensure?

No, mentoring is not part of certification or licensure for principals.

Is funding provided by the state to support the mandate?

No, the state doesn't provide funding for mentoring.

HISTORY

Why was the program started?

The program was started in 1997 to provide support to new administrators in the Bridgeport Public Schools. In the beginning, it was only for new principals. In 2001, Linda Hartzer expanded and extended the program to provide support for assistant principals as a separate cohort and later to provide differentiated support to new principals in Year 1 and Year 2. In 2003, in a less formal way, the program included curriculum leaders and special education administrators.

GOALS

What are the goals of the program?

The goals of the program are to

- Provide a network of new administrators within the Bridgeport Public Schools
- Provide professional development for new administrators
- Provide mentoring and coaching
- Support the Bridgeport Administrator Evaluation Plan
- Train and retain urban educators

(The State Department of Education has required all districts to revise their district administrators' evaluation plans to provide induction support separate from evaluation of more experienced administrators. It doesn't require official mentoring, although the state guidelines for administrator evaluation recommend mentoring.) In Bridgeport, the majority of administrative appointments come from within the system.

PROGRAM DESIGN

Who designed the mentor program?

Bill Glass and Fran Rabinowitz were the former executive directors of teaching and learning in Bridgeport and designed the original program. Linda Hartzer, the program administrator, came in 2001 and revised and expanded the program, which included mentoring and the components described below.

What are the components and recommended schedule of the program?

The components of the program are as follows:

- New administrators complete a needs assessment survey. They rank order their priority of topics, which determines the sequence and sessions that will be offered.
- There are separate programs for principals in Years 1 and 2, as well as a program for new assistant principals or curriculum leaders in Years 1 and 2.
- The program format varies depending on who is hired each year. In the first year, principals typically met monthly, as a whole group, during the year. In years when there were fewer new principals, such as in 2003, when there were two first-year principals, the program administrator met individually with the first-year principals each month during the school year.
- Second-year principals meet quarterly as a group or individually, depending on the size of the group.
- First- and second-year principals participate in on-site coaching. The program administrator meets with them at their schools, discusses issues, and walks their buildings visiting classrooms with them. She may observe a staff meeting, and coaches them regarding anything the new principals request. (The program administrator does the mentoring of all new principals and assigns mentors to assistant principals and curriculum leaders in like positions within the district. She also runs the Administrative Intern Program for selected teachers who have, or will have, their administrator certification by the end of the year and aspire to administrator positions within the Bridgeport Public Schools. A component of the intern program requires that the interns are assigned to schools and mentored by the principal of that school, thus tapping on the pool of veteran principals.)
- District or outside presenters also address topics at the sessions offered to the new principals. For example, the finance director addresses budgeting issues and the human resources director addresses personnel issues.
- Resource books and articles are purchased for the new administrators.
- New administrators also participate in the Cooperative Educational Services (CES) Regional Service Center New Administrator Induction Program. Professional development offerings are designed to be complementary to both programs.
- New administrators and their mentors participate in a mentor–mentee professional development workshop day offered by the Connecticut Association of Schools (CAS) Principals Center.

Are there any programs that complement the mentor program?

The Bridgeport administrators are part of CES, a Regional Education Service Center that provides professional development. The CES New Administrator Induction Program offerings are designed to complement the Bridgeport induction and mentor program for new principals.

PROGRAM ADMINISTRATION

Who coordinates the program?

Linda Hartzer is the program administrator.

How is information communicated to shareholders?

The program administrator communicates with shareholders in a variety of ways:

- She works with the associate superintendent and the executive director of teaching and learning in the Bridgeport Schools, who will periodically attend the sessions to observe or address the new principals.
- She meets with the superintendent to give program updates.

- She sends e-mail and has phone calls with participants.
- She has face-to-face meetings.

Who coordinates the integration of this program with other professional development opportunities or requirements in the school or district?

The program administrator works with the associate superintendent and the executive director of teaching and learning. The program administrator is also a member of the Teaching and Learning Cabinet, which includes the associate superintendent, the executive director, curriculum leaders, and assistant superintendent. They meet every three weeks.

PARTICIPATION IN THE PROGRAM

Who is served?

The program serves new principals, assistant principals, curriculum leaders, and the special education administrators.

Is the participation of new principals voluntary or mandatory?

Participation in the program is mandatory.

How long is the program?

The program lasts for two years.

WHO PROVIDES THE MENTORING AND INDUCTION?

What are the criteria for being a mentor?

The program administrator provides the mentoring and induction for new principals. Current administrators in like positions mentor new assistant principals and curriculum leaders. The criteria to be a mentor for the assistant principals, curriculum leaders, and special education administrators are listed below. Each mentor has to

- Be an experienced administrator from within the district who is in a like position
- Have good interpersonal skills and competent job performance

Are mentors full-time principals or retired principals?

The program administrator, a part-time consultant, is the mentor to new principals. Mentors of assistant principals and curriculum leaders are full-time employees in the district.

Are mentors from the same district as new principals?

Mentors are from the same district.

How are mentors selected?

Mentors of assistant principals and curriculum leaders are invited to participate based on interpersonal skills, experience, and job performance.

How are matches made between mentors and new principals?

The program administrator mentors all new principals. Mentors of assistant principals and curriculum leaders are matched based on being in like positions as well as possessing the skills needed by the new administrators.

WHAT IS EXPECTED OF MENTORS?

What are the job responsibilities of mentors?

Mentors have monthly face-to-face meetings with the new administrators. They also communicate by telephone and e-mail between their meetings.

Is the relationship between the mentor and the new principal confidential?

Yes, the relationship between the mentor and the new principal is confidential.

Are observation and coaching requirements of mentors?

Coaching and observation are done on request.

Do mentors formally evaluate new principals?

No, mentors do not formally evaluate new administrators.

How much time are mentors expected to work with new principals (weekly, monthly, and for how long)?

The amount of time mentors spend with new principals varies, depending on the number of new administrators. One year, there were seven new principals in Year 1 in the program and eight principals in Year 2. There were also 17 new assistant principals in Years 1 and 2. That year the program administrator was able to visit each new principal one to two times during the school year, because she was 0.5 FTE that year. In 2003–2004, with only two new principals, the program administrator visited them at least monthly, more frequently if there was a need.

When do mentors meet with the new principals?

Mentors and new principals meet at mutually agreed-upon times—sometimes during the day and other times after the school day.

WHAT SUPPORTS ARE AVAILABLE FOR MENTORS?

Are mentors remunerated?

The program administrator was paid as a part-time administrator to develop and facilitate the New Administrator Induction Program for principals, assistant principals, and curriculum leaders and the Administrative Intern Program. Mentoring is a part of all three programs.

Mentors of assistant principals, curriculum leaders, and interns are not remunerated financially. They are recognized and receive a gift.

Are mentors trained? If so, by whom?

Beginning in 2003, Bridgeport mentors are part of the CES regional training program for administrator mentors. There were two half-day training sessions: one in early fall and one in January. The program administrator and the CES person who is the Beginning Educator Support and Training Program (BEST) facilitator for the region developed the administrator mentor training.

Is there professional development for mentors after the initial training? If so, who provides it?

There is no additional professional development specifically for mentors after the two half-day trainings. However, one of the professional development sessions offered by CAS is intended for both mentors and new administrators to attend together.

Do mentors meet regularly with other mentors? If so, how often and for how long?

Yes, mentors meet with other mentors twice during the school year for 90 minutes at each meeting.

Is there any other ongoing support for mentors? If so, who provides it?

The program administrator supports mentors at the district level. The associate superintendent and the executive director may also respond to requests for support.

Are any other resources available for mentors?

CES offers professional development sessions that mentors may choose to participate in.

Are mentors supervised? If so, by whom and how frequently?

Yes, the program administrator does ongoing supervision of mentors. The associate superintendent and the executive director supervise the program administrator throughout the school year.

WHAT IS EXPECTED OF NEW PRINCIPALS REGARDING THEIR PARTICIPATION IN THE MENTORING PROGRAM?

How often do new principals meet with their mentors and for how long?

New principals meet with their mentors for at least two hours each month.

Are there other people with whom the new principal meets for mentoring and support?

Other people who are present at monthly meetings, from within or outside the district, also support mentees.

Is formative assessment of new principals required? If so, when, how, and by whom?

Formative and summative assessment of new principals is done by their evaluators and is not part of the mentoring program.

Are new principals required to prepare a portfolio?

No, new principals are not required to prepare a portfolio.

ARE ADDITIONAL SUPPORTS AVAILABLE FOR NEW PRINCIPALS?

Is any other professional development provided? If so, when and by whom?

CES and CAS offer additional professional development to principals throughout the state.

Do new principals meet regularly with other new principals?

New principals meet at the sessions offered by Linda Hartzer, the program administrator, in Bridgeport and at CES sessions.

What resources are required for the mentoring program?

The mentoring program requires resources for a part-time facilitator or principal mentor plus $4,000 for books, materials, resources, conferences, and meetings.

FUNDING

What are the funding sources?

The program is funded through the district budget and grant money.

Who requests the funding?

The associate superintendent and the executive director request the funding.

EVALUATION OF THE PROGRAM

Is the program evaluated formatively? Summatively? Who does the evaluation?

The executive director and the superintendent do formative evaluations throughout the school year. The end-of-year evaluation is summative. It includes anonymous feedback from the new administrators and mentors on written surveys.

Who sees the results?

The program administrator, the associate superintendent, and the executive director see the results of the evaluation.

RECRUITMENT, HIRING, AND RETENTION OF NEW STAFF

How many new principals are recruited and hired each year?

New principals were hired in the Bridgeport Public Schools as follows:

- 2001–2002: 8 new principals (17 assistant principals in Years 1 and 2)
- 2002–2003: 7 new principals (10 assistant principals in Years 1 and 2, 1 curriculum leader)
- 2003–2004: 3 new principals (7 assistant principals in Years 1 and 2, 1 curriculum leader)
- 2004–2005: 4 new principals (4 assistant principals, 1 curriculum leader)
- 2005–2006: Many anticipated retirements

Are there any data that correlate the mentoring program with the retention of new principals?

No principals have left their positions in Bridgeport after participating in the program.

Are there any data that correlate the mentoring program with the performance of the new principals?

Anecdotally, as reported by district central office administrators, connections are made between the mentoring program and the performance of the new principals. To date, the overall performance of new administrators has been assessed as successful by the assistant superintendents, who are the evaluators of new principals.

What are the indicators of program success?

Anecdotally, new administrator satisfaction and feedback from the assistant superintendents, the executive director of teaching and learning, and the associate superintendent are the indicators of success. Some of the comments that were received are as follows:

I valued the opportunity to discuss/share experiences with my administrator peers.

Thank you. Great support! Very informative and applicable.

Mentor program is wonderful! Great resource!

I valued that someone recognized the need for a new administrators support program.

MODEL 3.3

New Administrator Induction Program
Leadership Institute at Cooperative Educational Services (CES), CT

Linda Hartzer, Program Director
40 Lindeman Drive, Trumbull, CT 06611
203-365-8847   lhartzer@ces.k12.ct.us

Nancy Cetorelli, Executive Director
Esther Bobowick, Assistant to the Executive Director

Urban/suburban/rural school	All	Grade levels of school	All
Student population	Not applicable	Per pupil expenditure	Not applicable
Mentoring is/is not mandated for ongoing certification/licensure	Mentoring is not mandated	Mentoring program is/is not funded by the state	Mentoring is not funded
Unique feature of program	Regional network of collegial support; includes all positions in administration; includes expanded definition of "new"	Duration of program for new principals	Two years

Mentors are
   Full-time principals
      from same district
      from another district
Retired principals
	Mentors are typically full time from the same district; occasionally retired principals are utilized	Mentor selection criteria exist/do not exist
		
		Mentor matching process exists/does not exist
			Each district selects its own mentors
			
			Mentor matching process does exist and is determined by each district

Mentors are trained/not trained for role Mentors receive/do not receive ongoing support	Mentors are trained Mentors receive ongoing support	Mentors are/are not part of a team to support new principals	Mentors are part of a team to support new principals
Coaching is/is not a component	Coaching is encouraged, not required	Daily/weekly/yearly expectations for mentor	Mentors have monthly meetings with new principals
Mentors evaluate/do not evaluate the new principals	Mentors do not evaluate	Portfolio is required/is not required	Portfolio is not required
Mentor remuneration	District mentors are not renumerated; outside mentors are renumerated	Higher education affiliation	None
Cost of program	$550 per new administrator	Funding	Leadership Institute and districts
Years program in existence	One year	Full-time/part-time program coordinator/program coordination is part of another role in system/organization/state	Part-time director

STATE MANDATES

Is mentoring mandated for new principals?
No, mentoring is not mandated for new principals.

Is mentoring part of certification or licensure?
No, mentoring is not part of certification or licensure.

Is funding provided by the state to support the mandate?
No, the state does not provide any funds for mentoring.

HISTORY

Why was the program started?
This program was started in 2003–2004 in response to the State Department of Education requirement for districts to revise their administrator evaluation plans and to include a differentiated component for new administrators. The Cooperative Educational Services (CES) New Administrator Induction Program supports the districts in the CES region to address the induction components of their new administrator evaluation plans as well as provides a regional network of support for all new administrators, that is, principals, assistant principals, and curriculum leaders.

GOALS

What are the goals of the program?
The goals of the CES New Administrator Induction Program are to

- Support district administrator evaluation plans
- Provide a regional network of collegial support for
  - New administrator cohort
  - New administrators by "like" position
  - Mentors and support teams

- Allow district facilitators to learn and share successful induction practices and programs
- Provide mentor training that is specifically designed for mentors of administrators
- Provide professional development that may be required or recommended as part of the new state guidelines
- Provide a forum for successful practitioners from across the region to share their expertise with all new administrators
- Provide an opportunity to become a regional community of learners

PROGRAM DESIGN

Who designed the mentor program?
Linda Hartzer, the program administrator, designed this program in collaboration with district facilitators. Every district that participates in the program has a district facilitator. The program administrator meets with the district facilitators to discuss and review the program components and decide what workshops would best address the components of the district administrator evaluation plans and support their new administrators.

Districts within the CES region pay a fee to belong to the Leadership Institute at CES, whose purpose is to support the professional development of administrators in the region. The Leadership Institute voted to fund half the cost of this program for participating districts.

What are the components and recommended schedule of the program?

The components of the program include the following:

- One-to-one mentors for each new administrator

Each district designates the mentors for all of their administrators. It is recommended that the mentors are not the evaluators of the new administrators.

- Training for the mentors of the new administrators
- Support teams, designated by the district, in addition to the mentors, to respond to the needs of each new administrator
- Five professional development sessions that are offered over the course of the school year

In addition to content, there are opportunities for new administrators to network with administrators in like positions.

- A free voucher for new administrators to attend one of the CES administrator workshop series, which allows for differentiation based on needs and/or interests of each participant
- CEUs awarded for participation in the program

Are there any programs that complement the mentor program?

The following complement the New Administrator Induction Program:

- CES administrator workshop series
- Connecticut Association of Schools (CAS) Administrator Mentor/Mentee Program designed for principals
- Orientation sessions provided by the individual school districts

PROGRAM ADMINISTRATION

Who coordinates the program?

Linda Hartzer coordinates the program.

How is information communicated to shareholders?

Information is communicated when

- The program administrator meets with the district facilitators
- The district facilitators communicate with their superintendents, new administrators, and respective mentors
- The executive director of CES meets with the superintendents
- The superintendents attend the first session of the program with the mentors and district facilitators

Who coordinates the integration of this program with other professional development opportunities or requirements in the school or district?

The district facilitators coordinate the integration of this program with other professional development opportunities and requirements in the district.

PARTICIPATION IN THE PROGRAM

Who is served?

The program serves all new administrators in a district or in their position during their first and second years.

Is the participation of new principals voluntary or mandatory?

If the district has determined that it will participate in this program, participation of the district's new administrators is mandatory. Some sessions may be optional, depending on the experience of the new administrator and the approval of the district facilitator.

How long is the program?

This is a two-year program.

WHO PROVIDES THE MENTORING AND INDUCTION?

What are the criteria for being a mentor?

Each district selects the mentors for its new administrators. Typically, they assign administrators in like positions, when possible. They choose administrators with experience and expertise to be the mentors.

Are mentors full-time principals or retired principals?

In most cases, the mentors are full-time administrators in the district. Occasionally, the district hires retired administrators to mentor the new administrators.

Are mentors from the same district as new principals?

Mentors are usually from the same district; it could be otherwise if the district so decided.

How are mentors selected?

The district selects mentors for its own administrators.

How are matches made between mentors and new principals?

Mentors are matched with new administrators based on the

- Experience and expertise of the mentors
- New administrators and mentors being in like administrative positions
- Needs and style of the new administrators

WHAT IS EXPECTED OF MENTORS?

What are the job responsibilities of mentors?

Each mentor is expected to meet with the new administrator at least once a month. In addition, the new administrators contact their mentors by telephone and e-mail between meetings.

Is the relationship between the mentor and the new principal confidential?

The mentoring relationship is typically confidential; this is determined by the district.

Are observation and coaching requirements of mentors?

Observation is encouraged, not required.

Do mentors formally evaluate new principals?

No, mentors do not formally evaluate new administrators.

How much time are mentors expected to work with new principals (weekly, monthly, and for how long)?

Mentors are expected to meet at least monthly with the new administrators.

When do mentors meet with the new principals?

Mentors and new administrators meet at mutually determined times.

WHAT SUPPORTS ARE AVAILABLE FOR MENTORS?

Are mentors remunerated?

While mentors within districts are recognized and appreciated, they are typically not remunerated. Mentors from outside the district (retired administrators) are remunerated.

Are mentors trained? If so, by whom?

The mentors are trained by the program administrator and Lyn Nevins, the Beginning Educator Support and Training Program (BEST) facilitator.

Is there professional development for mentors after the initial training? If so, who provides it?

There are currently two training sessions for mentors. A follow-up session for previously trained mentors is also offered.

Do mentors meet regularly with other mentors? If so, how often and for how long?

Beyond the training sessions, mentor support meetings are encouraged at the district level.

Is there any other ongoing support for mentors? If so, who provides it?

The district facilitator supports the mentors if they have other needs and/or concerns. Central office personnel also support mentors within their own districts.

Are any other resources available for mentors?
The program coordinator provides articles to the mentors, as well as talking points, which are suggested topics defined by season.

Are mentors supervised? If so, by whom and how frequently?
District facilitators supervise the mentors, as determined in each district.

WHAT IS EXPECTED OF NEW PRINCIPALS REGARDING THEIR PARTICIPATION IN THE MENTORING PROGRAM?

How often do new principals meet with their mentors and for how long?
New administrators meet with their mentors at least monthly, with telephone and e-mail contacts in between.

Are there other people with whom the new principal meets for mentoring and support?
Districts can designate a support team, based on the needs of each new administrator.

Is formative assessment of new principals required? If so, when, how, and by whom?
Districts determine the required assessments of new principals.

Are new principals required to prepare a portfolio?
Districts determine whether portfolios are required.

ARE ADDITIONAL SUPPORTS AVAILABLE FOR NEW PRINCIPALS?

Is any other professional development provided? If so, when and by whom?
Professional development is offered at the district level, as well as through CAS.

Do new principals meet regularly with other new principals?
All new administrators meet during the five sessions, both for the content and in job-alike groups afterward.

What resources are required for the mentoring program?
Year 1 of the program cost is $550 per participant.

FUNDING

What are the funding sources?
The Leadership Institute pays $300 and the district pays $250 perparticipant.

Who requests the funding?
CES bills the participating districts.

EVALUATION OF THE PROGRAM

Is the program evaluated formatively or summatively? Who does the evaluation?

The program coordinator meets with the district facilitators four times a year to elicit input, feedback, and assess the program. The executive director meets regularly with the superintendents, and their feedback is ongoing. New administrators complete anonymous evaluations at the end of the program.

Who sees the results?

The program coordinator, district facilitators, executive director, and the assistant to the executive director see the program evaluation.

RECRUITMENT, HIRING, AND RETENTION OF NEW STAFF

How many new principals are recruited and hired each year?

Last year, there were 62 new administrators (not all principals) from 11 districts.

Are there any data that correlate the mentoring program with the retention of new principals?

The program has only been in existence one year. No data is yet available.

Are there any data that correlate the mentoring program with the performance of the new principals?

At this time there aren't any data correlating the program with the performance of the new administrators.

What are the indicators of program success?

Feedback from all the participants is very favorable, so much so that the new administrators, district facilitators, and district superintendents requested a second year of the program.

The following are comments from new administrators:

It makes me proud to be part of this network as well as part of my school district.

The superintendents' panel was one of the most valuable sessions I ever attended!

I really valued sharing mutual issues with my counterparts in different towns.

Comments from mentor training:

I only wish I had this opportunity when I began.

Great sessions! I really valued the time to reflect on what I will be doing as a mentor.

I appreciated the clarification of the mentor role . . . being able to share experiences with other administrators in terms of being "new". . . knowing the concerns of new administrators . . . listening to my colleagues and exchanging ideas.

Comments from the program coordinator:

What makes this program more likely to be successful and unique is the involvement of the districts and allowing for some differentiation. It is also a program that supports all administrators, not just principals, and there is a definite benefit of having opportunities for networking of all new administrators to come together regardless of position.

New administrators may be new to the position of administrator, new to a district, or new to a position in the same district. These multiple definitions of *new* may expand the thinking about what new administrators need to be supported.

Most people assume that if you are experienced in the role, then you don't need support. That is a misconception. The cultures and expectations of districts can be so different that it is just as important to mentor principals new to a district. We don't often think of mentoring positions above principals. Assistant superintendents and directors also need mentors.

MODEL 3.4

Leadership Initiative for Transformation (LIFT)
Chicago Public Schools

Sallie Penman, Director
Illinois Administrators Academy–Chicago
221 North LaSalle Avenue, Suite 1550, Chicago, IL 60601
312-263-1976   sdpenman@class.cps.k12.il.us

Urban/suburban/rural school	Urban	Grade levels of school	K–12
Student population	43,419	Per pupil expenditure	$8,482
Mentoring is/is not mandated for ongoing certification/licensure	Mentoring is not mandated for certification of licensure	Mentoring program is/is not funded by the state	Mentoring is not funded by the state
Unique feature of program	Program is part of a group of academies to support principals	Duration of program for new principals	One year
Mentors are Full-time principals from same district from another district Retired principals	Mentors are full-time principals and/or recently retired principals from the Chicago Public Schools	Mentor selection criteria exist/do not exist Mentor matching process exists/does not exist	Mentor selection criteria do exist Mentor matching process does exist
Mentors are trained/not trained for role Mentors receive/do not receive ongoing support	Mentors are trained for their role Mentors do receive specific ongoing support	Mentors are/are not part of a team to support new principals	Mentors are among several support providers for new principals
Coaching is/is not a component	Cognitive coaching is a component of the program	Daily/weekly/yearly expectations for mentors	Mentors participate in monthly trainings with new principals
Mentors evaluate/do not evaluate the new principals	Mentors do not evaluate new principals	Portfolio is required/not required	Portfolios are required by area area instructional officers
Mentor remuneration	$1,500/per protégé	Higher education affiliation	None
Cost of program	$262,500 plus LIFT staff salaries	Funding	Internally
Years program in existence	Nine years	Full-time/part-time program coordinator/program coordination is part of other role in system/organization/state	There is a full-time program coordinator

STATE MANDATES

Is mentoring mandated for new principals?

Mentoring is not mandated by the State of Illinois. It is mandated in the Chicago Public Schools (CPS). It didn't start out as a mandated program. Those who participated in the voluntary principal mentoring program had a much easier transition into the principalship. After a couple of years, the school district mandated this program for all new principals.

Is mentoring part of certification or licensure?

No, mentoring is not part of certification or licensure.

Is funding provided by the state to support the mandate?

No, funding is not provided by the state for mentoring.

HISTORY

Why was the program started?

In the past, the CPS had a principals' exam that aspirants who were certified needed to take. If aspirants passed the test, they were put on a list and assigned to principalships as they became open in the system. In fact, there was a period of time when surrounding districts required candidates to take the principals' exam in Chicago before they could be selected for their districts.

The Chicago School Reform Law of 1988 drastically changed the way principals were selected. Local Schools Councils (LSCs) were created and given the authority to select principals. LSCs had the authority to hire whomever they chose (providing the aspirant had a state administration certification). Many new principals went directly from the classroom to the principalship with little or no experience in school administration. By 1995, over 83 percent of the CPS principals had three years or less of experience. New principals could not rely upon neighboring principals for advice or counsel because neighboring principals were as inexperienced as they were. Alarmed at the decline in student achievement and seeing a need for action, five organizations with education and civic interest collaborated in the development of the Leadership Initiative for Transformation (LIFT).

GOALS

What are the goals of the program?

The goals of the LIFT program are to

- Support beginning principals in their first year as instructional and administrative leaders of their schools.
- Identify and train experienced principals to serve as coaches/mentors for beginning principals
- Foster a culture within the CPS that nurtures and encourages principals to strive for excellence and have high expectations for the staff and students in their charge

PROGRAM DESIGN

Who designed the mentor program?

Five organizations collaborated to design the LIFT Program. They included (1) Leadership for Quality Education (LQE) (composed of business and foundation people who wanted to help the schools) under the aegis of the Chicago Civic Committee, (2) the Chicago Principals and Administrators Association, (3) the Illinois Administrators Academy–Chicago, acting for the CPS, (4) Kellogg School of Management–Northwestern University, and (5) the Center for School Improvement.

What are the components and recommended schedule of the program?

The components of the program are as follows:

- The year starts with a four-day summer orientation, at which day-to-day information is shared, including available resources through the central office, where everything is, where to go for information, who to see, and school opening exercises.

- There is a coaching triad (one coach/mentor per two new principals, or protégés). Within the triad, protégés engage in reflective dialogue and receive individual and collegial counsel and support.

- There are one-, two-, and three-day monthly retreats, depending on the needs of the protégés. The coaches/mentors are trained next to their protégés.

- Intersession assignments are given between the monthly professional development days.

- The mentoring is job-embedded experiences.

- There is CPS calendar-related curriculum. The curriculum for the retreats is calendar related, that is, what's coming up is taught two months in advance. For example, before the budget is due, protégés are given intensive instruction on how to do their budgets online. It's all "just in time" training. Topics include day-to-day operations; local school finances; human resource management; curriculum, instruction, and assessment; and collaboration and political skills.

- Coaches/mentors and protégés are required to observe at each other's schools at least once.

- The general curriculum includes
  - School Operations and Day-to-Day Operations
  - Managing Local School Finances
  - Human Resource Management
  - Curriculum, Instruction, and Assessment
  - Collaboration and Political Skills for School Leaders
  - Self-Assessment of Leadership Style and Potential

Are there any programs that complement the mentor program?

Chicago has a continuum of leadership development programs. The following academies were created in the CPS, for different reasons, at different times. They are all part of Chicago Leadership Academies for Supporting Success (CLASS), and they are all sponsored by the CPS:

- Leadership Academy and Urban Network for Chicago (LAUNCH): training program for aspiring principals
- LIFT: program for new principals
- Chicago Academy for School Leaders (CASL): program for veteran principals
- Illinois Administrators Academy–Chicago: program for administrators to get state-mandated professional development. (This academy is also part of a state network of academies created by the State of Illinois in 1986.)

State professional development mandates must take place across all levels of experience for the purpose of recertification. They are totally separate from what the CPS require. Both coaches/mentors and protégés are able to fulfill their state-mandated professional development through their participation in the LIFT program. This is also true for participants in the other leadership academies.

Professional development is not intended to be an add-on; therefore, the director of the Illinois Administrators Academy-Chicago works in collaboration with the directors of the LIFT and other programs to form a seamless job-embedded connection between the state and local professional development mandates.

PROGRAM ADMINISTRATION

Who coordinates the program?

The program is coordinated by Dr. Arthur Fumarolo, who is the director of the LIFT program. Dr. Fumarolo can be reached at the following addresses and telephone number:

aafumarolo@class.cps.k12.il.us
221 North LaSalle Avenue, Suite 1550
Chicago, IL 60601
312-263-1976

How is information communicated to shareholders?

Information is communicated to shareholders via program mailings, the CPS Intranet, and the CLASS Web site. There is close communication between other departments in the CPS and the LIFT program. The LIFT Steering Committee, which has representation from the central office and the area instructional officers and current principals, is another way that information is communicated.

Who coordinates the integration of this program with other professional development opportunities or requirements in the school or district?

The director of LIFT does this, with assistance from the steering committee. There is a master district calendar, and professional development is scheduled around other principal responsibilities that are pressing on the principals' time.

PARTICIPATION IN THE PROGRAM

Who is served?

All first-year principals, be they new to the profession or new to the CPS, are part of the LIFT program.

Is the participation of new principals voluntary or mandatory?

Participation in the LIFT program is mandatory. In the beginning, the program was voluntary, yet the vast majority of beginning new principals participated.

How long is the program?

The LIFT program is one year long.

WHO PROVIDES THE MENTORING AND INDUCTION?

What are the criteria for being a mentor?

Coaches/mentors are successful principals with at least four years of experience in the principalship. Principals must have received a second four-year contract. At the end of the fourth year of a principal's contract, the Local Schools Council (LSC) may offer the principal another four-year contract. The second contract is evidence that the principal is experiencing success on the job.

Are mentors full-time principals or retired principals?

Coaches/mentors are full-time principals or recently retired principals. Retired principals may continue mentoring if they were mentors while they were principals in the district. Retired principals may only mentor for three years after their retirement.

Are mentors from the same district as new principals?

Yes, coaches/mentors are from within the CPS. CPS is one district.

How are mentors selected?

There is an application process. Coaches/mentors are selected by the LIFT Steering Team, consisting of the program director, the Chicago Principals and Administrators Association, key administrators from the central office, Area Instructional Officers (AIOs), and a selection of veteran principals.

How are matches made between mentors and new principals?

Matches between coaches/mentors and new principals are made in different ways each year. Sometimes they are matched by the proximity of their schools; other times they are matched because they have similar student bodies and/or issues. They are always matched by levels (e.g., elementary-elementary, middle-middle, high school-high school).

WHAT IS EXPECTED OF MENTORS?

What are the job responsibilities of mentors?

Coaches/mentors sign a contract agreeing to do the following:

- Attend appropriate coach development sessions
- Attend and actively participate in all LIFT professional development sessions
- Provide an average of one hour of contact time with each protégé per week in addition to the time spent at LIFT sessions
- Visit each protégé's school at least once before the November retreat (first retreat) and host a visit from each protégé before the December session
- Maintain and submit monthly reports of activities with protégés
- Be ready to act as facilitator or presenter at LIFT sessions upon request
- Maintain and honor the confidentiality of the coach–protégé relationship
- Commit to providing the support and guidance necessary to make LIFT protégés successful principals

Is the relationship between the mentor and the new principal confidential?

Yes, generally speaking. In all of the training programs, what is discussed in the training room stays in the training room. Mentors and new principals try to solve any problems themselves. If someone else needs to be brought in, mentors will do so. Mentors might go to the director of LIFT; things are usually worked out within the program.

Are observation and coaching requirements of mentors?

Yes. Coaches/mentors must visit each protégé's school so that they can observe them on the job and provide the support and guidance necessary to make LIFT protégés successful principals.

Do mentors formally evaluate new principals?

No, mentors do not evaluate principals.

How much time are mentors expected to work with new principals (weekly, monthly, and for how long)?

Coaches/mentors work with each protégé an average of one hour of contact time per week in addition to the time spent at LIFT sessions.

When do mentors meet with the new principals?

Meetings between coaches/mentors and new principals are up to them (time and place that works best for the mentor and protégé). Some meet on weekends, others meet mornings or evenings. Some mentors and protégés have been known to use e-mail more than face-to-face meetings. The monthly sessions are always a time to meet because they participate in the trainings together.

WHAT SUPPORTS ARE AVAILABLE FOR MENTORS?

Are mentors remunerated?

LIFT coaches/mentors are paid $1,500 per protégé for the year.

Are mentors trained? If so, by whom?

In the past, each program director arranged the training for their coaches/mentors. The coaches/mentors from each of the CLASS programs were trained in a different manner, a manner consistent with the specific needs of the program. In fiscal year 2005, all of the coach-mentors for LIFT, LAUNCH, and CASL will be trained in a cognitive coaching process. The goal is for the mentoring-coaching language to be the same across programs. This training will be done by the program directors from the CLASS program (the CLASS program directors have been trained by Bob Garmston).

Is there professional development for mentors after the initial training? If so, who provides it?

Coaches/mentors participate in professional development alongside their protégés. They also participate in the professional development provided by their AIOs, which keeps them abreast of changes in CPS policies, procedures, and initiatives. Training specific to individual programs is done as the need arises.

Do mentors meet regularly with other mentors? If so, how often and for how long?

No, coaches/mentors do not meet regularly other than in the monthly trainings. Usually they meet once or twice at the beginning of the school year. Additional meetings are scheduled as needed.

Is there any other ongoing support for mentors? If so, who provides it?

Yes, there is ongoing support for coaches/mentors. They can go to the LIFT director if they need anything, they can go to other LIFT coaches, and as principals in the district they have access to ongoing central office and/or area office support provided to any district principal.

Are any other resources available for mentors?

No, there aren't any additional resources for coaches/mentors provided through LIFT. However, CPS provides resources for the coaches/mentors who are current principals for carrying out their job responsibilities and assisting their protégés with carrying out theirs.

Are mentors supervised? If so, by whom and how frequently?

There is a reporting system, in which coaches/mentors submit monthly reports to the program director documenting their coach-mentoring activities. In addition, at the end of the year, the protégés complete a survey on their mentors, which goes to the program director.

WHAT IS EXPECTED OF NEW PRINCIPALS REGARDING THEIR PARTICIPATION IN THE MENTORING PROGRAM?

How often do new principals meet with their mentors and for how long?

Meetings between coaches/mentors and new principals are up to them (i.e., a time and place that works best for both of them). Some meet on weekends, others meet mornings or evenings. New principals meet with their coaches/mentors at least monthly for training.

Are there other people with whom the new principal meets for mentoring and support?

AIOs also support the new principals. There are over 600 schools in Chicago. The district is divided into clusters and areas. Each area is headed by an AIO who holds monthly professional development sessions with all of his or her principals.

Is formative assessment of new principals required? If so, when, how, and by whom?

No, formative assessment of new principals is not part of the LIFT program.

Are new principals required to prepare a portfolio?

All CPS principals do a portfolio that is shared with their AIOs as part of the evaluation process.

As of 2004, as part of a new process for selecting principals candidates, a portfolio is now required before a candidate's name is placed in the principal pool.

ARE ADDITIONAL SUPPORTS AVAILABLE FOR NEW PRINCIPALS?

Is any other professional development provided? If so, when and by whom?

Professional development that is required by the state is offered to all principals through the Illinois Administrators Academy-Chicago. AIOs provide professional development to the principals in their areas. Various district-level professional development is provided (e.g., from the Office of Specialized Services, the Law Department, or the Office of Accountability).

Do new principals meet regularly with other new principals?

New principals informally see each other during the monthly LIFT meetings as well as during their monthly AIO meetings.

What resources are required for the mentoring program?

The program costs amount to $262,500, not including LIFT staff salaries, as follows:

- Coaches/mentors $120,000
- Consultants: $21,000
- Professional services: $5,000
- Noninstructional services: $2,500

- Overnight residential cost: $100,000
- Meeting space cost: $9,000
- Office supplies: $5,000

FUNDING

What are the funding sources?
The CPS fund the LIFT program as well as the other CLASS programs.

Who requests the funding?
Funding is internally allocated.

EVALUATION OF THE PROGRAM

Is the program evaluated formatively? Summatively? Who does the evaluation?
The LIFT program is evaluated through session evaluations and feedback from the new principals at the end of the program. Every few years, the CLASS program is formally evaluated by an outside evaluator.

Who sees the results?
The director and the Steering Committee see the results of the evaluations. Results are shared with the CLASS Advisory Board as well as district-level administration.

RECRUITMENT, HIRING, AND RETENTION OF NEW STAFF

How many new principals are recruited and hired each year?
There were 60 new principals in fiscal year 2003 and 70 in fiscal year 2004. In fiscal year 2005 and 2006, approximately 200 new principals are projected to be hired.

There is no a principal shortage in Chicago; there are a surplus of people who want to be principals. There are over 4,000 employees with the administrative certificate. The major concern at this time is identifying and preparing a pool of strong principal candidates.

Are there any data that correlate the mentoring program with the retention of new principals?
It is difficult to correlate the LIFT program and principal retention, because local school councils may choose not to renew a principal's contract because they want someone else to be the principal.

Are there any data that correlate the mentoring program with the performance of the new principals?
There are no formal data correlating the LIFT program with new principals' job performance. When the program began, it was voluntary. The district noticed that principals who went through LIFT seemed to have far fewer problems. That is when the school system passed a mandate requiring all new principals to participate in LIFT.

What are the indicators of program success?
A number of principals who went through the LIFT program were nominated and/or selected as Outstanding Leaders (an award program funded by the district and private foundation funds for

several years). Some former LIFT participants (mentors and protégés) are now serving the district as AIOs, chief education officers, and chief officers of large programs.

Two LIFT principals commented as follows:

As a new principal, I knew I needed guidance. LIFT was able to furnish what I needed and many times provided me the help that I didn't realize that I needed.

—Jerry D. Mandujano, Principal, McAuliffe Elementary School

In addition to being a wonderful support program for new principals, the program allowed me to form a professional network of principals that I have associated with over the years.

—Donna R. Nelson, Principal, Murphy Elementary School

MODEL 3.5

New Principal Induction Program
Sheridan School District
Englewood, CO

Mike Poore, Superintendent
Sheridan School District
P.O. Box 1198, Englewood CO 80150
720-833-6616   poorem@sheridan.k12.co.us

Urban/suburban/rural school	Rural and urban	Grade levels of school	Pre-K–12
Student population	1,861	Per pupil expenditure	$6,718
Mentoring is/is not mandated for ongoing certification/licensure	Induction is mandated	Mentoring program is/is not funded by the state	Not funded
Unique feature of program	Mentoring within very small rural/urban district	Duration of program for new principals	Two years
Mentors are Full-time principals from same district from another district Retired principals	Superintendent and assistant superintendent	Mentor selection criteria exist/do not exist Mentor matching process exists/does not exist	Do not exist Does not exist
Mentors are trained/not trained for role Mentors receive/do not receive ongoing support	Mentors are not trained Mentors do not receive ongoing support	Mentors are/are not part of a team to support new principals	Mentors are the team to support new principals
Coaching is/is not a component	Coaching is a component	Daily/weekly/yearly expectations for mentors	Four times/month meetings + as needed
Mentors evaluate/do not evaluate the new principals	Superintendent evaluates the new principals	Portfolio is required/is not required	Portfolio is required for the state induction
Mentor remuneration	None: Central Office administrators mentor	Higher education affiliation	Principals may take offerings at area IHEs
Cost of program	$10,000	Funding	Within school district budget
Years program in existence	One year	Full-time/part-time program coordinator/program coordination is part of another role in system/organization/state	Coordination is done by superintendent and assistant superintendent

Used with permission of Mike Poore, the Sheridan School District, CO.

STATE MANDATES

Is mentoring mandated for new principals?

No, mentoring is not mandated for new principals.

Is mentoring part of certification or licensure?

Induction is required to move from a provisional license to a professional license. When students finish a program through a university and begin a new job, they are given a provisional license for three years. During those three years, they must be part of an induction program, and then they can get the professional license. There are a variety of different ways of doing induction.

Is funding provided by the state to support the mandate?

No, funding is not provided by the state.

HISTORY

Why was the program started?

There has always been support for principals in the Sheridan schools. After the legislation requiring induction was enacted, the program became formalized. The turnover in the Sheridan district is high because the salaries are relatively low. In 2003–2004, four of the five principals were in their first or second year. The fifth principal returned from retirement to work for the year.

GOALS

What are the goals of the program?

The goals of the program are to provide, in a timely way, a broad array of support on a variety of issues that principals will encounter so that they get what they need when they need it.

PROGRAM DESIGN

Who designed the mentor program?

Mike Poore, the superintendent, designed the induction program with Karla Esser, the director of curriculum and instruction. Sheridan is a small district with less than 2,000 students. Sheridan is in metro-Denver. The only schools that are of similar size are charter schools, which are set up differently and don't have the same demographics. Schools like Sheridan are not located nearby. For example, it's hard to find a high school with 550 kids and 80 percent of them receiving free or reduced lunch.

What are the components and recommended schedule of the program?

The components of the program are as follows:

- Leadership training is done twice a month for two to three hours. The superintendent and the director of curriculum and instruction offer the training on topics that principals need at that time. For example, the first round of support will be how to do open houses so that the mission is exhibited and parents are getting into the classrooms. The second round of support will be about how to utilize data. Goal setting for the upcoming year and budget decisions are topics that will be done in the spring. Sometimes they bring in outside people to help with the training.

- The superintendent and the director of curriculum and instruction mentor the principals. For the superintendent, it means going into their schools twice a month to address the issues they're having, as a support mechanism. It's not the superintendent coming to them with things he wants them to do; it's the superintendent coming to hear and help address their concerns, either immediately or to set up training down the line. For example, the superintendent spoke with a new principal three times during one day about custody issues, restraining orders, and physical attacks on staff. A positive aspect of the size of the district is that there is a direct tie between the new principals and the superintendent. The director of curriculum and instruction does the same type of things twice a month with each principal.
- A retreat of all the principals from Sheridan with the Edison School principals, including assessment tools, communication tools, and professional development opportunities, takes place.

Are there any programs that complement the induction program?

Programs that complement the induction program are as follows:

- The Colorado Association of School Executives (CASE) offers a variety of trainings and courses, including a one-day training for new principals.
- The Department of Education offers a one-day training for new principals.
- Colleges and universities in the area offer classes in support of principals to get beyond what they had in their master's programs.
- The Principal Center helps train principals.
- The Board of Cooperative Educational Services (BOCES) offers programs. Sheridan pays a fee to be in two different BOCES. In so doing, they can bring in programs to the district or send people to them.

PROGRAM ADMINISTRATION

Who coordinates the program?

The superintendent coordinates the program.

How is information communicated to shareholders?

Communication is direct face-to-face, telephone, and e-mail.

Who coordinates the integration of this program with other professional development opportunities/requirements in the school/district?

The superintendent and the director of curriculum and instruction confer about supporting principals, sometimes about individuals and sometimes for all of them as a group.

PARTICIPATION IN THE PROGRAM

Who is served?

All the principals are supported; four of the five are in their first two years, and the fifth is back from retirement for a year.

Is the participation of new principals voluntary or mandatory?

Technically, it is mandatory, since the superintendent is offering it.

How long is the program?

The program is for two years.

WHO PROVIDES THE MENTORING AND INDUCTION?

What are the criteria for being a mentor?

The superintendent and the director of curriculum and instruction are the mentors for most of the principals. There isn't a formal selection process for mentors.

Are mentors full-time principals or retired principals?

Not applicable.

Are mentors from the same district as new principals?

Not applicable.

How are mentors selected?

The superintendent and the director of curriculum and instruction may attract and bring in people who could meet a specific new principal's need.

How are matches made between mentors and new principals?

The superintendent and the director of curriculum and instruction each mentor all of the principals.

WHAT IS EXPECTED OF MENTORS?

What are the job responsibilities of mentors?

The superintendent and the director of curriculum and instruction each meet with each principal twice a month. They give principals a lot more direct attention, because that is what new principals need.

Is the relationship between the mentor and the new principal confidential?

The relationship is designed to be supportive. Since the superintendent evaluates the principals, the mentoring relationship cannot be considered confidential.

Are observation and coaching requirements of mentors?

The superintendent does observations and coaching as part of evaluation. The director of curriculum and instruction observes each principal and debriefs with them afterward.

Do mentors formally evaluate new principals?

The superintendent evaluates all the principals.

How much time are mentors expected to work with new principals (weekly, monthly, and for how long)?

The superintendent and the director of curriculum and instruction each work with each principal twice a month and as needed. With outside mentors, should they be needed, the time together is negotiated between the principals and those mentors.

When do mentors meet with the new principals?
They meet at mutually agreed-upon times.

WHAT SUPPORTS ARE AVAILABLE FOR MENTORS?

Are mentors remunerated?
Not applicable.

Are mentors trained? If so, by whom?
Not applicable.

Is there professional development for mentors after the initial training? If so, who provides it?
Not applicable.

Do mentors meet regularly with other mentors? If so, how often and for how long?
The superintendent and the director of curriculum and instruction regularly meet twice a week, and they always talk about mentoring the new principals. In fact, 30–40 percent of their time is spent talking about what they can do to support the principals.

Is there any other ongoing support for mentors? If so, who provides it?
Not applicable.

Are there any other resources available for mentors?
Not applicable.

Are mentors supervised? If so, by whom and how frequently?
Not applicable.

WHAT IS EXPECTED OF NEW PRINCIPALS REGARDING THEIR PARTICIPATION IN THE MENTORING PROGRAM?

How often do new principals meet with their mentors and for how long?
New principals individually meet with the superintendent and then with the director of curriculum and instruction twice a month plus on an as-needed basis.

Are there other people with whom the new principal meets for mentoring and support?
Principals meet with others, depending on the things they are being challenged by. For example, they might meet with the person in charge of facilities and technology or the CFO in the system for developing a budget or thinking of ways to better manage their activity accounts.

Is formative assessment of new principals required? If so, when, how, and by whom?
The superintendent discusses progress on goals with each principal every couple of months. These conversations are not written. The superintendent also asks the principals to do a self-evaluation midyear and to answer the questions, What has gone well and what are the challenges? This may be a little scary for the new principals, but they know that the superintendent and the director of

curriculum and instruction are just trying to help them get better. The principals don't appear reluctant to do this self-assessment.

Are new principals required to prepare a portfolio?

Yes, a portfolio is part of the induction they are required to do.

ARE ADDITIONAL SUPPORTS AVAILABLE FOR NEW PRINCIPALS?

Is any other professional development provided? If so, when and by whom?

There is professional development available to principals from the Department of Education, the Principal Center, universities and colleges, and CASE.

Do new principals meet regularly with other new principals?

The superintendent and the director of curriculum and instruction encourage the principals to meet by levels. Elementary principals meet once a week, partly because they are involved with a large Reading First grant. Secondary principals meet once a month. The assumption is that they listen to and support each other.

What are the resources required for the mentoring program?

The superintendent allocates approximately $10,000 for the professional development and support of principals. These include all costs for training. Principals pay their own member fees, and the district pays the additional costs for training or courses.

FUNDING

What are the funding sources?

The funding is from the district professional development budget or from grants.

Who requests the funding?

The superintendent allocates the funds to support the new principals.

EVALUATION OF THE PROGRAM

Is the program evaluated formatively? Summatively?
Who does the evaluation?

The superintendent and the director of curriculum and instruction are always asking if the principals are getting what they need and if they need anything else.

Who sees the results?

The superintendent and the director of curriculum and instruction discuss the new principals 30–40 percent of the time they meet.

RECRUITMENT, HIRING, AND RETENTION OF NEW STAFF

How many new principals are recruited and hired each year?

In the district, four to five principals are in their first or second year.

Are there any data that correlate the mentoring program with the retention of new principals?

It's too early to say whether the support of new principals will impact their retention.

Are there any data that correlate the mentoring program with the performance of the new principals?

The superintendent and the director of curriculum and instruction think their extra support of principals is making an impact; it's difficult to separate their work in induction from their work as superintendent and assistant superintendent.

What are the indicators of program success?

The superintendent hired two people from one of the largest districts in the area. Those principals said they couldn't believe the amount of access and help they were receiving. They were unaccustomed to having a superintendent's ear and availability. They felt that it is extraordinary. They said that when they were in the large district, they had felt like they were out on an island, whereas now the support was steady and accessible.

The superintendent sums up his philosophy: "I think that the trick for the supervisor of new principals is how far do you let them out of the corral, how much leash are you able to give them? You don't want them to go so far out that they go off the cliff when they didn't even know they were near the cliff. And you have to let them experience things and have pluses and minuses and then deal with it."

MODEL 3.6

Principal Induction Program
Wake Leadership Academy
Raleigh, NC

Dr. Joseph Peel
Director of the Wake Leadership Academy
3600 Wake Forest Road, Raleigh, NC 27611
919-850-8783   jwpeel@wcpss.net

Urban/suburban/rural school	Urban and suburban	Grade levels of school	PreK–12
Student population	114,000	Per pupil expenditure	$6,700
Mentoring is/is not mandated for ongoing certification/ licensure	Internships are part of earning a master's degree, which is required for certification	Mentoring program is/ is not funded by the state	Funds from the state are available for some students to get their master's degree in school administration
Unique feature of program	Half day of media training for new administrators; monthly topical presentations on topics of need	Duration of program for new principals	One year
Mentors are Full-time principals from same district from another district Retired principals	New principals are not assigned mentors; they are assigned buddies	Mentor selection criteria exist/do not exist Mentor matching process exists/does not exist	Not applicable Not applicable
Mentors are trained/not trained for role Mentors receive/do not receive ongoing support	Not applicable Not applicable	Mentors are/are not part of a team to support new principals	Not applicable
Coaching is/is not a component	Coaching is not a component	Daily/weekly/yearly expectations for mentor	Not applicable
Mentors evaluate/do not evaluate the new principals	Not applicable	Portfolio is required/is not required	Not required
Mentor remuneration	Not applicable	Higher education affiliation	None
Cost of program	$10,000	Funding	Wake School District and business community
Years program in existence	Six years	Full-time/part-time program coordinator/program coordination is part of another role in system/ organization/state	Coordination and presentations are part of the responsibilities of the Wake Leadership Academy coordinator

Used with permission of Joseph W. Peel, Wake Leadership Academy, NC.

STATE MANDATES

Is mentoring mandated for new principals?

No, mentoring is not mandated for new principals.

Is mentoring part of certification or licensure?

Principals need to get a master's degree in school administration to be certified; internships are part of the master's program. Full-time students do a year-long internship. Part-time students negotiate with the university about their internships. Internships are always around the Interstate School Leaders Licensure Consortium (ISLLC) standards.

Is funding provided by the state to support the mandate?

The state provides some funding for students to get their master's degree in school administration. There is a Principal Fellows program in which students' tuition is paid by the state and they are given an allowance for living expenses. Then in the second year they are hired as an intern and are paid a salary. They work four days a week in a school and one day in seminars. The state pays for that as well. This is a program in which the successful applicants for this scholarship program agree to give four years of service back to the state.

The Public School Forum is a privately funded group that is a think tank and does public policy research. It was established by the business community on state and regional levels. They are the ones who are contracted by the state to run the Principal Fellows program. Joanne Norris is at the Public School Forum in Raleigh.

HISTORY

Why was the program started?

The program was started in 1998. The school district and the Wake Educational Partnership considered the fact that many principals were retiring, and that to continue to improve schools, principals are key. It is important to support them during their first year and help them to be successful.

Wake is a large district, with 135 schools. There are many administrators leaving and being hired, and this is an opportunity to establish collaborative networks of new administrators. Typically, administrators meet other administrators from the 20–25 schools in the one of six feeder areas that they are assigned.

GOALS

What are the goals of the program?

The goals of the program are to

- Retain the good people that are hired as principals
- Provide professional development for new administrators related to the topics they need to know in order to survive and be effective, such as school finance and special education
- Develop a support system for new administrators as well as introduce them to a variety of district leaders and district services in an organized way
- Inculcate the new principals into the culture

PROGRAM DESIGN

Who designed the mentor program?

Dr. Joseph Peel, director of the Wake Leadership Academy, designed the program.

What are the components and recommended schedule of the program?

The components of the program are as follows:

- The new administrators meet from July through May. They typically meet once a month except in September and December, when they meet twice a month.
- The first meeting is a day-long meeting; the remainder are morning meetings from 8:15 to 11:30 a.m.
- Meeting presentations are on the topics of need. Different people present on the topics, based on their specialties. For example, the school attorney will present on the law and special education students and other legal issues; the assistant superintendent of human resources will present on working successfully with marginal teachers.
- New principals are assigned buddies by the area superintendents. They do not have mentors.
- When funding permits, mentors might be hired to work with new principals.

Are there any programs that complement the mentor program?

Yes, there is a Principals Executive Program, which is part of the University of North Carolina at Chapel Hill, and is a statewide induction program headed by Dr. Brad Sneeden. Of 21 new principals in one year, 1 or 2 also participated in this program.

PROGRAM ADMINISTRATION

Who coordinates the program?

The director of the Wake Leadership Academy coordinates the program.

How is information communicated to shareholders?

The director of the Wake Leadership Academy communicates with participants by e-mail.

Who coordinates the integration of this program with other professional development opportunities or requirements in the school or district?

The director of the academy coordinates the Principal Induction program with the many other Leadership Academy offerings. The director also coordinates the Leadership Academy, which offers many topics for all principals.

PARTICIPATION IN THE PROGRAM

Who is served?

The Principal Induction program serves all new principals in the Wake School District.

Is the participation of new principals voluntary or mandatory?

Participation is mandatory.

How long is the program?

The program lasts one year.

Who provides the mentoring and induction?

Not applicable. Mentoring is not part of the program at this time.

What is expected of mentors?

Not applicable.

What supports are available for mentors?

Not applicable.

WHAT IS EXPECTED OF NEW PRINCIPALS REGARDING THEIR PARTICIPATION IN THIS PROGRAM?

How often do new principals meet with their mentors and for how long?

Not applicable.

Are there other people with whom the new principal meets for support?

The director of the academy and topical presenters and the area superintendents are all resources for the new principals.

Is formative assessment of new principals required? If so, when, how, and by whom?

The area superintendents evaluate the new principals.

Are new principals required to prepare a portfolio?

No, a portfolio is not required.

ARE ADDITIONAL SUPPORTS AVAILABLE FOR NEW PRINCIPALS?

Is any other professional development provided? If so, when and by whom?

New principals may participate in any of the sessions offered by the Leadership Academy.

Do new principals meet regularly with other new principals?

New principals meet at the monthly meetings.

What resources are required for the program?

The additional resources needed for the Principal Induction program are $10,000, which pays for an outside consultant to do an intensive half day of media training. He is a videographer, and he prepares principals to be comfortable in front of the media. They work on "What is my story and how do I tell it" and learn how to market their schools in a high-profile community.

The director of the academy's salary for the Principal Induction program is included in his salary as director of the Leadership Academy.

FUNDING

What are the funding sources?

The school district and the business community fund the Principal Induction program. The district and the local education foundation, Wake Education Partnership, fund the Leadership Academy.

Who requests the funding?

The director of the academy requests the funding.

EVALUATION OF THE PROGRAM

Is the program evaluated formatively? Summatively? Who does the evaluation?

The director of the academy conducts an evaluation of the program through a questionnaire.

Who sees the results?

The director of the academy shares the results with the superintendent and the area superintendents.

RECRUITMENT, HIRING, AND RETENTION OF NEW STAFF

How many new principals are recruited and hired each year?

Twenty-one new principals were hired this year. Sixty-five new principals have been hired within the last four or five years. Part of the growth comes from opening seven new schools. A large part of the growth is due to retirement and turnover.

Are there any data that correlate the program with the retention of new principals?

In the last three years, only one new principal left the district.

Are there any data that correlate the program with the performance of the new principals?

No, there are not any data correlating the program with the performance of the new principals.

What are the indicators of program success?

The indicators of success for the program are clear through the positive evaluations by the new principals. In addition, the cohesive relationships that are formed is valuable. Many new principals call the director of the academy if they have a problem because the director has been a principal and a superintendent and has been with the district for a long time.

State Models

MODEL 4.1

Arkansas Beginning Administrator Induction Program

Kristi Pugh, Administrator Licensure Program Advisor
Arkansas Department of Education
#4 State Capital Mall, Room 405B, Little Rock, AR 72207
501-682-9850   kpugh@arkedu.k12.ar.us

Urban/suburban/rural school	Not applicable	**Grade levels of school**	Not applicable
Student population	Not applicable	**Per pupil expenditure**	Not applicable
Mentoring is/is not mandated for ongoing certification/ licensure	Mentoring is mandated	**Mentoring program is/is not funded by the state**	Mentoring is funded at $1,200 per new principal/mentor pair
Unique feature of program	Mentoring is mandated and funded by the state	**Duration of program for new principals**	Minimum of one year, maximum of three years
Mentors are **Full-time principals** **from same district** **from another district** **Retired principals**	Mentors are typically full-time principals from the same district; recently retired principals are also eligible, and sometimes mentors are from out of district	**Mentor selection criteria exist/do not exist** **Mentor matching process exist/do not exist**	Mentor selection criteria do exist Mentor matching process does exist
Mentors are trained/not trained for role **Mentors receive/do not receive ongoing support**	Mentors are trained Mentors do not receive ongoing support	**Mentors are/are not part of a team to support new principals**	Mentors are not part of a team to support new principals
Coaching is/is not a component	Coaching is a component	**Daily/weekly/yearly expectations for mentors**	Mentors are expected to work with new principals on a weekly basis
Mentors evaluate/do not evaluate the new principals	Mentors do not evaluate	**Portfolio is required/is not required**	Portfolios are not required in this program
Mentor remuneration	$400/year	**Higher education affiliation**	None
Cost of program	$200,000	**Funding**	State
Years program in existence	Four years	**Full-time/part-time program coordinator/program coordination is part of another role in system/organization/state**	Program coordination is part of other role in state

Used with permission of Kristi Horrell Pugh, Administrator Program Advisor, Arkansas Department of Education, Columbus, OH.

STATE MANDATES

Is mentoring mandated for new principals?

Yes, mentoring is mandated for new principals.

Is mentoring part of certification or licensure?

Yes, each beginning building-level and curriculum/program administrator must participate in the Arkansas Beginning Administrator Induction Program for a minimum of one year and a maximum of three years. Mentoring is one component of the licensure system that moves a candidate from an Initial Administrator license (three-year nonrenewable) to a Standard Administrator license (five-year renewable).

Is funding provided by the state to support the mandate?

Yes, each beginning administrator (BA)-administrator mentor (AM) pair receives $1,200 per year. The BA is provided $800 in professional development funding, and the AM receives a stipend of $400 for mentoring services.

HISTORY

Why was the program started?

The mission of the program is to establish and maintain high, rigorous standards for what administrators should know and be able to do to result in increased student achievement. Along with the state-adopted performance-based standards-driven licensure system, the mentoring program was put in place to provide support and guidance for new administrators, retain administrators in the profession, and ultimately produce better instructional leaders for greater student achievement.

GOALS

What are the goals of the program?

Administrators in Arkansas play a key leadership role in the education of all students, being responsible for daily management operations and, most important, instructional leadership for all. The purpose and goal of the licensure or mentoring system is to produce a cadre of high-quality instructional leaders possessing the knowledge, skills, and disposition as they relate to everyday leadership of teachers and students, again, ultimately leading to greater student achievement.

PROGRAM DESIGN

Who designed the mentor program?

Stakeholders from around the state designed the program, and included practicing administrators and representatives from the administrators' organizations and associations as well as representatives from the Arkansas Department of Education (ADE) and the institutions of higher education.

What are the components and recommended schedule of the program?

Each BA attends a one-day training with her or his mentor and then attends two one-day regional follow-up sessions (one each semester). Each AM attends a two-day training held statewide.

Are there any programs that complement the mentor program?

No, there aren't any other programs that specifically complement the mentor program.

PROGRAM ADMINISTRATION

Who coordinates the program?

Kristi Pugh, administrator licensure program advisor, coordinates the program.

How is information communicated to shareholders?

The administrator licensure program adviser hosts a variety of meetings throughout the state with school districts, educational service cooperatives, institutions of higher education, and administrator organizations and associations. Information is also distributed through the ADE's Director's Memos.

Who coordinates the integration of this program with other professional development opportunities or requirements in the school or district?

The administrator licensure program advisor coordinates the integration of this program with other professional development opportunities or requirements in the school or district.

PARTICIPATION IN THE PROGRAM

Who is served?

The program serves all beginning building-level administrators (principals, assistant principals, vice principals), curriculum or program administrators, special education program administrators, gifted and talented education program administrators, career and technical and talented educational program administrators, career and technical education program administrators, content area specialist program administrators and curriculum administrators holding an initial administrator license, those employed under an administrator completion program (ALCP), and those holding a standard principal license with less than one year of administrative experience.

Is the participation of new principals voluntary or mandatory?

Program participation is state mandated.

How long is the program?

The mentoring program is a minimum of one year and a maximum of three years.

WHO PROVIDES THE MENTORING AND INDUCTION?

What are the criteria for being a mentor?

Administrator mentors must be licensed administrators (preferably with three years of experience), trained in the Arkansas Administrator Mentor Model, with same grade-level experience sought by the beginning administrator.

Are mentors full-time principals or retired principals?

Most administrator mentors are full-time practicing administrators. Recently retired administrators also qualify to become mentors.

Are mentors from the same district as new principals?

The program recommends that the AM and BA work in the same building. However, with the diversity of school districts and schools, some AMs may work in another school building or another school district.

How are mentors selected?

AMs are selected in a variety of ways. The AM may self-select to attend the mentor training, the superintendent may choose mentors, or the district project director may choose administrators to be mentors.

How are matches made between mentors and new principals?

The BA may choose an AM that she or he already knows and respects, the superintendent may make the match, or the district project director may make the match. Ultimately, the district program director will make sure the match is made and will report the pair to the ADE.

WHAT IS EXPECTED OF MENTORS?

What are the job responsibilities of mentors?

Mentors are responsible for support and guidance of BAs. They coach and give formative feedback to BAs for their growth.

Is the relationship between the mentor and the new principal confidential?

Yes, the information shared between the two should remain between them. Information shared cannot be used for any type of evaluation of the BA.

Are observation and coaching requirements of mentors?

Yes, observation and coaching are required of mentors.

Do mentors formally evaluate new principals?

No, mentors do not formally evaluate new principals.

How much time are mentors expected to work with new principals (weekly, monthly, and for how long)?

There is not a specified amount of time that mentors are expected to work with new principals. They are asked to communicate on a weekly basis, if not daily.

When do mentors meet with the new principals?

When mentors and new principals meet varies with each pair. It depends on whether they are in the same building and/or the same district or whether they have to travel to visit with one another. Each pair sets up its own schedule to best meet the BA's needs.

WHAT SUPPORTS ARE AVAILABLE FOR MENTORS?

Are mentors remunerated?

Yes, each AM receives $400 per BA per year.

Are mentors trained? If so, by whom?

Yes, the ADE conducts mentor training. The ADE trains AM trainers, who then conduct two mentor trainings per year.

Is there professional development for mentors after the initial training? If so, who provides it?

Yes, Day 2 of the state training is specifically geared to provide professional development opportunities for each. They also have opportunities within their district, educational cooperative areas, and other state-sponsored trainings.

Do mentors meet regularly with other mentors? If so, how often and for how long?

No, mentors don't meet regularly with other mentors.

Is there any other ongoing support for mentors? If so, who provides it?

No, this program doesn't provide opportunities for other ongoing support for mentors.

Are any other resources available for mentors?

No, there aren't other resources available for mentors.

Are mentors supervised? If so, by whom and how frequently?

No, mentors aren't supervised.

WHAT IS EXPECTED OF NEW PRINCIPALS REGARDING THEIR PARTICIPATION IN THE MENTORING PROGRAM?

How often do new principals meet with their mentors and for how long?

The frequency of meetings between new principals and their mentors varies with each BA-AM pair. It depends on whether they are in the same building and/or same district, or whether they have to travel to visit with one another. The pair sets up its own schedule to best meet the BA's needs.

Are there other people with whom the new principal meets for mentoring and support?

Yes, each semester the BAs meet in regional follow-up meetings with one another.

Is formative assessment of new principals required? If so, when, how, and by whom?

No, formative assessment of new principals is not required.

Are new principals required to prepare a portfolio?

Yes, new principals are required to prepare a portfolio. However, it is not tied to the mentoring program. New principals are required to prepare a portfolio during their program of study in their preparation program.

ARE ADDITIONAL SUPPORTS AVAILABLE FOR NEW PRINCIPALS?

Is any other professional development provided? If so, when and by whom?

Yes, new principals have professional development opportunities within their district, educational cooperative areas, and other state-sponsored training.

Do new principals meet regularly with other new principals?

Yes, new principals meet with other new principals once a semester, during the regional follow-up meetings.

What resources are required for the mentoring program?

The program cost $200,000 in fiscal year 2004 and included the following:

- Mentor training
- New principal orientation
- Ongoing professional development for mentors and/or new principals
- Food for conferences and meetings
- Materials
- Remuneration for mentors
- Reimbursement at 50 percent for new principals taking the School Leaders Licensure Assessment
- Travel and lodging for mentors

FUNDING

What are the funding sources?

The state appropriates money for induction and mentoring.

Who requests the funding?

The program director of the Office for Professional Quality Enhancement requests the funding for the program.

EVALUATION OF THE PROGRAM

Is the program evaluated formatively? Summatively? Who does the evaluation?

All program participants (BA, AM, presenters, trainers) evaluate the program.

Who sees the results?

Everyone may see the results of the evaluation. However, the program coordinator, trainers, and presenters use the information to constantly tweak the program to make it as effective as possible.

RECRUITMENT, HIRING, AND RETENTION OF NEW STAFF

How many new principals are recruited and hired each year?

The program has trained about 400 BAs.

Are there any data that correlate the mentoring program with the retention of new principals?

The program is in the beginning stages of collecting data.

Are there any data that correlate the mentoring program with the performance of the new principals?

There is no data yet that correlate the mentoring program with the performance of the new principals.

What are the indicators of program success?

The feedback given from the BA and the AM as to how they have benefited from the program and have incorporated the information into their practice indicates the success of the program.

MODEL 4.2

Indiana Principal Leadership Academy

Becca Lamon, Associate Director
IPLA Indiana Department of Education
Room 229, State House, Indianapolis, IN 46204
317-232-9004   blamon@doe.state.in.us
www.doe.state.in.us/ipla

Urban/suburban/rural school	Not applicable	Grade levels of school	Not applicable
Student population	Not applicable	Per pupil expenditure	Not applicable
Mentoring is/is not mandated for ongoing certification/ licensure	Mentoring is mandated for ongoing licensure	Mentoring program is/is not funded by the state	The IPLA is funded by the state
Unique feature of program	There is a voluntary leadership academy, ongoing coursework for licensure, and optional coaching	Duration of program for new principals	One to two years
Mentors are Full-time principals from same district from another district Retired principals	Coaches are full-time principals or recently retired principals from different districts than the new principals	Mentor selection criteria exist/do not exist Mentor matching process exist/do not exist	Coach selection criteria do not exist Coaches are matched by grade level/subject area and geographical proximity to new principals
Mentors are trained/not trained for role Mentors receive/do not receive ongoing support	Coaches are trained for the role Mentors receive ongoing support	Mentors are/are not part of a team to support new principals	Mentors and coaches are part of a team to support new principals
Coaching is/is not a component	Mentoring is a component for two years; coaching is an optional component the second year	Daily/weekly/yearly expectations for mentors	Mentors meet with new principals during the course of two years. Coaches meet with new principals once a month for six months if new principals opt to work with a coach during their second year in the principalship
Mentors evaluate/do not evaluate the new principals	Mentors and coaches do not evaluate new principals	Portfolio is required/not required	State licensure requirements for portfolios have been suspended at this time
Mentor remuneration	$600/year	Higher education affiliation	None
Cost of program	$487,000	Funding	$487,000+ funding from Academy Alumni Association
Years program in existence	16 years	Full-time/part-time program coordinator/ program coordination is part of another role in system/organization/ state	There is typically a full-time executive director and an associate director. The executive director position is currently vacant

STATE MANDATES

Is mentoring mandated for new principals?

Mentoring is mandated for administrators as of 2003. Mentors are still being trained.

Is mentoring part of certification or licensure?

There is a stipulation about mentoring through the Indiana Professional Standards Board, which controls licensure. A trained mentor must mentor a new principal during her or his first two years. The only stipulation is that the mentor can't be in the same district as the new principal. The mentoring is more like collaborative networking—someone to fall back on when the new principals are having issues. There isn't any curriculum. Mentors are paid for their duties as mentors. They are paid $600 for the year, not per mentee. They could be mentoring five people and still get $600. Mentors don't have to be current practitioners. They must hold an administrator's license.

The Professional Standards Board is not connected to the Department of Education (DOE). It has half-day training seminars. The Indiana Principal Leadership Academy (IPLA) has been running a coaching program, independent of the Professional Standards Board, and the coaches have been licensed as mentors. The IPLA is one of the ways that mentors can become licensed in the state.

Is funding provided by the state to support the mandate?

The state provides $487,000 for the IPLA.

HISTORY

Why was the program started?

In 1985 the Indiana General Assembly passed House Enrolled Act 1236, which called for the establishment of a Principal Leadership Academy. In the initial discussions, it was agreed that a principals' academy should be a unique, innovative approach to professional development. To develop the concept, a think tank of over 70 people met during the summer of 1986. The think tank consisted of elementary school, middle school, and high school educators; university and college representatives; business leaders; superintendents; and parents. The challenge was to create a vision for the IPLA (see www.doe .state.in.us/ipla/history.html).

The IPLA is a division of the DOE. Initially, it offered a professional development program for Indiana public school principals. The goal was to improve student achievement by improving public school administration. Now assistant principals are included, and in fiscal year 2005 there is a pilot of the inclusion of some nonpublic school administrators. Through a grant, seven nonpublic school administrators have been accepted.

The IPLA is the overall program. Originally, 25 people entered the program, four times a year. Currently, 100 participants start each June. There have been over 1,800 graduates of the program. The academy also offers professional development opportunities for any educator in the state as well as manages the Indiana Promise grant, through the Wallace Foundation.

GOALS

What are the goals of the program?

The goals of the program are to

- Identify and select principals who have demonstrated a potential for professional self-growth and to develop that potential through an intensive and exciting program

- Create a self-perpetuating cadre of school administrators to serve as facilitators and trainers for other administrators and teachers
- Create an excitement for continuous growth of academy graduates
- Ensure school effectiveness by developing leaders of instructors as well as managerial technicians
- Strengthen leadership skills through exposure to an in-depth application of such administration themes as leadership styles, school culture, school improvement, and communication

PROGRAM DESIGN

Who designed the mentor program?

The IPLA was designed by a collaboration of many people. State Superintendent of Education H. Dean Evans initiated the idea that there was a need to develop programs to support education in the state of Indiana. Jerry DeWitt was a primary developer of the program.

What are the components and recommended schedule of the program?

The components of the program are as follows:

- The IPLA lasts for 18 days over a two-year period. The first day is for orientation and the last day is for graduation.
- Participants take 16 units of Leadership, Culture, Communication, and Teaching and Learning. Within each component are standards that are a combination of the ISLLC standards and the Indiana standards (see the standards on the IPLA Web site).
- A group of trained facilitators participate with each group. Part of their job is working on IPLA curriculum development, along with the executive director and the associate director. That curriculum is presented through national speakers, Indiana practitioners, and also the facilitators.
- One hundred participants are divided into network groups. They are divided by level of administration: elementary, middle, and high school. This promotes networking among the principals. Efforts are made to ensure that no one from the same district is in the same group and that no facilitator is from the same group. Facilitators are in charge of their own group and, together with the nine facilitators, are in charge of the 100 participants.
- Participants pay $110 for the 18 days, which covers the cost of food that isn't covered by funding. School districts cover travel, hotel, and per diem costs.
- Participants meet for two days each in June, November, February, and April plus an extra day in June for the orientation and an extra day in April for the graduation.
- IPLA publishes a quarterly magazine, which was named the Association of Supervision and Curriculum Development (ASCD) newsletter of the year in 2001. All the back issues are on the IPLA Web site. Becca Lamon, the associate director of the IPLA, is the editor of the quarterly magazine. Last year's themes included Overcoming the Barriers of Poverty and Looking at Achievement Gaps.

Are there any programs that complement the mentor program?

IPLA is a professional development program for administrators. It is not a mentoring program per se. It is a program to support new principals. There are some organizations that have workshops with similar goals. For example, Indiana NEXT provides technology professional development. The DOE offers training in looking at data. The Indiana Association of School Principals offers workshops and a two-day conference in November. They have a new principal program and a new administrator workshop in the summer. Steve Heck, the director, can be reached at 800-258-2188.

PROGRAM ADMINISTRATION

Who coordinates the program?

The executive director and the associate director coordinate the IPLA.

There is a Blue Ribbon design team that helps with curricular changes. There is an advisory board, as required by the law, composed of legislators, administrators (superintendents and principals), parents, business partners, university partners, and the executive and associate directors of IPLA.

How is information communicated to shareholders?

IPLA posts information on Supermail, which is the superintendents' electronic mailing system, through the DOE Web site. Past participants are encouraged to tap someone on the shoulder to introduce them to the IPLA. State testing data indicate districts with low student-achievement scores. The IPLA staff meets with the superintendents of those districts, who in turn send new principals.

Who coordinates the integration of this program with other professional development opportunities or requirements in the school or district?

It isn't coordinated. The DOE has just initiated the technical assistance plan. DOE units are starting to collaborate, in response to the No Child Left Behind act. No one in the DOE is doing the same things to support new principals.

PARTICIPATION IN THE PROGRAM

Who is served?

There is an application process of assistant principals and principals who want to participate in the IPLA. Assistant administrators (30 percent of the participants in the program) are now included, and the remaining 70 percent of the participants in the program are elementary and secondary principals. Priority is given to those principals who are sent by their superintendents over those who are self-selecting to apply to the IPLA program. Thus far, anyone who has applied has been accepted. Only assistant principals have been wait-listed. Any principal who applies is accepted.

Is the participation of new principals voluntary or mandatory?

The IPLA is voluntary, unless required by individual superintendents.

How long is the program?

The program lasts 18 months.

WHO PROVIDES THE MENTORING AND INDUCTION?

The facilitators do some mentoring. Second-year participants have a choice of doing assignments, journaling, and watching those programs or being assigned a coach. Those coaches are people who have gone through a coaching training program and have become coaches. This was a pilot program in 2004. If they choose coaching, their coach will visit them once a month from September through

February. The IPLA definition of coaching versus mentoring is that mentoring provides solutions and materials.

There are assignments and requirements to fulfill outside the 18 days. Some of it is journaling and an online streaming video professional development program. *IPLA Today* is a publication that features little 20–30-minute interviews with local administrators, on specific topics, interviewed by the associate director or the executive director at the DOE studio. Participants are assigned to watch several of them. It's an internal program.

What are the criteria for being a coach?

The former executive director selected the coaches. They are not necessarily administrators. Coaches participate in a five-to-seven-day training. Some issues don't require administrative experience, for example, time management or communication problems.

Are coaches full-time principals or retired principals?

Out of 50 coaches, 2 are retired principals and the other 48 are practicing administrators. They are becoming coaches to practice a skill they want to use with their own faculties. Everyone is benefiting.

Are coaches from the same district as new principals?

Coaches are never from the same district as new principals.

How are coaches selected?

At this point in the program, anyone willing to go through the training may do so.

How are matches made between coaches and new principals?

Matches between coaches and new principals are made by grade levels or subject areas and with regard to geographic proximity.

WHAT IS EXPECTED OF COACHES?

What are the job responsibilities of coaches?

Coaches are required to meet with the new principals once a month for six months.

Is the relationship between the coach and the new principal confidential?

The relationship between the coach and the new principal is totally confidential.

Is observation a requirement of coaching?

Coaches are not required to observe new principals. If new principals request it, coaches will observe them.

Do coaches formally evaluate new principals?

No, coaches do not evaluate new principals.

How much time are coaches expected to work with new principals (weekly, monthly, and for how long)?

Coaches meet with new principals for approximately one hour a month.

When do coaches meet with the new principals?

Coaches and new principals mutually agree upon convenient meeting times.

WHAT SUPPORTS ARE AVAILABLE FOR COACHES?

Are coaches remunerated?

Coaches are typically paid $600 for the year, regardless of the number of new principals they coach.

Are coaches trained? If so, by whom?

Yes, coaches are trained by Larry Huggins, a trainer with Huggins and Associates in Vashon, Washington. Ontological coaching is a particular way to look at a problem, asking and exploring what are the perceived barriers and solutions from that person's viewpoint. The goal is to get that person to look at the problem by observing in three ranges of experience: actions, results, and observations.

Is there professional development for coaches after the initial training? If so, who provides it?

The pilot program was in 2004. In 2005, participants will be getting two additional days of training. There is also coaching for coaches, with plans to connect coaches in a coaching situation to other coaches, in other words, peer coaching for coaches.

Do coaches meet regularly with other coaches? If so, how often and for how long?

Coaches see each other during the five to seven days of training.

Is there any other ongoing support for coaches? If so, who provides it?

No, there isn't any other ongoing support for coaches.

Are any other resources available for coaches?

No, there aren't any other resources for coaches.

Are coaches supervised? If so, by whom and how frequently?

No, coaches aren't supervised.

WHAT IS EXPECTED OF NEW PRINCIPALS REGARDING THEIR PARTICIPATION IN THE IPLA PROGRAM?

How often do new principals meet with their coaches and for how long?

New principals typically meet with their coaches for one hour per month for six months.

Are there other people with whom the new principal meets for mentoring and support?

New principals may belong to the IPLA program. They may opt to have a coach in their second year. In their first year, they have to have a state mentor through the licensure board.

Is formative assessment of new principals required? If so, when, how, and by whom?

Formative assessment of new principals is not required as part of the IPLA.

Are new principals required to prepare a portfolio?

Initially, the new licensure program required a portfolio system. There were difficulties when this was being piloted, so for now it is on hold.

ARE ADDITIONAL SUPPORTS AVAILABLE FOR NEW PRINCIPALS?

Is any other professional development provided? If so, when and by whom?

IPLA offers some additional programs that are open to any educational administrators in the state. The DOE and professional organizations also offer professional development sessions.

Do new principals meet regularly with other new principals?

There aren't any regularly scheduled meetings for new principals.

What resources are required for the coaching program?

On average, the cost to put on a session—hotel, food, facility, support staff— is approximately $50,00 for every two-day session.

FUNDING

What are the funding sources?

The funding sources for the IPLA are as follows:

- The Indiana legislature appropriated $487,000 this year for the IPLA. In the past, it was $500,000. The majority of the money supports the academy.
- The Alumni Association. Participants in the academy liked the program so much that they wanted more the following year. So they formed the association and funded a two-day conference that isn't part of the academy. It was open to 500 participants, and academy participants did not receive preferential acceptance. The cost to participants was $150, plus their own food, travel, and lodging. The money made from this two-day conference helps support the academy.

Who requests the funding?

The legislature appropriates the money, and the Alumni Association offered to sponsor a two-day conference.

EVALUATION OF THE PROGRAM

Is the program evaluated formatively? Summatively? Who does the evaluation?

Academy participants use a Scantron to give rank-order responses to eight questions. They are also given an opportunity to write about plusses, changes, and what they will take back from the academy. In addition, facilitators do their own evaluations of their sessions.

Who sees the results?

Facilitators, staff, and presenters see the results of the evaluations. Participants see the numerical results.

RECRUITMENT, HIRING, AND RETENTION OF NEW STAFF

How many new principals are recruited and hired each year?

Not applicable.

Are there any data that correlate the program with the retention of new principals?

There is interest in the retention issue and a desire to create a study of it.

Are there any data that correlate the coaching program with the performance of the new principals?

Program staff believe there is a connection between the IPLA and principal retention; the data haven't yet been collected.

What are the indicators of program success?

The indicators of program success are

- Evaluations
- Word of mouth
- The desire of participants for more days after the academy was over
- Utilization of the materials by the participants
- The duration of the program, which has sustained itself for 16 years
- Requests for coaching; last year, out of 104 participants, 94 requested coaching

MODEL 4.3

Mississippi Beginning Principal Mentorship Program and the Beginning Principals Network

Joan Haynie, Division Director
Office of Leadership Development
Beginning Principals Network
359 North West Street
P.O. Box 771, Jackson, MS 39205
601-359-3506   jhaynie@mde.k12.ms.us

Urban/suburban/rural school	Not applicable	Grade levels of school	Not applicable
Student population	Not applicable	Per pupil expenditure	Not applicable
Mentoring is/is not mandated for ongoing certification/licensure	Mentoring is not mandated	Mentoring program is/is not funded by the state	Is sometimes funded by the state
Unique feature of program	Training for mentors and new principals; 90 contact hours between mentors and new principals	Duration of program for new principals	One year

Mentors are
Full-time principals
  from same district
  from another district
Retired principals
	Mentors are full-time and/or retired principals	Mentor selection criteria exist/do not exist
		
		Mentor matching process exists/does not exist
			Selection criteria are stated in the law.
			
			The matching process does exist, at the discretion of each region

Mentors are trained/not trained for role Mentors receive/do not receive ongoing support	Mentors are trained; Mentors receive ongoing support	Mentors are/are not part of a team to support new principals	Mentors are part of a team to support new principals
Coaching is/is not a component	Coaching is a component	Daily/weekly/yearly expectations for mentor	90 contact hours during the year
Mentors evaluate/do not evaluate the new principals	Mentors do not evaluate	Portfolio is required/is not required	Portfolios are not required
Mentor remuneration	Varies by each program	Higher education affiliation	Varies by each program
Cost of program	$131,000 to start it	Funding	State legislature
Years program in existence	Five years	Full-time/part-time program coordinator/program coordination is part of another role in system/organization/state	Coordination is part of another role

Used with permission of Pamela M. Felder, the Beginning Principals Network.

STATE MANDATES

Is mentoring mandated for new principals?

The program was established by legislative mandate (MS Code 37-9-251). However, participation is voluntary.

Is mentoring part of certification or licensure?

No, mentoring is not part of certification.

Is funding provided by the state to support the mandate?

The legislature provided full funding for the first year of the program but reduced it by 50 percent during the second and third years. Although not funded for fiscal year 2005, it is hoped funding will be restored in fiscal year 2006.

HISTORY

Why was the program started?

The Beginning Principal Mentorship Program was established to provide first-year principals with continued and sustained support from a formally assigned mentor during their first full year of principal service.

GOALS

What are the goals of the program?

The goals of the program are to

- Support new principals
- Retain the beginning principals

PROGRAM DESIGN

Who designed the mentor program?

The School Executive Management Institute within the Mississippi Department of Education designed the program according to specifications in the Mississippi Code. Based on an application process, the state funded one mentorship program in each of five congressional districts within the state.

What are the components and recommended schedule of the program?

The components of the program are as follows:

- It provides 90 contact hours between the beginning principals and the mentors. These could include training at which they both participate, one-on-one visits to the school, and telephone conversations.
- Training is embedded in the program. There is training of the mentors and the beginning principals.

Are there any programs that complement the mentor program?

Orientation for School Leaders is a 10-day training program required of all entry-level administrators, regardless of their position. This training provides an introduction and orientation to leading Mississippi schools.

The Beginning Principals Network provides current information and continuing support for first-year principals. Content is determined by the expressed needs of each group.

A selection of additional training programs offered through the School Executive Management Institute provides opportunities for principals to increase their knowledge and skills in leading school improvement.

PROGRAM ADMINISTRATION

Who coordinates the program?

Barbara Miller coordinates the Beginning Principal Mentorship Program and the Orientation School Leaders training. Pamela Felder and Joan Haynie coordinate the Beginning Principals Network.

How is information communicated to shareholders?

Information is communicated in a variety of ways, including

- Meetings of the shareholders
- The requests for proposals (RFPs)
- Consortia in each congressional district
- University communiqués
- Consortium of school districts
- Flyers
- E-mail
- Face-to-face conversations
- Telephone calls
- Newsletters

Who coordinates the integration of this program with other professional development opportunities or requirements in the school or district?

Professional development coordinators, or curriculum coordinators, will often integrate the professional development offerings in their district with the offerings by the state in their region.

The state does the majority of professional development offerings for administrators, who must renew their license every five years.

PARTICIPATION IN THE PROGRAM

Who is served?

The Beginning Principal Mentorship Program was designed for eligible beginning principals in Mississippi. To participate in the program, beginning principals need to possess an administrator's license, be employed as a principal by a public school district, and have served fewer than 90 consecutive days as a licensed principal.

Is participation of new principals voluntary or mandatory?

Participation in the Beginning Principals Network and the Beginning Principal Mentorship Program is voluntary.

How long is the program?

The program is for one year.

WHO PROVIDES THE MENTORING AND INDUCTION?

What are the criteria for being a mentor?
Mentor principals must

- Possess a standard administrator's license
- Be employed by or retired from a public school district
- Have successfully served for three or more years as a licensed principal in any public school
- Demonstrate mastery of administrative skills and subject matter knowledge
- Attend training provided by the Mississippi Department of Education and the mentoring program within their congressional district

Are mentors full-time principals or retired principals?
Mentors are full-time and/or retired principals.

Are mentors from the same district as new principals?
Mentors are not usually from the same school district. Sometimes principals may request someone from their district, though that is not typical.

How are mentors selected?
Mentorship program coordinators in each congressional district select mentors according to established criteria.

How are matches made between mentors and new principals?
Matches of mentors and beginning principals are made according to the needs of the beginning principal and the level of the principal.

WHAT IS EXPECTED OF MENTORS?

What are the job responsibilities of mentors?
Formal assistance provided by a mentor principal to a beginning principal includes

- Direct administrative observation and consultation
- Assistance in administrative planning and preparation
- Support in implementation and delivery of principal administrative responsibilities
- Support in the administrative functions of school leadership

A minimum of 90 hours, over the course of a year, of direct contact between mentor principals and beginning principals, including observation and assistance with administrative duties, or both, during the school day, is required.

Is the relationship between the mentor and the new principal confidential?
Yes, the relationship between the mentor and the new principal is confidential.

Are observation and coaching requirements of mentors?
Yes, observation of the beginning principal and consultation by the mentor are required in the program.

Do mentors formally evaluate new principals?
No, mentors do not evaluate new principals.

How much time are mentors expected to work with new principals (weekly, monthly, and for how long)?
Mentors meet with beginning principals a minimum of 90 contact hours.

When do mentors meet with the new principals?
Mentors meet with new principals during the school day, in their buildings, and at joint trainings.

WHAT SUPPORTS ARE AVAILABLE FOR MENTORS?

Are mentors remunerated?
Remuneration of mentors is determined by each mentorship program.

Are mentors trained? If so, by whom?
The state contracted with Dr. John Daresh to provide training for all mentors. Each program provides additional training as needed.

Is there professional development for mentors after the initial training? If so, who provides it?
Dr. Daresh has provided three follow-up trainings for mentors.

Do mentors meet regularly with other mentors? If so, how often and for how long?
The state does not facilitate regularly scheduled meetings of mentors. However, each regional program may do so.

Is there any other ongoing support for mentors? If so, who provides it?
Regional programs may choose to support mentors.

Are any other resources available for mentors?
Additional resources for mentors are at the discretion of the program coordinators.

Are mentors supervised? If so, by whom and how frequently?
The coordinator of each regional program oversees mentor activities.

WHAT IS EXPECTED OF NEW PRINCIPALS REGARDING THEIR PARTICIPATION IN THE MENTORING PROGRAM?

How often do new principals meet with their mentors and for how long?
New principals meet with their mentors for a minimum of 90 contact hours during the school year.

Are there other people with whom the new principal meets for mentoring and support?

No other people are required to mentor or support the new principals.

Is formative assessment of new principals required? If so, when, how, and by whom?

Principals are required to be evaluated by the local district. However, procedures and criteria are local options.

Are new principals required to prepare a portfolio?

No, new principals are not required to prepare a portfolio.

ARE ADDITIONAL SUPPORTS AVAILABLE FOR NEW PRINCIPALS?

Is any other professional development provided? If so, when and by whom?

The School Executive Management Institute (SEMI) also offers the Beginning Principals Network to provide current information and continuing support for first-year principals. Content is determined by the expressed needs of each group. Four to five full-day sessions are held during the school year. Completion applies to license renewal.

SEMI also offers a number of additional training programs from which principals can select to increase their knowledge and skills in leading school improvement.

Do new principals meet regularly with other new principals?

Principals who join the network meet regularly. Several regional school district consortia also host meetings for principals.

What resources are required for the mentoring program?

The resources required are

- Travel: Reimbursement for expenses
- Personnel services: Honoraria for mentors, fees for facilitators and presenters
- Contractual: Meeting space, equipment rental, and printing
- Commodities: Instructional materials, supplies, and refreshments

Each project proposed a budget based on their goals and plans. Initially, funds were distributed equally to each program. The next time, the funds were distributed to each program according to the number of principals served. They budgeted their allocations within the categories.

FUNDING

What are the funding sources?

The legislature funded the program in fiscal years 2000, 2001, and 2004, as follows:

- Fiscal year 2000: Development and delivery of training for 33 beginning principals and 24 mentors. Grants to five congressional districts totaled $131,363.

- Fiscal year 2001: Mentoring program awarded continuation. Grants to the five congressional districts totaled $75,000.

- Fiscal year 2002: Development of customized online professional development training through a contract with ACTV in order to reach a larger audience.

- Fiscal year 2003: Completion and distribution of three customized online professional development training modules for beginning principals. Piloted the Beginning Principals Network for 25 first-year principals.

- Fiscal year 2004: Continued the Beginning Principals Network for career-level principals in their first year. Provided online professional development training modules for all beginning principals. Reinstatement of the Beginning Principal Mentoring Programs in the five congressional districts; grants totaled $60,000.

Who requests the funding?

The Department of Education requests funding for the program from the legislature annually.

EVALUATION OF THE PROGRAM

Is the program evaluated formatively? Summatively? Who does the evaluation?

Barbara Miller, the coordinator of the program, evaluated the mentorship program in the second year through a telephone survey. She called each new principal for feedback.

In addition, each program evaluates itself. The training was evaluated in written responses.

Who sees the results?

A report is presented to the Mississippi legislature annually.

RECRUITMENT, HIRING, AND RETENTION OF NEW STAFF

How many new principals are recruited and hired each year?

This information is not available.

Are there any data that correlate the mentoring program with the retention of new principals?

This information is not available.

Are there any data that correlate the mentoring program with the performance of the new principals?

This information is not available.

What are the indicators of program success?

Comments about the program from participants include the following:

The importance to me was hearing others' problems, solutions, etc. They are all the same, but we don't know that always. . . . I would like to have a follow-up meeting next year.

The information from the State Department was very informative. The presenters were very good—State Department, other principals, and outside presenters. The network should be continued for beginning principals because it does give them a lot of support.

The network was helpful for me because as a first-year principal, I needed the support of others who were experiencing some of the same feeling situations. I believe I have developed a network of references who I can contact for help in the future. Much of the information has been useful. I certainly think that next year's group of first-year principals would benefit from the program.

I think the most useful thing for me was being in a collaborative atmosphere and being able to share problems and triumphs in a nonthreatening atmosphere.

MODEL 4.4

Ohio Entry-Year Program for Principals

Deborah Miller, Liaison to the Entry-Year Program for Principals
Ohio Department of Education
25 South Front Street, Mailstop 504, Columbus, OH 43215
614-728-6914   deborah.miller@ode.state.oh.us

Urban/suburban/rural school	Not applicable	Grade levels of school	Not applicable
Student population	Not applicable	Per pupil expenditure	Not applicable
Mentoring is/is not mandated for ongoing certification/ licensure	Mentoring is mandated	Mentoring program is/is not funded by the state	Is funded by the state
Unique feature of program	Performance-based professional development	Duration of program for new principals	Two years

Mentors are
Full-time principals
    from same district
    from another district
Retired principals
	Mentors are full-time or recently retired administrators from different districts or same district, if so requested by superintendent	Mentor selection criteria exist/do not exist
		
		Mentor matching process exists/does not exist
			Selection criteria do exist
			
			Matching process does exist

Mentors are trained/not trained for role Mentors receive/do not receive ongoing support	Mentors are trained Mentors do receive ongoing support	Mentors are/are not part of a team to support new principals	Mentors are part of a team to support new principals
Coaching is/is not a component	Coaching is a component	Daily/weekly/yearly expectations for mentor	Expectations in terms of time are not stated
Mentors evaluate/do not evaluate the new principals	Mentors do not evaluate	Portfolio is required/is not required	Portfolio is required
Mentor remuneration	$750 for two years	Higher education affiliation	None
Cost of program	$800,000 for entire state	Funding	Ohio DOE
Years program in existence	Two years that it has been required following a four-year pilot program	Full-time/part-time program coordinator/ program coordination is part of another role in system/organization/ state	There are three regional coordinators and one state liaison who do this work as part of their total job description

Used with permission of Deborah Miller, the Ohio Department of Education.

STATE MANDATES

Is mentoring mandated for new principals?

Yes, there is a statute requiring a structured program of support, including mentoring, for entry-year principals and assistant principals.

Is mentoring part of certification or licensure?

Yes, mentoring is required to move from a two-year provisional principal license to a five-year professional license.

Is funding provided by the state to support the mandate?

Yes. The state provides funds to cover the registration cost and fees—approximately $1,300 for program costs per entry-year principal.

Mentors are given $500 for their first year of service and $250 for the second year with the entry-year principal(s) with whom they work. Mentors are paid for each entry-year principal they mentor.

HISTORY

Why was the program started?

Effective instructional leadership in each school building is seen as a key element in the quest for student success. However, today's principals face a myriad of managerial responsibilities that can easily become overwhelming and cause them to overlook their most important responsibility—instructional leadership to increase teacher effectiveness and student learning. This program is designed to provide support to principals in the early stages of their careers, to increase their effectiveness in instructional leadership and management, and to attract more quality educators to this important professional role.

GOALS

What are the goals of the program?

The goals of the program are to

- Provide leadership and learning support systems for entry-year principals and assistant principals
- Provide a collaborative learning community to share best practices and ideas with higher education's principal preparation programs
- Create a statewide community of learners to best assist in reshaping the role of the principal to meet the challenges of the 21st century
- Fulfill the requirements for Ohio Administrative Code 3301-24909, Performance-Based Licensure for Administrators

PROGRAM DESIGN

Who designed the mentor program?

The Ohio Entry-Year Program for Principals began in 1997 when representatives from four Ohio universities (Ashland University, Kent State University, Ohio State University, and the University of Dayton) received grants to begin entry-year programs for principals in a competitive Ohio Department of Education (ODE) Entry-Year grant process. Two of the pilot programs were based around administrative portfolio development, while the third program focused on a first-year handbook for principals.

A portfolio was used to measure the performance of principals in each of the six Interstate School Leaders Licensure Consortium (ISLLC) Standards for School Leaders.

ODE grants were made available to five regions of the state (central, northwest, northeast, southeast, and southwest) beginning in fiscal year 2000. Institutions of higher education were required to work with each other in order to qualify for funding. The intent was to design consortia across the state. The Ohio Entry-Year Program for Principals pilot was funded from 1999 through 2003 in the same five regions.

What are the components and recommended schedule of the program?

The Ohio Entry-Year Program for Principals is organized into three regions of the state, with a coordinator for each region. Entry-year principals are paired for their first two years with a mentor who is a practicing or recently retired principal and who has completed the mentor training program. The mentors receive a stipend for their services. Each region hosts activities to provide professional development for whole and/or cluster groups. Activities are based on the ISLLC standards.

Each entry-year principal (EYP) enrolls in the entry-year program and selects a content track, which includes the following:

- Beginning Administrators' Program, developed by the Ohio Association of Secondary School Administrators
- Standards Aligned Instructional Leadership (SAIL), developed by the Ohio Association of Elementary School Administrators

The components of the Ohio Entry-Year Program for Principals are as follows:

- Preassessment: The EYP's portfolio will utilize the ISLLC School Leaders' Self-Inventory. This inventory is available through the Council of Chief State School Officers (CCSSO) in their *Collaborative Professional Development Process for School Leaders* booklet.
- With the help of their mentors, participants use the results from their inventory to develop a personal learning plan.
- Mentoring support is two years.
- The program works with mentors to give them a minimum of six structured meeting times for mentors and EYPs to come together on a regional or subregional basis. Each of those meetings would be on one of the ISLLC standards. Mentors communicate with new principals during school visits, online, and through the logs kept by the new principals.
- Mentors and entry-year principals and assistant principals receive a copy of *The Portable Mentor.*
- Personal learning plan, which the mentors help the EYP create, using the information from their self-assessment and school improvement plan, becomes a focal point of their program.
- Professional Practice Portfolio, which is the documentation of their professional growth, is a very important requirement regardless of the track chosen by each EYP. This portfolio shows the growth in each of the ISLCC standards.
- Postassessment, using the ISLLC School Leaders Self-Inventory, determines their growth.
- The content includes
  - Instructional Leadership
  - Ohio Academic Content Standards
  - Impact of Leadership on Student Achievement
- End-of-program assessment is required.

Are there any programs that complement the mentor program?

There are many programs throughout the state that are based on the ISLLC standards. They are offered by educational service centers and regional professional development centers. There are also programs through SAIL that extend beyond the entry year. These are also available for veteran and experienced principals.

PROGRAM ADMINISTRATION

Who coordinates the program?

Deborah Miller is the ODE liaison, and there are three regional coordinators. Deborah hosts the planning meetings, prepares the agendas, and gets program approval for content tracks.

How is information communicated to shareholders?

An entry-year information packet for principals is electronically sent out in the beginning of the school year to all superintendents, fiscal agents of the districts, and entry-year coordinators. Each school district is required to have an entry-year program and someone who is coordinating that program. (In most districts, it's a part-time position, though in very large districts there may be several entry-year coordinators.)

Who coordinates the integration of this program with other professional development opportunities or requirements in the school or district?

The entry-year coordinators assume responsibility for the integration of professional development opportunities and requirements in the school districts with the entry-year program.

PARTICIPATION IN THE PROGRAM

Who is served?

Principals and assistant principals are required to complete the entry-year program if they are employed full time in the same assignment under a two-year provisional principal license effective in 2003 or later in their area of licensure for at least 120 days. Successful completion of the Entry-Year Program for Principals allows the EYP to advance to a five-year professional principal license.

Is the participation of new principals voluntary or mandatory?

It is mandatory for EYPs to successfully complete the entry-year program to advance to the five-year license.

How long is the program?

The program lasts two years.

WHO PROVIDES THE MENTORING AND INDUCTION?

What are the criteria for being a mentor?

The criteria for being a mentor are as follows. A mentor

- Must be a current or recently retired administrator, with some type of principal experience
- Must have familiarity with ISLLC standards
- Must have completed the ODE day-long mentor training, which includes an overview of the content tracks, components of the program, and adult learning theory and training

Are mentors full-time principals or retired principals?

Mentors are full-time or recently retired administrators who have experience as building principals.

Are mentors from the same district as new principals?

It is strongly recommended that mentors be from the same county so they may make on-site visits. The regional coordinators confer with the district superintendents before assigning a mentor. A superintendent may want in-district mentors, and if so, they will be trained in October.

How are mentors selected?

In the summer of 2003, the ODE trained over 200 mentors and now has 260 mentors in the database. The regional coordinators make the mentor selection based on the matching factors cited below, as well as by speaking with the superintendents.

How are matches made between mentors and new principals?

Each EYP is assigned a trained mentor who will provide guidance and support during the entry-year program. Regional coordinators will contact district superintendents to discuss assigning trained mentors for EYPs. Additional mentor training sessions will be available if superintendents wish to assign administrators who have not received previous training.

Geographic proximity, similar school level (elementary or secondary), and needs of the EYP as suggested by the district superintendents are the considerations for matches made by the regional coordinators. All the regional coordinators come to the mentor trainings, so they each have basic knowledge of the mentors in their region.

WHAT IS EXPECTED OF MENTORS?

What are the job responsibilities of mentors?

The job responsibilities of the mentors are to

- Schedule individual visits with mentees as determined by mentees' needs
- Document mentoring activities through minutes or logs submitted after activities
- Attend regional mentor-mentee meetings as scheduled
- Attend state-sponsored mentor training meetings as scheduled
- Attend mentor-mentee subregional cluster group meetings as scheduled
- Conduct self-appraisal activities and feedback opportunities as needed
- Assist mentees in the review of their content option requirements as needed
- Assist mentees in the review of their Professional Practice Portfolio as needed
- Develop the personal learning plan, based on the self-assessment data and school data
- Assist in assembling the performance-based portfolio, including help with the reflection questions and documentation
- Participate in the evaluation of the project as needed

Is the relationship between the mentor and the new principal confidential?

Yes, the relationship is confidential, and that is part of the mentor training.

Are observation and coaching requirements of mentors?

Observation and coaching are desirable though not requirements. Some coaches are too far away to observe, since mileage is not paid.

Do mentors formally evaluate new principals?

Mentors do not evaluate new principals.

How much time are mentors expected to work with new principals (weekly, monthly, and for how long)?

At this time, there are not any stated time parameters for mentors, though they do keep a log of their meetings.

When do mentors meet with the new principals?

Mentors and new principals meet at mutually agreed-upon times. There are also six regional or subregional meetings over the two-year period required for EYPs and optional for mentors.

WHAT SUPPORTS ARE AVAILABLE FOR MENTORS?

Are mentors remunerated?

Yes, mentors receive $500 the first year and $250 the second year for each EYP.

Are mentors trained? If so, by whom?

Fred Lindley, who is also one of the regional coordinators, does the mentor training. The materials are provided; mentors pay for their lodging and travel expenses.

Is there professional development for mentors after the initial training? If so, who provides it?

After the initial mentor training, there are updated postings on the ODE Web site, as well as a database for communication. When more funds are available, the intent is to provide continued training for mentors. Any assigned mentors are welcome to attend the new training to learn any updates on the program since they were initially trained.

Do mentors meet regularly with other mentors? If so, how often and for how long?

Mentors do not regularly meet with other mentors at this time.

Is there any other ongoing support for mentors? If so, who provides it?

The mentors and EYPs may attend regional and subregional sessions together. These sessions are not required of mentors, yet mentors report that when they are able to attend, they are getting as much out of them as the EYPs.

Are any other resources available for mentors?

Online resources and publications are available for mentors. A mentoring section on the entry-year Web site is a goal.

Are mentors supervised? If so, by whom and how frequently?

Mentors agree to complete the terms of the agreement and also keep a log of their meetings with the EYP. The mentors and the EYPs complete anonymous surveys at the end of the program, which also give feedback on mentors.

WHAT IS EXPECTED OF NEW PRINCIPALS REGARDING THEIR PARTICIPATION IN THE MENTORING PROGRAM?

How often do new principals meet with their mentors and for how long?
Mentors and new principals decide the frequency of their meetings.

Are there other people with whom the new principal meets for mentoring and support?
The entry-year coordinators in each district are also supports for the EYPs.

Is formative assessment of new principals required? If so, when, how, and by whom?
The self-assessment at the beginning of the program is the formative assessment of the EYPs.

Are new principals required to prepare a portfolio?
Each EYP must document professional development and growth during the entry-year program in a Professional Practice Portfolio. The portfolio is submitted for performance-based assessment in March of the second year. EYPs receive guidance and support creating their portfolios from their mentors and through regional meetings.

ARE ADDITIONAL SUPPORTS AVAILABLE FOR NEW PRINCIPALS?

Is any other professional development provided? If so, when and by whom?
The ODE and the two principals' associations, elementary and secondary, offer many programs throughout the year.

Do new principals meet regularly with other new principals?
Because of the required programs, EYPs get together in their content track meetings or their regional meetings.

What resources are required for the mentoring program?
The resources (for fiscal year 2005, $800,000 is budgeted) for the two-year program (for 150–200 EYPs per year) are the following:

- $1,100 per EYP to cover content track for professional development (which goes to the principals' associations as providers)
- $750 over two years for mentor stipends for each EYP served
- $40,000–$50,000 for mentor training over the two years
- $300,000 ($100,000 each) for the regional sites for salaries, materials for participants, office expenses, and meeting costs
- $5,000 per year for each subregional liaison

FUNDING

What are the funding sources?
The ODE funds the program registration costs for each EYP. Travel and lodging expenses are the responsibility of the EYP.

Who requests the funding?

School districts do not request funding for the Entry-Year Program for Principals. The ODE disburses all funds directly to the content providers and mentors.

EVALUATION OF THE PROGRAM

Is the program evaluated formatively? Summatively? Who does the evaluation?

A program review each spring includes

- A panel of some of the trained mentors, who discuss the components of the program with the coordinators
- Online or paper survey results from mentors and mentees
- A compilation of the results by an independent consultant and shared at the end of August

Who sees the results?

All the content providers, regional coordinators, and ODE staff on the project see the results of the evaluation.

RECRUITMENT, HIRING, AND RETENTION OF NEW STAFF

How many new principals are recruited and hired each year?

In 2003–2004, there were 154 EYPs. In 2004–2005, approximately 200 EYPs are projected.

Are there any data that correlate the mentoring program with the retention of new principals?

The program just started as a required program. The results from the pilot were very positive. People who participated in the entry-year program, specifically the portfolio and mentoring pieces, tended to stay in the profession. Many have made collateral moves, staying in the profession of educational administration.

Are there any data that correlate the mentoring program with the performance of the new principals?

One comment was, "The entire program contributed to my success as an EYP this year."

What are the indicators of program success?

Said one principal, "All the components in the program are important in their own right. However, the most important component is to have face-to-face contact on a regular basis to discuss routine events, situations, and scenarios."

MODEL 4.5

Tennessee Academy for School Leaders (TASL)

Dennis Bunch, Director
710 James Robertson Parkway, 4th Floor
Andrew Johnson Tower, Nashville, TN 37243-0376
615-532-6205   Dennis.Bunch@state.tn.us

Urban/suburban/rural school	Not applicable	Grade levels of school	Not applicable
Student population	Not applicable	Per pupil expenditure	Not applicable
Mentoring is/is not mandated for ongoing certification/ licensure	Mentoring is mandated	Mentoring program is/is not funded by the state	Not funded
Unique feature of program	New principals pick their mentors	Duration of program for new principals	Two years
Mentors are Full-time principals from same district/ from another district Retired principals	Mentors are full-time principals from another district	Mentor selection criteria exist/do not exist Mentor matching process exists/does not exist	Mentor selection criteria do exist Mentors matching process does exist
Mentors are trained/not trained for role Mentors receive/do not receive ongoing support	Mentors are trained Mentors receive ongoing support	Mentors are/are not part of a team to support new principals	Mentors are part of a team to support new principals
Coaching is/is not a component	Coaching is a component	Daily/weekly/yearly expectations for mentor	Monthly meetings are expected
Mentors evaluate/do not evaluate the new principals	Mentors do not evaluate	Portfolio is required/is not required	Not required
Mentor remuneration	None	Higher education affiliation	None
Cost of program	$199,000	Funding	DOE
Years program in existence	10 years	Full-time/part-time program coordinator/program coordination is part of another role in system/organization/ state	Full-time director

Used with permission of Dennis Bunch, the Tennessee Academy for School Leaders.

STATE MANDATES

Is mentoring mandated for new principals?

No, mentoring is not mandated through legislative action, the Tennessee Department of Education, or the State Board of Education rules and regulations.

Is mentoring part of certification or licensure?

Yes, every new-to-the-role school administrator begins with a Beginning Administrators License (BAL). To earn a Professional Administrators License (PAL) they are required to have had a mentor as part of the transition process.

Is funding provided by the state to support the mandate?

There is not a mandate, and there is no funding for mentoring.

HISTORY

Why was the program started?

The program was started to support new principals.

GOALS

What is the goal of the program?

The goal of the program is to help new administrators earn the PAL. New administrators must complete items on a checklist. Every one of those items is built into the Beginning Principals Academy (BPA); there are also other items integral to the principalship. (This program does not license. It does every component on the checklist but doesn't sign off on their application. The University of Memphis signs off on the checklist.)

PROGRAM DESIGN

Who designed the mentor program?

Dr. Marty Alberg and Dr. Dean Butler, in conjunction with the Department of Education, developed the BPA to fulfill the requirements for moving from the BAL to the PAL. The directors for the Tennessee Association of School Leaders (TASL) had a hand in designing the program. Elizabeth Vaughn-Neely was the first to bring the mentors together to meet before they were assigned to the protégés. Dennis Bunch, the director of TASL, now does training for the mentors, prior to the training for new principals, who are called protégés in this program.

What are the components and recommended schedule of the program?

The components of the program are as follows:

- The BPA is a two-year program.
- Tennessee requires 72 hours of professional development for administrators every five years; that's nine days in a five-year cycle. The BPA makes the most of those days. They break the days into four two-day sessions, fall and spring each of the first two years.
- Each mentor has a maximum of five protégés; typically it is a 4:1 ratio. The protégés self-select their mentors.

- The year 2004 marked the 10th cohort and the 10th year of the BPA. The program has been refined and remodeled regarding who delivers the content. BPA responds to the request of participants for specific information in certain areas. BPA will not cover material it covered in the Assistant Principals Academy (APA) such as time management, conflict resolution, issues of fit—professional attitudes profile—to see how they will fit into the principalship. Principals who have never been assistant principals may attend some of the APA for some of the pieces they may want to study. If they get into the survival mode in October and November and haven't reached disillusionment yet, they are starting to reach for tools. They may come to APA and go through the program for strategies to use in specific situations they face at work. Those academies run in different months: two days in the fall and two days in the spring. The BPA is in August and April, the APA in September and March.

Curriculum Components:

- Data Analysis
- Tennessee School Improvement Planning
- Communications
- Dealing With the Media
- Team Building
- Leadership Styles and Theory
- Tennessee School Improvement Planning Process (TSIP) Evaluation and Effectiveness
- School Law
- Tennessee School Climate Inventory (TSCI) Initial Application: TSCI Debriefing/Interpretation
- TSCI Second Application: TSCI Debriefing and Interpretation
- Myers-Briggs Type Inventory (MBTI) Administration: MBTI Interpretations
- School Safety
- Teacher Evaluations: Positive and Negative Feedback Sessions
- Introduction to the ISLLC standards
- Principal Self-Assessment Survey (PSAS) Application: PSAS Debriefing and Interpretation
- Politics and Ethics in the Principalship

Are there any programs that complement the mentor program?

The entire spectrum of TASL supports principals. That spectrum includes

- The promotion of student achievement through excellence in school leadership
- Induction academies for beginning principals, assistant principals, and directors
- Data-driven decision making
- A $2.7 million grant from Gates Institute for School Leaders
- Professional learning communities

PROGRAM ADMINISTRATION

Who coordinates the program?

The TASL office coordinates the program. Dennis Bunch came to the department in 2000 to head the BPA.

How is information communicated to shareholders?

Information is shared through

- The TASL Web site: www.k-12.state.tn.us/tpd/tasl.htm
- Trifold brochures, which are sent to professional development centers, urban centers, and DOE presenters
- Word of mouth

Who coordinates the integration of this program with other professional development opportunities or requirements in the school or district?

The superintendents and supervisors coordinate the integration of this program with their professional development opportunities and requirements. The larger systems can custom tailor their programs to complement the TASL program. It is therefore very important for TASL to make its efforts known to them so they are not trying to replicate TASL's services.

PARTICIPATION IN THE PROGRAM

Who is served?

First- or second-year principals from Memphis City to Bristol City are served by the academy. Mentoring is now available for beginning supervisors in the Beginning Supervisors Academy. Supervisors are in the central office. Their program is very much the same thing as BPA.

Is the participation of new principals voluntary or mandatory?

Participation is voluntary. This is one way to do all of the 72 hours of professional development required for certification from the same provider.

How long is the program?

This program lasts two TASL years: fall through spring and the next fall through spring.

WHO PROVIDES THE MENTORING AND INDUCTION?

What are the criteria for being a mentor?

Mentors are experienced principals who display evidence of student achievement (growth) at their schools, as based on state testing data.

Are mentors full-time principals or retired principals?

Mentors are active, full-time principals.

Are mentors from the same district as new principals?

No, protégés are encouraged to not select a mentor from their district.

How are mentors selected?

Mentors are selected by the TASL director, with approval by the superintendent of schools.

How are matches made between mentors and new principals?

Protégés select their own mentors. There is a storyboard for each mentor that includes the following information about each mentor: demographics, personal information, and information about their schools. The storyboard is the first introduction to the potential population of mentors. Protégés look at each of the storyboards in a "wall walk." Then the mentors come and introduce themselves, one at a time, to the group. The protégés select their mentors after these two ways of learning about the mentors.

WHAT IS EXPECTED OF MENTORS?

What are the job responsibilities of mentors?

The director of the program describes the responsibilities of the mentors as delivering the world to the new principals. Mentors are the ears. There is a distinct difference between coaches and mentors. Coaches can keep the protégés at arm's length and protect them. TASL wants mentors to start as coaches. A mentor will welcome the protégés. The more time they spend with the protégés, the more phone calls they make, the closer they get. The mentors no longer keep the protégés at arm's length. At this point, they are not only functioning as coaches, they are mentors.

Is the relationship between the mentor and the new principal confidential?

The relationship is almost completely confidential. There is one piece of documentation on the checklist that mentors have to make public. The director of TASL reads the document. They have a conversation in front of the other protégés in their mentor's group. This conversation is about the protégé's strengths and weaknesses. The mentor and protégé look at the weaknesses together and make an Individual Professional Development plan (IPD). This IPD is required of every principal transitioning from the BAL to the PAL. This happens in the middle of the two years. Mentors have a list of TASL offerings outside the program. They become action steps. The IPD is signed by the mentor, protégé, and superintendent.

Are observation and coaching requirements of mentors?

Coaching is required. First, the protégés become finely tuned managers. Then they can be instructional leaders. Mentors do not observe.

Do mentors formally evaluate new principals?

No, they do not formally evaluate new principals. Protégés may request informal evaluations.

How much time are mentors expected to work with new principals (weekly, monthly, and for how long)?

Typically, the mentor and protégé meet monthly over a two-year period; it varies at different times of the year. These meetings may include phone calls and e-mails as well as an on-site visit.

When do mentors meet with the new principals?

They meet during the two-day sessions, for a total of eight days. The ninth day is a site visit at which the protégé goes to the mentor's school.

WHAT SUPPORTS ARE AVAILABLE FOR MENTORS?

Are mentors remunerated?

Mentors are not remunerated. Expenses are reimbursed for attending the two-day sessions.

Are mentors trained? If so, by whom?

The director trains the mentors in the TASL office. Before the initial meeting with protégés, there is a one-day training for mentors.

Is there professional development for mentors after the initial training? If so, who provides it?

No, there is no additional professional development.

Do mentors meet regularly with other mentors? If so, how often and for how long?

No, mentors do not meet regularly with other mentors.

Is there any other ongoing support for mentors? If so, who provides it?

There is a mentor liaison, a recent retiree, who is very active in the state organization. His job is to maintain frequent contact with the mentors to assess their needs.

Are any other resources available for mentors?

Other resources for mentors include Web sites, the DOE, and the electronic community. There are field service centers (FSCs), which are three regional offices in each of three grand divisions. The personnel are available to answer questions and also to do on-site training.

Are mentors supervised? If so, by whom and how frequently?

To support mentors, there is now a mentor liaison because it is important to stay in constant contact with the mentors. The liaison assesses the strengths of the mentors and what makes them the best mentors. The purpose of the assessment is to strengthen the program, not to evaluate the mentors.

WHAT IS EXPECTED OF NEW PRINCIPALS REGARDING THEIR PARTICIPATION IN THE MENTORING PROGRAM?

How often do new principals meet with their mentors and for how long?

New principals meet with their mentors on a monthly basis.

Are there other people with whom the new principal meets for mentoring and support?

New principals are also supported by the DOE and nonpublic organizations that offer services for schools.

Is formative assessment of new principals required? If so, when, how, and by whom?

Formative assessment of new principals is included in the conversation between the mentor and the protégé in preparing the IPD. The IPD is signed by the superintendent.

Are new principals required to prepare a portfolio?

The BPA doesn't require a portfolio; some districts do.

ARE ADDITIONAL SUPPORTS AVAILABLE FOR NEW PRINCIPALS?

Is any other professional development provided? If so, when and by whom?

Professional development is provided by TASL. It is also offered through other organizations, such as the state affiliates of the national organizations such as the Association for Supervision and Curriculum Development (ASCD) and the National Staff Development Council (NSDC). Field service centers offer professional development programs. The Tennessee framework for evaluation training is required of principals.

Do new principals meet regularly with other new principals?

New principals meet with each other at the BPA; they do not meet outside the BPA because they are reluctant to leave their buildings.

What resources are required for the mentoring program?

The cost per cohort is $99,500 per year, and there is an elementary and a secondary cohort each year. It costs $68,050 for the 40 participants and $31,450 for the mentor training, lodging, and travel.

FUNDING

What are the funding sources?

The funds come from the Office of Professional Development, which is part of the Curriculum and Instruction Division in the DOE.

Who requests the funding?

The director of TASL requests the funding.

EVALUATION OF THE PROGRAM

Is the program evaluated formatively? Summatively?
Who does the evaluation?

There is an academy evaluation. Now TASL is working to link the evaluation of the academy to student achievement.

Who sees the results?

The TASL director, TASL board of control, the executive director, and the presenters all see the evaluations.

RECRUITMENT, HIRING, AND RETENTION OF NEW STAFF

How many new principals are recruited and hired each year?

No data set is currently available about new principal recruitment and hiring. TASL doesn't represent even half of the new principals in the state.

Are there any data that correlate the mentoring program with the retention of new principals?

Dennis Bunch, the director of TASL, is working on this for his dissertation.

Are there any data that correlate the mentoring program with the performance of the new principals?

Dennis Bunch is also working on this for his dissertation.

What are the indicators of program success?

Many of the participants in the earliest cohorts of the BPA are retired or in the central office. Some of the previous participants are still in principalships and are still maintaining their relationships with their mentors.

Says the TASL director, "New principals shouldn't need to invent wheels all the time. This program brings together master-level, experienced, successful principals, those who are successful in raising student achievement. They are giving back to the profession they love. Over two years, they gather far more than they could do on their own. The mentors relive their beginnings through the new principals' experience. It's definitely a win-win relationship."

Professional Association Models

MODEL 5.1

National Association of Elementary School Principals (NAESP)
Principals Advisory Leadership Services (PALS)

Fred Brown, Associate Executive Director
1615 Duke Street, Alexandria, VA 22314
703-684-3345 x. 275   fbrown@naesp.org

Urban/suburban/rural school	Not applicable	Grade levels of school	Not applicable
Student population	Not applicable	Per pupil expenditure	Not applicable
Mentoring is/is not mandated for ongoing certification/ licensure	Not applicable	Mentoring program is/is not funded by the state	Not applicable
Unique feature of program	Nationwide principal-mentor training and NAESP certification	Duration of program for new principals	One year
Mentors are Full-time principals from same district from another district Retired principals	Mentors are full-time principals or recently retired principals from same or different districts	Mentor selection criteria exist/do not exist Mentor matching process exists/does not exist	Mentors have more than five years of experience Protégés find their own mentors
Mentors are trained/ not trained for role Mentors receive/do not receive ongoing support	Mentors are trained Mentors receive ongoing support	Mentors are/are not part of a team to support new principals	Each district determines additional support for new principal
Coaching is/is not a component	Coaching is a component	Daily/weekly/yearly expectations for mentor	Mentors meet with new principal 72 hours during the year
Mentors evaluate/do not evaluate the new principals	Mentors do not evaluate	Portfolio is required/is not required	Portfolio documents are submitted every month
Mentor remuneration	Mentors are not remunerated, unless district offers payment to mentor	Higher education affiliation	Nova Southeastern University
Cost of program	Participants pay $750 for immersion institute	Funding	District/personal
Years program in existence	One and one-half years	Full-time/part-time program coordinator/program coordination is part of another role in system/ organization/state	Program coordination is part of another role in NAESP

STATE MANDATES

Not applicable.

HISTORY

Why was the program started?

The program was started because there was a growing need for principals to take the place of members who are retiring. There will be a critical shortage of principals in the very near future. Most principals leave the job within the first three years for lack of support from the central office.

The program is for new or newly appointed principals because many principals have been reassigned to a different level (such as high school, middle school, or elementary) when openings occur. They need a mentor on the level of their new assignment.

This program is also a way to involve retired principals who have a desire to share their knowledge and experience and to continue to be active educational professionals.

Thirty-eight states now require some form of mentoring for new administrators.

GOALS

What is the goal of the program?

The goal of the program is to establish the first national mentoring certification program for principal mentors.

PROGRAM DESIGN

Who designed the mentor program?

A committee of National Association of Elementary School Principals (NAESP) staff, practicing principals, and staff from Nova Southeastern University designed the program.

What are the components and recommended schedule of the program?

The components of the program are as follows:

- An experienced principal works with a new or newly assigned principal over the course of the first or second year to help her or him be successful.
- There is a three-and-one-half-day immersion institute, consisting of five components:

  1. Adult learning: Mentors need to understand what is required to work with adults (this is especially important for someone coming into a new situation)

  2. Art and science of mentoring, including effective communication skills and the nuts and bolts of mentoring

  3. Urban practitioner, including effective communication, working effectively with mentor, and understanding emotional intelligence

  4. NAESP's Leading a Learning Community program, which encompasses the Interstate School Leaders Licensure Consortium (ISLLC) standards

  5. Development of a positive school culture

- The mentor spends 72 contact hours with the protégée over the course of the year after the immersion institute. They do reflections, using the standards. They may be done with a new principal protégée from within the same district as the mentor or from a different state.
- Cohorts of five mentors work with a coach in a chat room once a month for a minimum of an hour on predetermined topics. There is also open time to share concerns. Cohorts are determined geographically so participants don't cross time zones.
- A portfolio based on the eight learning outcomes of the program is submitted monthly.
- There is a weekly participation in bulletin board discussions.
- A final project, written journal, or portfolio presentation of the mentoring experience and how it has impacted the mentor is used.

Mentors may complete the entire program to earn a National Principals Mentoring Certification, awarded by NAESP and Nova Southeastern University.

Mentors could opt to participate in the immersion institute without doing the rest, and then they would not earn the national mentoring certification. NAESP prefers that participants pursue the certification. It is hoped that after completing the program, participants will work with their state affiliates to develop and enhance mentoring programs in their state.

Thus far, there have been three cohorts, and 35 certifications have been awarded.

Are there any programs that complement the mentor program?

Participants may participate in programs at their state level as offered and are appropriate.

PROGRAM ADMINISTRATION

Who coordinates the program?

Fred Brown, associate executive director of Professional Outreach, coordinates the program.

How is information communicated to shareholders?

The program was piloted in 2003, and it was communicated by word of mouth. It was advertised nationally in 2004.

Who coordinates the integration of this program with other professional development opportunities or requirements in the school or district?

Not applicable.

PARTICIPATION IN THE PROGRAM

Who is served?

Mentors who are experienced or recently retired principals may participate in the Principals Advisory Leadership Services (PALS).

Is the participation of new principals voluntary or mandatory?

PALS is for experienced or recently retired principals to become nationally certified mentors. New principals may voluntarily work with these mentors after they are trained.

How long is the program?

The program lasts for one year. Participants may contact their coach in later years for consultation or support.

WHO PROVIDES THE MENTORING AND INDUCTION?

What are the criteria for being a mentor?

Mentors need to be fully certified principals with a minimum of five years of experience in the role.

Are mentors full-time principals or retired principals?

Mentors are full-time principals or recently retired principals (who were principals after No Child Left Behind was enacted).

Are mentors from the same district as new principals?

Mentors may be from the same district as the protégée, and they also may be from another district and/or state.

How are mentors selected?

Prospective mentors complete an online application on the NAESP Web site and write a 250-word statement on why they would be a good mentor.

Nearly everyone who applies is accepted, though they may be assigned to a future mentor training if the current training is full and they meet experience criteria.

How are matches made between mentors and new principals?

Mentors find their own new principal protégés.

WHAT IS EXPECTED OF MENTORS?

What are the job responsibilities of the mentor?

The job responsibilities of mentors are as follows:

- Mentors are expected to do 72 contact hours with the new principals.
- Mentors participate in a guided chat room at least once a month. This is an opportunity for discussion, with a coach, among each cohort of mentors. In this way, the instruction continues throughout the year while the mentors are guiding the protégé.

Is the relationship between the mentor and the new principal confidential?

Yes, the relationship between the mentor and the new principal is confidential.

Are observation and coaching requirements of mentors?

Mentors are available to observe if they are requested to do so by the new principal. For example, they might observe a faculty meeting and then debrief it with the new principal. Mentors are available to support new principals. They may spend time in the schools, looking for signs of success, and noticing the tenor of the school.

Do mentors formally evaluate new principals?

No, mentors do not evaluate new principals.

How much time are mentors expected to work with new principals (weekly, monthly, and for how long)?

Mentors spend 72 contact hours with the new principals.

When do mentors meet with the new principals?

Mentors and new principals meet at mutually convenient times.

WHAT SUPPORTS ARE AVAILABLE FOR MENTORS?

Are mentors remunerated?

No, mentors are not remunerated through this program. It is possible that the districts of the new principals might remunerate the mentors.

Are mentors trained? If so, by whom?

Mentors participate in the three-and-one-half-day immersion institute, and they pay $750 plus their own travel expenses.

This program works on the assumption that principals who are prospective mentors in a given state will bring with them the knowledge of the state standards and testing protocols, for example.

Is there professional development for mentors after the initial training? If so, who provides it?

There are trainings four times a year offered by NAESP.

The program is using former participants, who earned national mentoring certification from the program, to be coaches for future cohorts of prospective mentors.

Do mentors meet regularly with other mentors? If so, how often and for how long?

There aren't any scheduled meetings.

Is there any other ongoing support for mentors? If so, who provides it?

Mentors participate in monthly chat rooms, in their cohorts of five, with their coach.

Are any other resources available for mentors?

Resources for mentors include the following:

- Mentors receive a binder with all of the Power Points used in the training, and the tool kit. The tool kit includes interview questions to help mentors get a grasp of the new principal's needs, Emotional I quotients, and action plan forms. It also has pieces written by experienced principals about the first day of school, the first week of school, and at other benchmarks during the school year.
- Mentors receive a 40 percent discount on courses through Nova Southeastern University.
- Mentors get 26 hours of online learning free through NAESP's online partner, Educational Impact. Educational Impact has a standards document—*Leading Learning Communities*. These are standards of what principals should know and be able to do. It is a 20-hour online piece that includes authors Roland Barth and Tom Sergiovanni, for example. Mentors can take it online free, while NASEP members would buy it. There is also a six-hour piece specifically on mentoring. Mentors can get CEUs from Educational Impact.

Are mentors supervised? If so, by whom and how frequently?

Mentors are not supervised.

WHAT IS EXPECTED OF NEW PRINCIPALS REGARDING THEIR PARTICIPATION IN THE MENTORING PROGRAM?

This is not a program for new principals. This program is to prepare and to nationally certify mentors through the NAESP and Nova Southeastern University.

How often do new principals meet with their mentors, and for how long?
New principals meet with their mentors a minimum of 72 contact hours during the year.

Are there other people with whom the new principal meets for mentoring and support?
This program doesn't provide other support to new principals beyond the skills of the mentor.

Is formative assessment of new principals required? If so, when, how, and by whom?
Mentors do not assess new principals. They may coach them, as requested.

Are new principals required to prepare a portfolio?
This program doesn't have any requirements for the new principals.

ARE ADDITIONAL SUPPORTS AVAILABLE FOR NEW PRINCIPALS?

Is any other professional development provided? If so, when and by whom?
Not applicable.

Do new principals meet regularly with other new principals?
Not applicable.

What are the resources required for the mentoring program?
This program is in the developmental stages, so the costs are not yet clear.

FUNDING

What are the funding sources?
Not applicable.

Who requests the funding?
Not applicable.

EVALUATION OF THE PROGRAM

Is the program evaluated formatively? Summatively? Who does the evaluation?
There is a final project, a compilation presentation of the mentoring experience and how it has impacted the prospective mentors.

Feedback from participants has been very positive. Evaluation forms are collected at the end of each day of the immersion institute.

Who sees the results?

Nova Southeastern University and NAESP see the results.

RECRUITMENT, HIRING, AND RETENTION OF NEW STAFF

How many new principals are recruited and hired each year?

Not applicable.

Are there any data that correlate the mentoring program with the retention of new principals?

Not yet.

Are there any data that correlate the mentoring program with the performance of the new principals?

Not yet.

What are the indicators of program success?

The indicators of success are that participants will

- Mentor at least one new or newly assigned principal during the internship year
- Effectively participate in online chats and conference calls with assigned coaches
- Submit reflections on preassigned topics to be evaluated by the assigned coaches
- Submit a summative document of experiences and learning for review by coaches and NAESP staff
- Complete separate and confidential satisfaction assessments to determine the effectiveness of the mentoring program

Eighty-five percent of participants have stated their satisfaction with PALS.

MODEL 5.2

Massachusetts Elementary School Principals Association (MESPA)
The Consulting Mentor Program: Guiding the Journey of New School Leaders

Nadya Aswad Higgins, Executive Director
MESPA, Massachusetts Elementary School Principals Association
28 Lord Road, Suite 125, Marlborough, MA 01752
508-624-0500   higginsn@mespa.org

Jim Brown, Assistant Executive Director
brownj@mespa.org

Urban/suburban/rural school	Not applicable	Grade levels of school	Not applicable
Student population	Not applicable	Per pupil expenditure	Not applicable
Mentoring is/is not mandated for ongoing certification/licensure	Mentoring is mandated for certification	Mentoring program is/is not funded by the state	Not funded by state
Unique feature of program	Multiple forms of contact, including joint training, on-site visits, and online communication	Duration of program for new principals	One year
Mentors are **Full-time principals** from same district from another district **Retired principals**	Mentors are full-time principals from different districts and/or recently retired principals	Mentor selection criteria exist/do not exist Mentor matching process exists/does not exist	Mentor selection criteria do not exist Mentor matching process does exist
Mentors are trained/not trained for role Mentors receive/do not receive ongoing support	Mentors are trained Mentors receive ongoing support	Mentors are/are not part of a team to support new principals	Mentors are not part of a team of support
Coaching is/is not a component	Coaching is not a component	Daily/weekly/yearly expectations for mentor	40 hours contact including 6 site visits and 5 hours of online communication
Mentors evaluate/do not evaluate the new principals	Mentors do not evaluate	Portfolio is required/is not required	Portfolio is not required
Mentor remuneration	$1,000	Higher education affiliation	None
Cost of program	$27,000 for 15 participants	Funding	Fee for service
Years program in existence	Several	Full-time/part-time program coordinator/program coordination is part of another role in system/organization/state	Program coordination is part of executive director's and assistant executive director's roles

STATE MANDATES

Is mentoring mandated for new principals?

Yes, mentoring is mandated for new principals.

Is mentoring part of certification or licensure?

Yes, mentoring is a certification requirement for every new administrative position. There are guidelines by the state for mentoring responsibilities and standards they have to meet.

Is funding provided by the state to support the mandate?

No, there isn't any funding to support the certification requirements.

HISTORY

Why was the program started?

The program was initiated in 1991. It involved training people to be mentors and meetings with mentors and mentees. The Massachusetts Elementary School Principals Association (MESPA) ran the program for two years, and it was very successful. When education reform in Massachusetts was passed in 1993, it was clear that the retired principals who were mentors were at a disadvantage because they hadn't worked under the mandates of the new law. That program was dropped for a few years because there were so many other things needed to help principals adjust to education reform.

In 2001, a new program was developed, similar to the one started in 1991. This program tried to give very practical strategies to new principals as they approached the challenges they were facing.

GOALS

What are the goals of the program?

This mentoring program is designed to provide support to mentees and professional development for mentors and mentees and to facilitate meetings and interschool visitations between mentors and mentees, in order that they may engage in professional dialogue about best practices.

PROGRAM DESIGN

Who designed the mentor program?

Nadya Asdwad Higgins, the executive director, and Chuck Christiansen designed the program that began in 1991. Nadya and Jim Brown, assistant executive director, designed the more recent program.

What are the components and recommended schedule of the program?

The components of the program for mentees (new principals) are 40 hours of support, including

- Individualized mentoring for each new principal in the program, which includes
  - Six one-hour visits by the mentor to the mentee's school for walk-abouts and reflection
  - Five hours of online communication between mentees and their mentors, plus as needed
- Joint training sessions (four half-day sessions) on the mentoring relationship. These sessions are designed to introduce consulting mentors and mentees to

- Assist in the development of positive professional relationships
- Identify standards for communication, visitations, and feedback as they relate to observation and problem solving
- Two full days of professional development from the MESPA Professional Development Program, which includes, but is not limited to, a Six-Point School Improvement Framework, Leadership, Curriculum, Data-Driven Decision Making, the Middle Level, and the annual MESPA Spring Conference
- Six visitation hours at schools that are identified by MESPA as having strong leadership and innovative programming and that are successfully implementing standards-based education
- Guidance by consulting mentors to mentees in creating professional development plans that are aligned to school and district goals for improving student learning
- Support in many areas, including
  - Improving teaching and learning
  - Creating professional learning communities
  - Building collaborative school cultures based on distributive leadership
  - Analyzing and using multiple assessment data to inform decision making
  - Creating and refining school improvement plans
  - Working effectively with school councils and other groups
  - Creating family-friendly schools
  - Implementing state and federal special education laws
  - Developing conflict-resolution and problem-solving strategies
  - Understanding and utilizing current research and promising practices

Are there any programs that complement the mentor program?

MESPA's Professional Development Program, which offers over 200 sessions each year, complements the Consulting Mentor Program.

PROGRAM ADMINISTRATION

Who coordinates the program?

Jim Brown, the assistant executive director, coordinates the program in consultation with Nadya Higgins, the executive director.

How is information communicated to shareholders?

Information is communicated through MESPA mailings to all elementary and middle-level school principals and school districts.

Who coordinates the integration of this program with other professional development opportunities or requirements in the school or district?

There isn't anyone who specifically coordinates this program with professional development opportunities or requirements in individual schools or districts.

PARTICIPATION IN THE PROGRAM

Who is served?

New principals are served by this program. The program is able to run when there are 12–15 participants. However, mentors are provided to principals even though the preferred number of enrollees is not reached. In this case, the program is adjusted a bit to meet their needs.

Is the participation of new principals voluntary or mandatory?

Participation in this program is voluntary.

How long is the program?

The program lasts one year.

WHO PROVIDES THE MENTORING AND INDUCTION?

What are the criteria for being a mentor?

Consulting mentors are experienced principals who have a proven record of successful administration.

Are mentors full-time principals or retired principals?

Consulting mentors are full-time principals or recently retired principals.

Are mentors from the same district as new principals?

Consulting mentors are not typically from the same district as the new principals.

How are mentors selected?

The coordinator selects consulting mentors after reviewing the applications, which include a written statement about the applicant's philosophy of education.

How are matches made between mentors and new principals?

In order to match consulting mentors and new principals, the coordinator reads all the statements of qualification by the mentors and the statements of need by the mentees. Matches are made based upon level of school, location, similar educational focus, and any other special consideration. Consultation with the executive director is made before final selections are made.

WHAT IS EXPECTED OF MENTORS?

What are the job responsibilities of the mentor?

Mentors are required to give 40 contact hours to mentees. These hours include

- Joint professional development sessions
- On-site visits and conversations
- Online communication
- Consultations to help mentees create professional development plans
- Year-end report of the mentoring experience

Is the relationship between the mentor and the new principal confidential?

Yes, the relationship between the consulting mentor and the new principal is confidential.

Are observation and coaching requirements of mentors?

Consulting mentors do six one-hour prescheduled visits. These visits include a joint walk-about and time for the consulting mentor and mentee to converse. Coaching is not a requirement because mentors are not formally trained as coaches.

Do mentors formally evaluate new principals?

Mentors do not evaluate new principals.

How much time are mentors expected to work with new principals (weekly, monthly, and for how long)?

Consulting mentors meet with new principals for 40 hours during the school year. Consulting mentors meet with their mentees during four half-day training sessions, for six on-site visitations to their schools, online for five hours, plus as needed during the year. Mentors also help mentees create professional development plans.

When do mentors meet with the new principals?

New principals meet with their consulting mentors at mutually agreed-upon times.

WHAT SUPPORTS ARE AVAILABLE FOR MENTORS?

Are mentors remunerated?

Consulting mentors are paid $1,000 to mentor a new principal for a school year.

Are mentors trained? If so, by whom?

A consultant hired by MESPA, Dr. Kenneth Chapman, trains consulting mentors on how to listen to people's issues and feelings and how to work with new principals in terms of leadership, management effectiveness, and problem solving.

Is there professional development for mentors after the initial training? If so, who provides it?

Consulting mentors participate with the new principals in the four joint training sessions.

Do mentors meet regularly with other mentors? If so, how often and for how long?

Mentors meet with other mentors at the joint training sessions. There are not any other scheduled meetings.

Is there any other ongoing support for mentors? If so, who provides it?

Consulting mentors confer with the coordinator or the executive director if they need support.

Are any other resources available for mentors?

No, there aren't any other resources for mentors.

Are mentors supervised? If so, by whom and how frequently?

Consulting mentors are contacted throughout the year by the coordinator but are not formally supervised. The end-of-the-year evaluations of the program are opportunities for feedback from the new principals.

WHAT IS EXPECTED OF NEW PRINCIPALS REGARDING THEIR PARTICIPATION IN THE MENTORING PROGRAM?

How often do new principals meet with their mentors and for how long?

New principals meet with their consulting mentors for 40 hours during the school year. They meet during four half-day training sessions, for six on-site visitations to their schools, and online for five hours plus as needed during the year.

Are there other people with whom the new principal meets for mentoring and support?

New principals get support from Dr. Kenneth Chapman and may get support from other administrators in their districts.

Is formative assessment of new principals required? If so, when, how, and by whom?

No formal assessment of new principals is required. However, the year-end report may give an assessment of the mentor's sense of the success of the mentor-mentee experience.

Are new principals required to prepare a portfolio?

New principals are required to create a professional development plan. They are not required to prepare a portfolio.

ARE ADDITIONAL SUPPORTS AVAILABLE FOR NEW PRINCIPALS?

Is any other professional development provided? If so, when and by whom?

New principals may participate in two full days of training through MESPA's Professional Development Program. New principals may also participate in any of the over 200 offerings that MESPA provides to principals in any given year. New principals may do half-day visits to other schools, arranged by MESPA.

Do new principals meet regularly with other new principals?

MESPA has a new principals' program in which they may participate, but that is not a required part of the mentoring program.

What resources are required for the mentoring program?

The program costs $27,000 for 15 participants, and includes

- Mentors, who are paid $1,000 for the school year to work with a mentee
- A trainer for the four half-day sessions
- In-kind service for the two full days of professional development from MESPA
- Food
- Materials
- Administration
- Advertising

FUNDING

What are the funding sources?

This is a fee-for-service program. The program cost is $1,800 for each new principal. The program runs when there are 15 participants enrolled.

Who requests the funding?

The new principals or their districts pay the fee for their participation.

EVALUATION OF THE PROGRAM

Is the program evaluated formatively? Summatively? Who does the evaluation?

Consulting mentors and new principals give feedback on the program.

Who sees the results?

The coordinator and the executive director see the feedback from the participants.

RECRUITMENT, HIRING, AND RETENTION OF NEW STAFF

How many new principals are recruited and hired each year?

This information is not available.

Are there any data that correlate the mentoring program with the retention of new principals?

This information is not available.

Are there any data that correlate the mentoring program with the performance of the new principals?

This information is not available.

What are the indicators of program success?

The success of the program is based on the following advantages:

- There is expressed value in having a safe environment outside the district for new principals to voice their concerns without getting involved in dangerous landscapes.
- Sometimes districts can be insular, passing on the same behaviors without broadening thinking.
- Confidentiality.

MODEL 5.3

New Jersey Principals and Supervisors Association (NJPSA)
New Jersey Leaders to Leaders (NJ-L2L)

Dr. Eloise Forster, Director of School Leadership Programs
Foundation for Educational Administration
12 Centre Drive, Monroe Township, NJ 08831
609-860-1200   emforster@njpsa.org

Urban/suburban/rural school	Not applicable	**Grade levels of school**	Not applicable
Student population	Not applicable	**Per pupil expenditure**	Not applicable
Mentoring is/is not mandated for ongoing certification/ licensure	Is mandated	**Mentoring program is/is not funded by the state**	Not funded
Unique feature of program	Combines intensive and sustained mentoring support with an intensive and sustained, standards-driven, job-embedded leadership development program	**Duration of program for new principals**	One to three years
Mentors are **Full-time principals** **from same district** **from another district** **Retired principals**	Mentors are recently retired principals, not from the same district as the new principals	**Mentor selection criteria exist/do not exist** **Mentor matching process exists/does not exist**	Mentor selection criteria do exist Mentor matching process does exists
Mentors are trained/not trained for role **Mentors receive/do not receive ongoing support**	Mentors are trained Mentors receive ongoing support	**Mentors are/are not part of a team to support new principals**	Mentors are part of a team to support new principals
Coaching is/is not a component	Coaching is a requirement	**Daily/weekly/yearly expectations for mentor**	Year 1: 45 hours Year 2: 30 hours Year 3: 15 hours
Mentors evaluate/do not evaluate the new principals	Mentors do evaluate	**Portfolio is required/is not required**	Portfolio is required
Mentor remuneration	Year 1: $1,500 Year 2: $1,000 Year 3: $500	**Higher education affiliation**	None
Cost of program	Cost to participants is $1,800 for Year 1, $1,300 for Year 2 $800 for Year 3	**Funding**	Washington Mutual Foundation
Years program in existence	Two years	**Full-time/part-time program coordinator/program coordination is part of another role in system/ organization/state**	Program coordination is part of another role

STATE MANDATES

Is mentoring mandated for new principals?

Yes, mentoring is mandated for new principals within the New Jersey Administrative Code.

Is mentoring part of certification or licensure?

Yes. New principals, assistant principals, directors, and assistant directors who hold certificates of eligibility for principal and are newly employed must complete the state-required residency requirement for standard certification, which includes being mentored.

New Jersey Leaders to Leaders (NJ-L2L) is designed to meet current and emerging state requirements for New Jersey's school leaders and their districts. NJ-L2L is aligned with

- Standard principal certification requirement for the residency and mentoring
- New Jersey Professional Standards for School Leaders, which are aligned with the national standards developed by the Interstate School Leaders Licensure Consortium (ISLLC)
- New Jersey professional development requirements for school leaders
- State expectations for the knowledge and use of educational technologies consistent with the national Technology Standards for School Administrators (TSSA)

Is funding provided by the state to support the mandate?

No, funding is not provided for mentoring or the residency requirement. The Foundation for Educational Administration (FEA) has successfully solicited public and private funding to support NJ-L2L and provide scholarships to new school leaders to offset NJ-L2L registration fees, which includes costs related to mentoring and professional development.

HISTORY

Why was the program started?

NJ-L2L is offered by the FEA. The FEA is a nonprofit organization that is affiliated with the New Jersey Principals and Supervisors Association (NJPSA). The FEA provides a range of professional development programs and services to further NJPSA efforts to support its members and effective school leadership in New Jersey. Both FEA and NJPSA have a vested interest in improving school leadership across the state and are concerned about retaining principals and supporting school leaders to be successful in their roles.

The state requires a one-year residency program for new administrators, which includes mentoring. State regulations and guidelines provide a general framework. There needed to be more consistency in the induction and continuing professional development of administrators. The focus is on the support structure that is needed for new administrators, even beyond their first year. The program is available to anyone who must meet the state's residency requirement and also to those in their second and third year as novice school leaders.

GOALS

What are the goals of the program?

The goals of the program are to

- Support and retain new administrators
- Help new administrators continue their professional growth and be most effective

- Help new administrators complete the state's residency requirement and receive standard certification
- Improve educational leadership in the state of New Jersey
- Prepare and support school leaders as agents of educational change and improvement and as instructional leaders who effectively guide their schools to attain high academic achievement for all students represented in New Jersey's diverse population

PROGRAM DESIGN

Who designed the mentor program?

Dr. Eloise Forster, director of School Leadership Programs at the Foundation for Educational Administration, designed the NJ-L2L program based on (a) an extensive review of the research on mentoring and retention of new administrators, (b) NJPSA and the New Jersey DOE surveys of school leaders in New Jersey related to their needs and experiences as new administrators, (c) review and alignment with state requirements and guidelines for the residency, and (d) consultations with the New Jersey DOE, school district personnel, and NJPSA members.

What are the components and recommended schedule of the program?

NJ-L2L is designed as a comprehensive three-year induction program and support system that provides an option for new school leaders to continue the program for a second and third year upon completion of their state-required residency. Each of the three years requires mentoring, continuing professional development, and a job-embedded project focused on improving schools, teaching, and learning.

NJ-L2L is a comprehensive mentoring and induction program and support system for new and novice school leaders that

- Combines intensive and sustained high-quality mentoring and support with an intensive and sustained standards-driven, job-embedded leadership development program
- Is guided by individualized professional growth plans and ongoing performance-based assessment
- Fulfills state requirements for completion of the state-required residency and eligibility for standard principal certification
- Is aligned with New Jersey's professional development requirements and standards for school leaders
- Is recommended by the American Council on Education (ACE) for three to four graduate credits per completed year of NJ-L2L
- Focuses on intensive and sustained support by trained mentors who are committed to a minimum number of mentoring contact hours as appropriate to each year of induction, as follows:
  - NJ-L2L Year 1 (state-required residency): 45 hours
  - NJ-L2L Year 2 (novice): 30 hours
  - NJ-L2L Year 3 (novice): 15 hours

Each year of NJ-L2L requires continuing professional development and job-embedded projects that are consistent with New Jersey's professional development requirements for school leaders.

Upon completion of each year of the program, participants receive NJ-L2L's School Leader Professional Development Certificate.

Orientation of New School Leaders and Mentors

The program begins with new school leaders and their mentors coming together for a full-day orientation, which provides a comprehensive overview of the NJ-L2L program, requirements for the state's residency, expectations and standards for performance and continual professional growth of effective school leaders, and self-assessment using instruments and methods aligned with the New Jersey Professional Standards for School Leaders. Mentors assist new school leaders in development of their individualized professional growth plans, which guide their continuing learning and development. The process for ongoing performance-based assessment, reflective practice, and requirements for their leadership portfolios are also introduced. Hands-on training is also provided on NJ-L2L's OnLine Learning Community, which new school leaders and their mentors use throughout the program to facilitate communication, collaboration, and sharing as a professional learning community.

Mentoring and Ongoing Support

Mentoring includes site visits, individual conferences, and inquiry group meetings with other new school leaders and mentors in a team mentoring approach that capitalizes on the individual strengths of each mentor.

Job-Embedded Professional Development

NJ-L2L supports standards-driven, inquiry-focused professional development during each induction year that is designed to further develop the leadership and pedagogical knowledge and skills and the personal dispositions required of effective school leaders. Mentors guide new or novice school leaders in planning professional development goals and experiences that are aligned with New Jersey residency and continuing professional development requirements for school leaders.

Are there any programs that complement the mentor program?

A range of FEA professional development programs and service(s), as well as school district offerings, complement the NJ-L2L program. The New Jersey EXCEL (Expedited Certification for Educational Leadership) is an alternative path to principal certification provided by FEA, and New Jersey EXCEL graduates typically continue in NJ-L2L once appointed to administrative positions.

PROGRAM ADMINISTRATION

Who coordinates the program?

Dr. Eloise Forster, director of School Leadership Programs, and Dr. Mary Reece, associate director for School Leadership Programs, coordinate the NJ-L2L program.

How is information communicated to shareholders?

Information is communicated through

- Statewide mailings to school districts
- NJPSA newsletters and professional journals
- NJPSA county officers and the statewide field service network
- Online FEA newsletters
- The NJPSA convention held annually in November
- The New Jersey DOE
- Word of mouth

Who coordinates the integration of this program with other professional development opportunities or requirements in the school or district?

A state-required district advisory panel, composed of two or more representatives in each participating district, works with NJ-L2L mentors to coordinate all facets of the program within the district.

PARTICIPATION IN THE PROGRAM

Who is served?

New and novice school leaders in New Jersey's public school districts are eligible to enter NJ-L2L during any of the first three years in their school leader positions.

Is the participation of principals voluntary or mandatory?

Participation in NJ-L2L is voluntary.

How long is the program?

The program lasts one to three years.

WHO PROVIDES THE MENTORING AND INDUCTION?

What are the criteria for being a mentor?

Educators with at least 10 years of combined experience as a principal or assistant principal and who have been retired from the principal position for less than five years are eligible to apply to be mentors. Applicants are selected based on their credentials, demonstration of positive leadership qualities, and recognized accomplishments as school leaders and practitioners in a range of school and district leadership positions. Mentors are expected to minimally possess and demonstrate the following characteristics, skills, and abilities:

- Knowledge and skills consistent with current research-based school leadership and instructional practice
- Personal dispositions reflecting the values, attitudes, and ethical practices expected of effective school leaders
- Excellent oral and written communication skills and human relationships skills
- High standards and expectations for themselves and the work of others
- Knowledge, skills, and disposition for effective mentoring

Are mentors full-time principals or retired principals?

The mentors are recently retired principals who have been retired for no more than five years.

Are mentors from the same district as new principals?

NJ-L2L mentors are not typically from the same district as the new school leaders.

How are mentors selected?

NJPSA provides retirement counseling and related services for prospective and retired principals. FEA, therefore, has access to this pool and advertises the opportunity for them to become mentors. FEA also uses its statewide network of county officers and field service representatives to recommend school leaders who meet NJ-L2L criteria for mentors. Recently retired principals may apply to become NJ-L2L mentors. However, FEA carefully selects mentors based on its criteria and personal knowledge or recommendations for selection.

How are matches made between mentors and new school leaders?

Matching of mentors and new school leaders is based on the experience of the mentors (e.g., grade levels, specialized schools, type of district), specific areas of interest, and geographic proximity, in consultation with sponsoring school districts and new school leaders and prospective mentors.

WHAT IS EXPECTED OF MENTORS?

What are the job responsibilities of mentors?

A minimum number of contact hours is required for each induction year, during which mentors are required to

- Conduct site visits to observe their new school leaders on the job and assess their performance as they carry out their day-to-day activities
- Conduct inquiry group meetings and team mentoring to provide collegial support and opportunities for new school leaders to discuss issues and concerns
- Provide feedback related to the mentees' performance and areas requiring further professional growth
- Guide mentees in their continuing professional development and completion of job-embedded school-based projects that are aligned with state professional development requirements for school leaders
- Provide ongoing support using NJ-L2L's OnLine Learning Community
- Complete state-required formative and summative evaluations for licensure and an NJ-L2L summative assessment at the end of each year

Is the relationship between the mentor and the new principal confidential?

The relationship is based on the level of openness and trust required for successful mentoring. However, mentors are required by the state to recommend the new school leaders for standard certification, suggest an additional year, or recommend that a new school leader should not be awarded standard certification. This recommendation is based on state guidelines and evaluation criteria and instruments that are required by the state to be shared with the district advisory panel. NJ-L2L expects and trains mentors to use their professional judgment related to the confidential nature of the relationship with their new school leaders.

Are observation and coaching requirements of mentors?

Yes, observation and coaching are requirements of mentors.

Do mentors formally evaluate new principals?

Yes, mentors are required by the state to formally evaluate the new school leaders during their residency at the end of their third, sixth, and ninth month. NJ-L2L also requires a summative assessment at the end of 12 months in Years 1, 2, and 3.

How much time are mentors expected to work with new principals (weekly, monthly, and for how long)?

Mentors are expected to work with new school leaders for a minimum number of contact hours per year, as follows:

NJ-L2L Year 1 (residency): 45 hours

NJ-L2L Year 2: 30 hours

NJ-L2L Year 3: 15 hours

When do mentors meet with the new school leaders?

Mentors and school leaders meet at mutually agreed-upon times, as well as at scheduled NJ-L2L training and support sessions. However, it is expected that communication and support will be ongoing via telephone and use of NJ-L2L's OnLine Learning Community.

WHAT SUPPORTS ARE AVAILABLE FOR MENTORS?

Are mentors remunerated?

Mentors receive a $1,500 stipend per assigned school leader for Year 1, $1,000 for Year 2, and $500 for Year 3.

Are mentors trained? If so, by whom?

There is mentor training that consists of a four-day initial training program, which must be completed for certification by FEA as an NJ-L2L mentor. Training is conducted by FEA staff.

Is there professional development for mentors after the initial training? If so, who provides it?

In order to retain active status as a certified NJ-L2L mentor, a one-day mentor recertification training is required annually. FEA also provides opportunities for mentors to participate in continuing professional development through its range of professional development workshops and conferences at no cost to the mentor.

Do mentors meet regularly with other mentors? If so, how often and for how long?

Mentors meet with other mentors on a regular basis for the inquiry group meetings where team mentoring is provided to new school leaders. FEA also brings mentors together to provide program updates and obtain feedback related to formative program evaluation and continuous improvement of the NJ-L2L program. Mentors also communicate regularly using NJ-L2L's OnLine Learning Community.

Is there any other ongoing support for mentors? If so, who provides it?

Ongoing support is available to mentors who have access to the director and associate director, administrative support, and technology support. NJ-L2L processes all documents required by the New Jersey DOE for mentors, new school leaders, and school districts.

Are any other resources available for mentors?

Other resources are available to mentors as required, such as technology training and facilities for meetings at NJPSA's state-of-the-art training facility.

Are mentors supervised? If so, by whom and how frequently?

Yes, mentors are supervised by the associate director for school leadership programs.

WHAT IS EXPECTED OF NEW SCHOOL LEADERS REGARDING THEIR PARTICIPATION IN THE MENTORING PROGRAM?

How often do new school leaders meet with their mentors and for how long?

New school leaders are expected to

- Complete a minimum number of contact hours with their mentors
- Complete pre– and post–self-assessments on which they base individualized professional growth plans in consultation with their mentors
- Engage in job-embedded professional development that is aligned with New Jersey Professional Standards for School Leaders and state professional development requirements for school leaders
- Develop a leadership portfolio
- Complete a job-embedded project that focuses on improving schools, teaching, and learning
- Present their job-embedded projects to other new school leaders in the NJ-L2L program

New principals meet with their mentors one-on-one for at least 50 percent of their minimum required number of contact hours and 50 percent in inquiry group meetings.

Are there other people with whom the new school leader meets for mentoring and support?

The new school leaders are also supported in inquiry groups of other new school leaders and their mentors for team mentoring and collegial support. Inquiry groups are designed to address the isolation felt by new school leaders and to utilize a team mentoring approach that capitalizes on the unique experiences and strengths of each mentor.

Is formative assessment of new school leaders required? If so, when, how, and by whom?

Yes, for the residency in Year 1, mentors conduct state-required formative evaluations for new school leaders at the end of their third and sixth month. Then mentors conduct summative evaluations at the end of the ninth month of the program and make their recommendation for state licensure.

Are new school leaders required to prepare a portfolio?

Yes, new school leaders are required to prepare leadership portfolios that provide evidence of their professional growth and completion of state-required experiences.

ARE ADDITIONAL SUPPORTS AVAILABLE FOR NEW SCHOOL LEADERS?

Is any other professional development provided? If so, when and by whom?

New school leaders and their mentors participate in continuing professional development on such topics as

- Using Data to Improve Schools and Student Learning Innovations
- Technology for School Leaders
- Staff Supervision, Evaluation, and Professional Development
- Addressing Needs of Diverse Student Population
- Creating a Safe and Orderly School Environment of Student Learning Innovations
- Managing the School as a Learning Community
- Engaging Families and Community in the Educational Process

Additional supports are available through FEA's range of professional development programs and services and the range of member services available through NJPSA (e.g., legal services).

Do new school leaders meet regularly with other new school leaders?

New school leaders meet with other new school leaders regularly in their inquiry groups.

What are the resources required for the mentoring program?

The program is not for profit. It is designed to be self-funded and self-sustaining. There is a registration fee of $1,800 for Year 1, $1,300 for Year 2, and $800 for Year 3.

The majority of the fee is for the mentor stipends. Approximately $300 per person covers all other costs.

FUNDING

What are the funding sources?

FEA was funded by the Washington Mutual Foundation for the 2003–2004 pilot program and continued funding during 2004–2005. These funds are used to support mentor training and provide scholarships to participants to offset registration fees. FEA has also received a federal School Leader Program grant, which provides scholarships to partner high-need school districts in the state. All participants or their districts are required to make a financial commitment of $500. Participants may receive $500–$1,500 scholarships toward the registration fees.

Who requests the funding?

Funding is requested through FEA.

EVALUATION OF THE PROGRAM

Is the program evaluated formatively? Summatively? Who does the evaluation?

The program is both formatively and summatively evaluated using state-approved Program Evaluation Standards and Design developed for NJ-L2L.

Who sees the results?

Evaluation results are reviewed internally by FEA staff for continuous program improvement, by the New Jersey DOE to continue state program approval, funding agencies as required, and others as appropriate.

RECRUITMENT, HIRING, AND RETENTION OF NEW STAFF

How many new school leaders are recruited and hired each year?

In 2003–2004, 34 new school leaders participated in NJ-L2L. As of October 2004, 46 new school leaders had registered for NJ-L2L. These numbers continued to grow when districts hired for the 2004–2005 school year.

Are there any data that correlate the mentoring program with the retention of new school leaders?

After only one year, data show that all participants were retained after their first year. In addition, several new assistant principals were promoted to principalships.

Are there any data that correlate the mentoring program with the performance of the new school leaders?

After only one year, data related to the impact of NJ- L2L on new school leader performance is not available. However, anecdotal data is promising:

An induction program is extremely important in the retention of new school administrators. To have a vehicle by which new school leaders can be part of a professional network of newly appointed school leaders, as well as a cadre of very experienced mentors provides a much needed service and opportunity for districts across the state. It is particularly beneficial for urban districts where retention of school leaders can be problematic.

—*Charles T. Epps Jr., Superintendent, Jersey City Public Schools*

Making the transition from being a teacher to an administrator has been an overwhelming experience. But it wasn't as bad as I thought because of the strong support I have received from NJ-L2L's many support systems. My mentor is a wonderful resource person, professional development activities are applicable to my new position, and opportunities to discuss the trials and errors of my new position with my colleagues in the program have been invaluable.

—*Angela Petrongolo, Assistant Principal, Washington Township Public Schools*

As a newly hired principal of a large high school district, I have found the NJ-L2L program to be a valuable resource of information with numerous opportunities to participate in professional development. I was provided an experienced mentor with a vast background in education who has met with me on a regular basis at work and who is available to discuss issues any hour of the day. I am also part of a smaller group that meets regularly to share and exchange information and ideas about what is actually happening in our daily work, not hypothetical situations. NJ-L2L will serve as a valuable resource for any new educational leader.

—*Anthony Mongelluzzo, Principal, Oakcrest High School, Mays Landing*

The NJ-L2L program represents an exemplary, comprehensive, and outcomes-based mentoring and professional development model for educational leaders. It is research-based, innovative, and specifically aligned to national and state standards and requirements. The NJ-L2L program has helped to ensure that our two new school administrators were provided with the sustained, job-embedded mentorship and professional development program that they needed. Our new administrators were certainly served well by their participation in NJ-L2L.

—*Brian P. Chinni, Supervisor for Curriculum & Instruction, Montvale Public Schools*

What are the indicators of program success?

Indicators of program success include

- Retention after one year
- Promotions
- Testimonials
- Pre– and post–self-assessment data
- Program evaluation data (especially related to the quality of the mentoring experiences and the benefits of such support)
- Impact data related to participating school leaders' performance as measured by improvements in schools, teaching, and learning

MODEL 5.4

Texas Elementary Principals and Supervisors Association (TEPSA)
First Time Texas Campus Administrator Program

Sandi Borden, Executive Director
501 East 10th Street, Austin, TX 78701
512-478-5268   sandi@tepsa.org

Urban/suburban/rural school	Not applicable	Grade levels of school	Not applicable
Student population	Not applicable	Per pupil expenditure	Not applicable
Mentoring is/is not mandated for ongoing certification/licensure	Mentoring is mandated	Mentoring program is/is not funded by the state	Not funded
Unique feature of program	The academy is a model that is replicated throughout the state	Duration of program for new principals	Two years

Mentors are
Full-time principals
   from same district
   from another district
Retired principals
	Mentors are full-time or recently retired principals from the same district	Mentor selection criteria exist/do not exist
		
		Mentor matching process exists/does not exist
			Mentor selection criteria do exist
			
			Mentor matching process does exists

Mentors are trained/not trained for role Mentors receive/do not receive ongoing support	Mentors are trained Mentors receive ongoing support	Mentors are/are not part of a team to support new principals	Mentors are part of a team of support
Coaching is/is not a component	Coaching is not a requirement	Daily/weekly/yearly expectations for mentor	In the first year, monthly meetings; in the second year, less frequent
Mentors evaluate/do not evaluate the new principals	Mentors do not evaluate	Portfolio is required/is not required	Portfolio is required
Mentor remuneration	Local decision	Higher education affiliation	None
Cost of program	Varies by region and district	Funding	TEPSA funded the development of the program. Local school districts, possibly with regional service centers, fund the local programs
Years program in existence	Three years	Full-time/part-time program coordinator/program coordination is part of other role in system/organization/state	Coordinators are throughout different geographic regions and are self-organized

Underwritten for Texas public school leaders through the generosity of the Board of Directors of the Texas Elementary Principals and Supervisors Association (TEPSA). Used with permission.

STATE MANDATES

Is mentoring mandated for new principals?

Yes, mentoring is mandated for administrators in their first year.

Is mentoring part of certification or licensure?

As of September 2002, certification for first-time campus administrators requires at least one year of support induction. Mentoring support is an expectation during this induction period.

Is funding provided by the state to support the mandate?

No, there is no funding provided by the state.

HISTORY

Why was the program started?

In 1998, the possible shortage of administrators was on the national horizon. The executive director of the Texas Elementary Principals and Supervisors Association (TEPSA), Sandi Borden, spoke with the TEPSA staff in anticipation of the rule that would be passed to require a year of supported induction. She presented her idea for a First Time Texas Campus Administrator Academy to the board and it was accepted. The program was piloted in 2001 and formally began in 2002.

GOALS

What is the goal of the program?

The goal is to create a quality induction support system for new campus administrators. The support is predicated on a servant leadership philosophy of administration: "In the root of the principal's role responsibilities are the roots of school leadership—a commitment to administer to the needs of the school or an institution by serving its purposes, by serving those who struggle to embody those purposes, and by acting as guardian to protect the institutional integrity of the school" (Sergiovanni, 1991, p. 88).

PROGRAM DESIGN

Who designed the mentor program?

Dr. Betty Jo Monk facilitated the development of the program with the TEPSA board and staff. A panel of secondary and elementary principals also assisted in the development of the program.

What are the components and recommended schedule of the program?

The First Time Texas Campus Administrator Academy is a two-year program. The first year of the program is specifically designed to comply with the requirements of the Texas Administrative Code that require that all campus administrators employed for the first time in Texas participate in at least a one-year induction period. The second year of the program is designed to facilitate the continued learning of both participants through engagement in a specific learning project.

Four academy meetings are scheduled for the first year of the induction period.

- Mentors participate in two days of mentor training and the first-time campus administrator participates in a one-day orientation session.

- Both mentoring partners participate in three one-day academy meetings during the first year of the induction period. One-day academy meetings are held in the middle of the fall semester, early in the spring semester, and near or following the end of the academic year. At the three one-day academy meetings, the partners participate together in sessions for mentors and first- time campus administrators, and they participate separately in sessions designated for a specific role (i.e., sessions specifically for mentors and sessions specifically for first-time campus administrators).

For the second year of the induction program, the first-time campus administrator and the mentor become learning partners and develop a learning plan focused on a project of mutual interest. The learning partners may also serve as resources to participants in their first year of the induction program. Two academy meetings are scheduled for the second-year learning partners. The learning partners participate in two one-day academy meetings: one in the fall semester and one in the spring semester. In addition, they work on a project together and present it at the final meeting of the academy.

Are there any programs that complement the mentor program?
Local school districts supplement the program with their own leadership training. There are several professional development training modules that are offered by the Texas Principals Leadership Initiative on many topics, including conflict management and leading learners.

PROGRAM ADMINISTRATION

Who coordinates the program?
A First Time Texas Campus Administrator Academy may be established by a variety of providers:

- Individual school districts
- Education service centers
- Induction collaboratives involving partnerships between school districts, education service centers, principal preparation programs, and professional administrator associations

The academy is established as a response to the need for a quality induction program for first-time campus administrators in school districts in a specific geographic region. Academy coordinators must go through a two-day overview training session to ensure that they adhere to the integrity of the program developed by TEPSA.

How is information communicated to shareholders?
Promotion of the academy occurs formally and informally. The academy coordinator, along with the members of the academy advisory board and school district administrators, is responsible for the promotion of the academy. Promotional information about the program such as fliers and brochures is prepared and disseminated within the constituent district(s). In-house media tools are used to inform individuals about the academy and its purpose. The academy coordinator makes presentations about the academy to stakeholder groups such as school boards, education service center staff, professional association groups, university or college faculty, aspiring administrators, and potential mentors.

Who coordinates the integration of this program with other professional development opportunities or requirements in the school or district?
Local district administrators coordinate the integration of this program with other professional development opportunities or requirements in the district.

PARTICIPATION IN THE PROGRAM

Who is served?

The First Time Texas Campus Administrator Academy is a two-year program for principals and assistant principals employed for the first time as campus administrators in Texas and their mentors. Based on the number of first-time campus administrators to be served by the academy provider, it may be desirable to structure separate academies for

- Individuals employed for the first time as principals
- Individuals employed for the first time as assistant principals
- Individuals with prior campus administrative experience employed for the first time as principals or assistant principals in Texas

Is the participation of principals voluntary or mandatory?

Participation of first-time campus administrators is mandatory, based on district decision to participate in the academy.

How long is the program?

The academy offers a two-year program.

WHO PROVIDES THE MENTORING AND INDUCTION?

What are the criteria for being a mentor?

The following are the criteria for being a mentor. Prospective mentors must

- Be certified to serve as a principal in Texas
- Have five or more years of experience as a principal in Texas
- Have experience as a principal within the last five years
- Be an administrator in good standing with the school district served
- Be recommended as a mentor by two or more individuals

Are mentors full-time principals or retired principals?

Mentors are full-time principals or principals who have retired within the previous five years of serving as a mentor.

Are mentors from the same district as new principals?

Mentors may be from within the same district as the first-time campus administrators they serve. The program recommends that the mentors be from another campus and not be the new administrator's supervisor.

How are mentors selected?

Mentors are selected by the local coordinators or regions or districts.

How are matches made between mentors and new principals?

The academy coordinator is responsible for the assignment of the mentoring partners. Each first-time campus administrator completes the First Time Campus Administrator Profile, and each potential mentor completes the First Time Campus Administrator Mentor Profile. After reviewing the profiles for the pool of mentors, each campus administrator is given the opportunity to express her or his preferences for a mentor. A mentor, upon confidential notification by the academy coordinator that a first-time campus administrator has indicated preference for her or him as a mentor, may accept or reject the request of the first-time campus administrator. Formal notification of the mentoring assignments is made by the academy coordinator.

The academy coordinator is the contact for each set of mentoring partners. In the unlikely event of problems between the first-time campus administrator and the mentor, the academy coordinator is contacted and the concerns are discussed confidentially. If the academy coordinator cannot resolve the concerns, the relationship is dissolved and the relationship with the mentoring partner is discontinued. The first-time campus administrator is assigned a new mentor. There should be no repercussions for either party if the relationship needs to be dissolved.

WHAT IS EXPECTED OF MENTORS?

What are the job responsibilities of mentors?

Mentors are expected to

- Participate in the two-day mentor training
- Participate in the four academy meetings in the first year of the program and the two academy meetings in the second year of the program
- Meet with the first-time campus administrator at least once a month and communicate more frequently by telephone and e-mail
- Develop a First Time Campus Administrator and Mentor Agreement with the first-time campus administrator
- Maintain documentation of the induction period contacts and activities

Is the relationship between the mentor and the new principal confidential?

The mentoring agreement that the first-time campus administrator and the mentor develop provides a foundation for the evolving relationship and includes a confidentiality requirement.

Are observation and coaching requirements of mentors?

Yes, observation and coaching are required of mentors.

Do mentors formally evaluate new principals?

The relationship between the first-time campus administrator and the mentor is not a supervisory relationship. In some cases, the mentor may be the immediate supervisor, although this is probably not to the advantage of either party. In the case where the mentor is also the immediate supervisor of the first-time campus administrator, the mentor must be particularly careful in differentiating between mentoring activities and supervision.

How much time are mentors expected to work with new principals (weekly, monthly, and for how long)?

Mentors are expected to work with the first-time campus administrator at least once a month during the first year as well as participate in the four academy meetings. In the second year, mentors may meet less frequently with their partners, and they participate in the two academy meetings. They also become learning partners jointly participating in a learning partner project, which is presented at the final academy meeting.

When do mentors meet with the new principals?

The meetings may occur in a variety of locations and settings, but must be face-to-face. In addition to the monthly face-to-face meetings, the partners are encouraged to talk frequently with each other and to meet as often as possible. The use of technology such as e-mail is encouraged as a means of communication but should not replace the face-to-face meetings.

WHAT SUPPORTS ARE AVAILABLE FOR MENTORS?

Are mentors remunerated?

Remuneration of mentors is decided by the local districts.

Are mentors trained? If so, by whom?

Yes, mentors have a two-day training at the beginning of the first year of the program, offered through the academy.

Is there professional development for mentors after the initial training? If so, who provides it?

Yes, mentors participate in four academy meetings in the first year and two academy meetings in the second year of the program. In planning the academy session for the first year, the academy coordinators build upon the information presented in the academy's mentor training and orientation sessions related to the roles of the learning leader model and "First-Year Responsibilities by Quarter" outline in the *Academy Handbook*. The four roles depicted in the roles of the learning leader model address transformational (leadership) and transactional (management) competencies needed by campus administrators. Plenary or role-specific sessions may be planned around the four roles (empowerer, innovator, integrator, and producer) or the competencies associated with the different roles. It is suggested that the coordinator plan at least one session related to the transformational area and one session related to the transactional area for each of the three academy meetings held during the year. The topics may be addressed in a variety of ways (e.g., book reviews, book studies, group sharing, panel discussions, and presentations by experts and/or practitioners).

The "First-Year Responsibilities by Quarter" also provides a rich set of topics for use in planning academy sessions. The coordinator may anticipate upcoming responsibilities and provide sessions where the mentors discuss how to help the first-time administrators in specific areas (e.g., enrollment projections). Working sessions where the mentors and first-time campus administrators work together to plan for upcoming responsibilities may be of value to both parties.

Do mentors meet regularly with other mentors? If so, how often and for how long?

Yes, mentors meet quarterly, as decided locally. In addition, the primary mentors meet with the secondary mentors as needed.

Is there any other ongoing support for mentors? If so, who provides it?

The four academies provide other support for mentors.

Are any other resources available for mentors?

There are many professional development offerings through the Texas Principals Leadership Initiative. Reimbursement for travel expenses is decided locally.

Are mentors supervised? If so, by whom and how frequently?

The academy coordinator supervises the mentors. The mentors are required to keep a record of contacts with the new principals; these and other forms are designed to generate frank discussions with the academy coordinator about the mentoring relationships.

WHAT IS EXPECTED OF NEW PRINCIPALS REGARDING THEIR PARTICIPATION IN THE MENTORING PROGRAM?

How often do new principals meet with their mentors and for how long?

First-time campus administrators meet with their mentors at least once a month, more often if possible. They also participate in four academy meetings during the first year and two academy meetings during the second year.

Are there other people with whom the new principal meets for mentoring and support?

In addition to the primary mentor assigned by the academy coordinator, each first-time campus administrator develops a mentoring support team for herself or himself. The members of the mentoring support team may include the immediate supervisor, central office representatives, college or university professors, and colleagues in similar roles. These other supports are considered secondary mentors and are respected helpers in the administrator's career development process. Typically, the role of the secondary mentor is more limited in scope and degree than that of the primary mentor. The primary mentor of the first-time campus administrator may seek the advice and assistance of secondary mentors on matters related to technical skill, knowledge, or processes. Peers, immediate supervisors, central office personnel, and preparation program faculty may serve as secondary mentors for a new campus administrator.

Is formative assessment of new principals required? If so, when, how, and by whom?

As required in the Texas Administrative Code, adopted by the State Board for Educator Certification (SBEC), each first-time campus administrator should complete an assessment process during the first year of employment as a principal or assistant principal. Individuals holding the Standard Principal Certificate or Standard Mid-Management must select an assessment from the approved list provided by the State Board for Educator Certification (SCEC). Following the required assessment, each principal or assistant principal must develop a professional growth plan. The results of the individual assessment and the professional growth plan will be used exclusively for professional growth purposes and may only be released with the approval of the individual assessed.

Are new principals required to prepare a portfolio?

Each first-time campus administrator is expected to maintain a journal for the two-year induction period. It is a method for recording thoughts, feelings, ideas, and activities. For a certificate renewal, a principal or assistant principal must complete and document continuing education hours. The first-time campus administrator is also expected to maintain a record of contacts with the mentor and/or mentoring team during the induction period. The first-time campus administrator should complete and file all documents required by the SBEC. The Record of Induction Experiences may be used in completing the required SBEC report.

The first-time campus administrator and mentor work together as learning partners during the second year of the program.

ARE ADDITIONAL SUPPORTS AVAILABLE FOR NEW PRINCIPALS?

Is any other professional development provided? If so, when and by whom?

There is a one-day orientation for first-time campus administrators. If possible, this day of orientation is held in the summer prior to the beginning of the school year. The primary focus of this orientation is related to the sharing of expectations for the induction and mentoring period. Each first-time campus administrator receives a *Campus Administrator Handbook* to use in the orientation session and to have as a resource throughout the induction/mentoring period.

In the second year of the mentoring and induction process, the mentoring partners collaborate with each other to research and/or investigate a problem of mutual interest. At the beginning of their second year, the partners provide the academy coordinator with a synopsis and time line for the project. At the end of the second year, the learning partners are encouraged to present their work during the final academy meeting for an academic year.

In planning their learning partner project, the mentoring partners are encouraged to engage in action research. The partners are encouraged to define the problem or topic they will study and decide on the purpose and goals of their study and their techniques for learning the problem or topic. No formal written report is required.

Do new principals meet regularly with other new principals?

First-time administrators meet four times a year at the academies as well as at regional or local school district sessions.

What are the resources required for the mentoring program?

TEPSA allocated $100,000 for the development and piloting of the program. The following are required and are provided at the local and/or regional level; costs are not available.

- Mentor training
- New principal orientation
- Ongoing professional development for mentors and/or new principals
- Food for conferences and meetings
- Materials
- Remuneration for mentors
- Project director's salary, or portion related to mentoring
- Hardware and audiovisual equipment

FUNDING

What are the funding sources?

The TEPSA Board allocated revenue for the development of the program. Districts must commit in writing to the participation of first-time campus administrators and mentors in the academy sessions and must be willing to provide the financial and/or technical support required by the academy. A signed agreement between the academy and each school district outlining the responsibilities of each party is executed prior to a district's participation in the academy. It is essential that mentors and first-time campus administrators perceive that mentoring and induction are viewed as a worthwhile use of professional time and that their districts support the academy as a professional development provider.

Who requests the funding?

Service centers or local districts request the funding from their own sources.

EVALUATION OF THE PROGRAM

Is the program evaluated formatively? Summatively? Who does the evaluation?

Evaluation has been anecdotal, with the director of TEPSA speaking with some of the academy coordinators throughout the state to see how their programs are going. Two doctoral students are surveying the first-time campus administrators and the mentors during fiscal year 2005.

Who sees the results?

The results are seen by

- The Texas Principals Leadership Initiative (a nonprofit collaborative, with Dr. Bobbie Edinns as executive director)
- Dr. Betty Jo Monk
- TEPSA staff and advisory group
- Texas State Board of Education

RECRUITMENT, HIRING, AND RETENTION OF NEW STAFF

How many new principals are recruited and hired each year?

In fiscal year 2005, 1,800–2,000 new principals were hired. In 1999, more than half of the campus administrators in Texas were 45 years old or older. In 2004, the campus administrators were equally divided by age among those who are in their '20s, '30s, '40s, '50s, and '60s.

Are there any data that correlate the mentoring program with the retention of new principals?

Surveys are being conducted in fiscal year 2005.

Are there any data that correlate the mentoring program with the performance of the new principals?

Surveys are being conducted in fiscal year 2005.

What are the indicators of program success?

The following indicate the success of the program:

As an SBEC board member, I realize the goal is to ensure the highest level of educator preparation and practice to achieve student excellence. While much as been made about the teacher shortage, we also face a principal shortage. This program goes a long way toward remedying that shortage.

—*Dr. Troy Simmons, Board Member, State Board for Educator Certification; Past President, Texas Association of School Boards*

The 1st Time Campus Administrators Academy provides the tools necessary to create and implement a supportive structure for those new to campus leadership . . . a great resource for school districts desiring to make a sound investment in their new leaders.

—*Dr. Mike Moses, Superintendent, Dallas Independent School District (ISD)*

Mentor and protégé emerge from the process as more knowledgeable professionals and it ensures the continuity of best practices while merging them with new ideas. I see mentoring as another facet of my own learning.

—*Nellie Morales, Principal, Ysleta ISD, 2001 Texas National Distinguished Principal*

Having the opportunity to establish a trustworthy, supportive mentorship with an experienced administrator who is knowledgeable and confident in the position is a lifeline for a first year administrator.

—*Lisa Conner, Principal, Edinburg Consolidated Independent School District (CISD)*

MODEL 5.5

National Association of Secondary School Principals (NASSP)
Selecting and Developing the 21st Century Principal

Dick Flanary, Director
Office of Professional Development Services
1904 Association Drive, Reston, VA 20191-1537
703-860-0200 x294   flanaryd@principals.org

Urban/suburban/rural school	Not applicable	**Grade levels of school**	Not applicable
Student population	Not applicable	**Per pupil expenditure**	Not applicable
Mentoring is/is not mandated for ongoing certification/licensure	Not applicable	**Mentoring program is/is not funded by the state**	Not applicable
Unique feature of program	Program is based on diagnostic assessment. NASSP works with sponsoring organizations to build their capacity to develop and implement a mentoring program	**Duration of program for new principals**	Duration is flexible depending on needs of individuals and organizations
Mentors are **Full-time principals** **from same district** **from another district** **Retired Principals** **Mentors are trained/not trained for role** **Mentors receive/do not receive ongoing support**	Mentors are full-time principals, typically from the same district Mentors are trained Mentors receive ongoing support	**Mentor selection criteria exist/do not exist** **Mentor matching process exists/does not exist** **Mentors are/are not part of a team to support new principals**	Mentor selection is determined by sponsoring organization Matching process is determined by sponsoring organization It depends on the sponsoring organization as to their designation for the mentor cadre
Coaching is/is not a component	Coaching is a component of the program. Mentors serve as resources to bring in coaches to assist protégés with specific skills	**Daily/weekly/yearly expectations for mentor**	Expectations for the mentors are established by the sponsoring organization.
Mentors evaluate/do not evaluate the new principals	Mentors do not evaluate new principals	**Portfolio is required/is not required**	It depends on the sponsoring organization
Mentor remuneration	It depends on the sponsoring organization	**Higher education affiliation**	It depends on the sponsoring organization
Cost of program	Dictated by number of mentors trained	**Funding**	Funding depends on the sponsoring organization
Years program in existence	Five years	**Full-time/part-time program coordinator/ program coordination is part of another role in system/ organization/ state**	Program coordination is part of role in NASSP

STATE MANDATES

Not applicable.

HISTORY

Why was the program started?

In response to calls for higher standards for school leaders and in anticipation of widespread principal shortages, the National Association of Secondary School Principals (NASSP) developed two skills assessment programs to support the mentoring of aspiring and practicing school leaders. These two skills assessment models provide diagnostic information about a person's strengths and weaknesses, and this information in turn provides a platform to begin a mentor or protégé relationship. Selecting and Developing the 21st Century Principal, a face-to-face skills assessment model, and the Individual Professional Skills Assessment Program, an online tool, present participants with a realistic job preview as they engage in a series of simulations. These two programs are designed to work in concert with NASSP's Mentoring and Coaching Developmental module.

GOALS

What is the goal of the program?

The goal of the program is to develop school leaders who have the skills and attributes required to lead their schools successfully and ensure student success.

PROGRAM DESIGN

Who designed the mentor program?

NASSP staff designed the program.

What are the components and recommended schedule of the program?

These skill assessment programs provide a diagnostic foundation for developing and sustaining effective mentoring programs for aspiring and practicing school leaders. Individuals and organizations benefit from a diagnostic-based mentoring relationship that

- Expands the knowledge base and skill level of potential school leaders and practicing school leaders
- Builds morale of protégés and mentors
- Fosters increased leadership productivity and effectiveness
- Reduces leadership turnover
- Promotes more leadership continuity in the system
- Provides cost-effective development experiences for aspiring school leaders
- Improves quality of school leadership
- Creates a better working environment for teachers
- Enhances learning environment for students

When the mentoring is used in conjunction with the Individual Professional Skills Assessment, there is a combination of face-to-face work and use of an online tool, which presents participants with a series of activities that simulate the job of a school principal to help determine the presence and strength of specific skills or proficiencies in prospective and current school leaders.

These data-driven tools provide each participant with accurate information about her or his leadership strengths and improvement needs that can be used to assist in a mentoring relationship to strengthen existing skills and develop new skills as well as plan career goals and personal and professional self-improvement activities.

Are there any programs that complement the mentor program?

Yes, the Individual Professional Skills Assessment complements the mentor program. It is built on a foundation of skills identified as critical for success in the principalship and is linked to the standards for school leaders developed by the Interstate School Leaders Licensure Consortium (ISLLC). These standards go beyond initial licensure to suggest that school leaders exhibit certain knowledge, dispositions, and standards for performance related to such areas as vision, school culture, organization and management, community involvement, integrity, and the larger political, social, economic, legal, and cultural context. The skills assessment program provides a diagnostic foundation for developing and sustaining effective mentoring programs for aspiring and practicing school leaders.

PROGRAM ADMINISTRATION

Who coordinates the program?

NASSP works with sponsoring organizations to train local personnel to conduct the program.

How is information communicated to shareholders?

Sponsoring organizations communicate the program design, schedule, and outcomes to their networks. NASSP promotes the program nationally through its publications and Web site.

Who coordinates the integration of this program with other professional development opportunities or requirements in the school or district?

Sponsoring organizations coordinate the program with other resources in the district, region, or state.

PARTICIPATION IN THE PROGRAM

Who is served?

A school district is served because the programs strengthen the ability of a district to identify and develop leadership talent.

Individuals benefit because the programs provide a diagnostic foundation for a mentoring relationship that, if successful, increases an individual's leadership capacity.

Is participation of new principals voluntary or mandatory?

The voluntary or mandatory status of the program is a decision of the sponsoring organization.

How long is the program?

The Selecting and Developing the 21st Century Principal skills assessment program is a one-day experience, and the Individual Professional Skills Assessment program, a self-paced program, can take up to five to six hours to complete the assessment portion and another five to six hours to complete the self-analysis portion.

The mentoring and coaching program involves a day and a half for mentor and coach training. The duration of the mentoring relationship is determined by the sponsoring organization and the individuals involved.

WHO PROVIDES THE MENTORING AND INDUCTION?

What are the criteria for being a mentor?

The criteria for being a mentor are as follows. A mentor

- Has demonstrated excellent leadership skills
- Has confidence in her or his own personal and professional development
- Enjoys providing support and encouragement to aspiring and new leaders
- Is knowledgeable about current educational practices and issues
- Has sufficient experience to be skillful as a school leader
- Possesses an understanding of the political and organizational dynamics in organizations
- Is committed to the mentoring process
- Is open to new ideas
- Is sensitive to the needs and concerns of others
- Possesses effective listening skills
- Has received mentor training

Are mentors full-time principals or retired principals?

Successful mentors are both practicing principals and recently retired principals. If mentors are retired, they must possess a relevancy related to the position for which they are providing mentoring or coaching.

Are mentors from the same district as new principals?

Generally, mentors are from the same district; however, some programs engage mentors from other districts.

How are mentors selected?

Mentors are selected based on their meeting the successful mentor criteria.

How are matches made between mentors and new principals?

The mentor or protégé matching process is based on a combination of factors. These factors include areas of developmental interests, developmental assets, and a previous connection for a mentor and protégé.

WHAT IS EXPECTED OF MENTORS?

What are the job responsibilities of the mentor?

Mentors' job responsibilities include

- Providing feedback
- Encouraging professional growth
- Helping protégés build a professional network
- Sharing their information and influence
- Challenging and giving responsibility
- Teaching specific skills
- Assisting protégés to develop an administrative perspective

Is the relationship between the mentor and the new principal confidential?

It is critically important for a mentor and protégé to have a trusting relationship. Trust assures a mentor and protégé that any confidential information will be secure.

Are observation and coaching requirements of mentors?

A mentor must have a means to assess a protégé's performance, whether through real-time coaching or postperformance coaching. Time variables make actual observations difficult sometimes; therefore, journaling and reflective logs are tools that assist a mentor in coaching a protégé.

Do mentors formally evaluate new principals?

Mentors are not a part of the formal evaluation process.

How much time are mentors expected to work with new principals (weekly, monthly, and for how long)?

The time segment varies, depending on the policies of the sponsoring organization. Some mentoring relationships can continue for years. Effective development is ongoing and not related to a specific time period.

When do mentors meet with the new principals?

Mentors meet with new principals as soon as possible to begin establishing the process.

WHAT SUPPORTS ARE AVAILABLE FOR MENTORS?

Are mentors remunerated?

Remuneration for mentors is an organizational decision.

Are mentors trained? If so, by whom?

Mentors should receive formal training. NASSP provides training to mentors in a sponsoring organization.

Is there professional development for mentors after the initial training? If so, who provides it?

Effective mentoring programs provide ongoing development and support to mentors to continue to build their capacity to be effective. NASSP provides ongoing support to mentors.

Do mentors meet regularly with other mentors? If so, how often and for how long?

Effective mentoring programs provide opportunities for mentors to meet regularly to share successes and strategies.

Is there any other ongoing support for mentors? If so, who provides it?

Generally, mentors in an organization develop an internal network of support.

Are any other resources available for mentors?

Mentors are only limited by their own imagination and work in generating additional resources for protégés. Job-embedded development has proven to be very effective, and there is no limitation to the job-embedded opportunities that mentors can create for protégés.

Are mentors supervised? If so, by whom and how frequently?

The mentoring relationship does not require supervision; it does require support, monitoring, and accountability.

WHAT IS EXPECTED OF NEW PRINCIPALS REGARDING THEIR PARTICIPATION IN THE MENTORING PROGRAM?

How often do new principals meet with their mentors and for how long?

The length and frequency of meetings between mentors and protégés is determined by the needs of the protégés and the ability of both the mentors or coaches and protégés to meet.

Are there other people with whom the new principal meets for mentoring and support?

Mentors assist protégés in determining the human and material resources available.

Is formative assessment of new principals required? If so, when, how, and by whom?

Formative assessment is a determination made by the sponsoring organization or school district.

Are new principals required to prepare a portfolio?

Portfolio development and/or evaluation is a determination of the school district.

ARE ADDITIONAL SUPPORTS AVAILABLE FOR NEW PRINCIPALS?

Is any other professional development provided? If so, when and by whom?

Principal professional development is provided by a myriad of organizations and groups. School districts, state departments of education, universities, and state and national professional organizations provide professional development.

Do new principals meet regularly with other new principals?

Yes, new principals generally meet regularly and establish an informal communication network.

What resources are required for the mentoring program?

Program costs vary, depending on the number of mentors to be trained and the programs established by the sponsoring organizations.

FUNDING

What are the funding sources?

Mentor programs can be funded internally or externally. Many national foundations have recently funded the development of aspiring and new principals.

Who requests the funding?
Sponsoring organizations seek their own funding.

EVALUATION OF THE PROGRAM

Is the program evaluated formatively? Summatively? Who does the evaluation?
Successful mentoring programs have a strong evaluative component that allows the organization to determine the success of the program. Evaluation is determined by the sponsoring organizations.

Who sees the results?
All of the individuals involved in the program see the results.

RECRUITMENT, HIRING, AND RETENTION OF NEW STAFF

How many new principals are recruited and hired each year?
Not applicable.

Are there any data that correlate the mentoring program with the retention of new principals?
No data are available at this time.

Are there any data that correlate the mentoring program with the performance of the new principals?
No data are available at this time.

What are the indicators of program success?
Indicators of success are determined and collected by sponsoring organizations.

MODEL 5.6

Association of Washington School Principals (AWSP)
Assessing and Developing the 21st Century Principal

Don Rash, Director of Principal Assessment and Mentoring
Association of Washington School Principals
1021 8th Avenue SE, Olympia, WA 98501
800-562-6100   don@awsp.org

Urban/suburban/rural school	N/A	Grade levels of school	N/A
Student population	N/A	Per pupil expenditure	N/A
Mentoring is/is not mandated for ongoing certification/licensure	Mentoring is not mandated	Mentoring program is/is not funded by the state	There is some funding for mentoring
Unique feature of program	A two-day assessment of principal leadership skills	Duration of program for new principals	One year
Mentors are Full-time principals from same district from another district Retired principals	Mentors are typically retired principals from another district	Mentor selection criteria exist/do not exist Mentor matching process exists/does not exist	Mentors are invited based on their reputation Mentor matching process does exist
Mentors are trained/not trained for role Mentors receive/do not receive ongoing support	Mentors are trained Mentors receive support as needed	Mentors are/are not part of a team to support new principals	Mentors are not part of a team to support new principals
Coaching is/is not a component	Coaching is a component	Daily/weekly/yearly expectations for mentor	Minimally, six full days of mentoring during the course of the school year
Mentors evaluate/do not evaluate the new principals	Mentors do not evaluate	Portfolio is required/ is not required	Portfolio is not required
Mentor remuneration	$1,500	Higher education affiliation	None
Cost of program	$650,000	Funding	Washington State legislature
Years program in existence	Five years	Full-time/part-time program coordinator/program coordination is part of other role in system/ organization/state	Program coordination is part of another role in the organization

STATE MANDATES

Is mentoring mandated for new principals?

No, mentoring is not mandated for new principals.

Is mentoring part of certification or licensure?

No, mentoring is not part of certification or licensure for new principals.

Is funding provided by the state to support the mandate?

Yes, there is some funding for mentoring. Though it is not mandated, there is support for principal assessment and mentoring through the state. Through biennium efforts with the Washington State legislature, support continues, and every biennium funding must be requested. The number of slots made available to participants is based on the amount of funding.

HISTORY

Why was the program started?

The Association of Washington School Principals (AWSP) initiated and administers this project to provide authentic feedback and support to both new and experienced building administrators. The program began in 1999.

GOALS

What are the goals of the program?

The goals of the program are to assess and develop the 21st-century principal. In essence, this program provides training in knowledge and skills to become a performance-based leader in a standards-based educational system.

PROGRAM DESIGN

Who designed the mentor program?

The AWSP has adopted a nationally researched, performance-based principal leadership assessment and mentoring process. It was initiated by the NASSP and is known in Washington State as Assessing and Developing the 21st Century Principal.

What are the components and recommended schedule of the program?

The components of the program are as follows:

- Two-day assessment. The principal leadership skills assessed are
  - Educational leadership, including setting instructional direction; teamwork; sensitivity; and development of others
  - Resolving complex problems, including judgment; results orientation; organizational ability
  - Communication, including oral and written communication
  - Developing self, including understanding own strengths and weaknesses
- One year of mentoring. At a minimum, it is the equivalent of six full days of mentoring. This includes on-site visits, telephone calls, e-mails, and preparation for meetings.

Are there any programs that complement the mentor program?

AWSP trains mentor principals.

PROGRAM ADMINISTRATION

Who coordinates the program?

Don Rash is the director of Assessing and Developing the 21st Century Principal.

How is information communicated to shareholders?

Information is communicated through membership communication, written and electronic, through the state's Office of Superintendent of Public Instruction and through the state's Elementary and Secondary Education Action (ESEA) leadership grant.

Who coordinates the integration of this program with other professional development opportunities or requirements in the school or district?

No one is charged with coordinating the integration of this program with other professional development opportunities or requirements in the school or district, but AWSP does work with school districts to make this an opportunity for their principals.

PARTICIPATION IN THE PROGRAM

Who is served?

This program is designed to serve participants who are in their first three years of building administration. Career principals can participate, but at district expense, whereas principals in their first three years are paid for by legislative allocation.

Is the participation of new principals voluntary or mandatory?

Participation in this program is voluntary.

How long is the program?

There is one year of mentoring.

WHO PROVIDES THE MENTORING AND INDUCTION?

What are the criteria for being a mentor?

The criteria for being a mentor are primarily that they are retired principals who have a record of success in education reform and student achievement.

Are mentors full-time principals or retired principals?

Mentors are usually retired principals.

Are mentors from the same district as new principals?

Mentors are not typically from the same district as new principals.

How are mentors selected?

AWSP invites mentors to participate in the program based on their success as principals.

How are matches made between mentors and new principals?

An attempt is made to match assessor-mentors with new principal participants who are geographically near one another. This reduces travel time and costs. Attempts are also made to match assessor-mentors with new principal participants who have experience at similar administrative levels (elementary, middle level, or high school).

WHAT IS EXPECTED OF MENTORS?

What are the job responsibilities of the mentor?

The responsibilities of the mentor are to

- Administer a performance-based assessment and write an assessment report describing the principal's leadership strengths and growth needs
- Review this confidential report with the participant in a feedback session
- Schedule future meetings and activities with the principal that will support the principal's professional growth plan over the next year

Is the relationship between the mentor and the new principal confidential?

Yes, the relationship is confidential.

Are observation and coaching requirements of mentors?

The mentor-assessor observes the principal in a two-day simulation of leadership challenges.

Do mentors formally evaluate new principals?

No, assessor-mentors do not formally evaluate participating principals. Mentors assess the principal's performance in simulated school settings that are used for multiple, individual, and group activities. Participants complete exercises and are assessed via a performance rubric. Exercises include case studies, "in basket" responses, and interviews. Mentors, who are trained assessors, observe the principals and measure the extent to which they meet the skill requirements of each exercise. Up to two days are required to complete the assessment exercises for each participant.

How much time are mentors expected to work with new principals (weekly, monthly, and for how long)?

At a minimum, mentors meet with new principals at least the equivalent of six full days. This is agreed upon between the principal and the mentor, based on the principal's professional growth plan, which they devise together.

When do mentors meet with the new principals?

Mentors and new principals meet at mutually agreed-upon times.

WHAT SUPPORTS ARE AVAILABLE FOR MENTORS?

Are mentors remunerated?

Yes, mentors are paid $250 per day for the six days of mentoring activities.

Are mentors trained? If so, by whom?

Assessor-mentors are trained in the Assessing and Developing the 21st Century Principal program by a trained trainer from the NASSP and AWSP.

Is there professional development for mentors after the initial training? If so, who provides it?

Yearly mentor meetings are planned.

Do mentors meet regularly with other mentors? If so, how often and for how long?

Mentors meet annually with each other.

Is there any other ongoing support for mentors? If so, who provides it?

Mentors receive ongoing support by AWSP at annual meetings.

Are any other resources available for mentors?

If resources are needed, an attempt is made to provide them.

Are mentors supervised? If so, by whom and how frequently?

Mentors are supervised by their site director and the director of assessment of the mentoring program.

WHAT IS EXPECTED OF NEW PRINCIPALS REGARDING THEIR PARTICIPATION IN THE MENTORING PROGRAM?

How often do new principals meet with their mentors and for how long?

New principals meet with their mentor for one year at a minimum, for the equivalent of six full days of mentoring. This includes on-site visits, telephone calls, e-mails, and preparation for meetings.

Are there other people with whom the new principal meets for mentoring and support?

Other supports for new principals are determined by the individual district and new principal.

Is formative assessment of new principals required? If so, when, how, and by whom?

The mentors are trained assessors who observe new principal participants, and a group of their peers perform a series of performance-based activities that simulate the tasks of a principal. New principals are observed as they demonstrate skills that have been identified as critical for professional success. These include the skills to

- Be an effective educational leader
- Resolve complex problems
- Communicate effectively
- Develop self and others

Are new principals required to prepare a portfolio?

Portfolio requirements are being considered because of new performance-based certification requirements.

ARE ADDITIONAL SUPPORTS AVAILABLE FOR NEW PRINCIPALS?

Is any other professional development provided? If so, when and by whom?

AWSP provides a very comprehensive professional development program that is available to all principals and principal interns.

Do new principals meet regularly with other new principals?

New principals do not meet regularly with other new principals as part of the assessment and mentoring program.

What resources are required for the mentoring program?

The program costs approximately $650,000 per year for 75 new principals. Prior to a state budget cut in 2003, the dollar amount was twice the above amount and twice the principals were able to be assessed and have mentors.

FUNDING

What are the funding sources?

The Washington State legislature funds this program. The amount funded determines the number of new principals who may be selected to participate.

Who requests the funding?

AWSP, through the Office of Superintendent of Public Instruction, requests the funds from the legislature.

EVALUATION OF THE PROGRAM

Is the program evaluated formatively? Summatively? Who does the evaluation?

Participants and assessor-mentors complete an evaluation at the end of the year of mentoring. Mentors keep a detailed log of items discussed, actions taken, and activities completed for each mentoring session.

Who sees the results?

Results of the program evaluation are shared with the site directors, reviewed by the director of the program, and then shared with the AWSP executive staff.

RECRUITMENT, HIRING, AND RETENTION OF NEW STAFF

How many new principals are recruited and hired each year?

Approximately 300 new principals throughout the state of Washington are recruited and hired each year.

Are there any data that correlate the mentoring program with the retention of new principals?

No, there are not any data correlating the mentoring program with the retention of new principals.

Are there any data that correlate the mentoring program with the performance of the new principals?

There are numerous very positive testimonials from participating principals and their superintendents.

What are the indicators of program success?

Anecdotal comments, including the following:

The assessment and mentoring [have] been quite valuable. I've gained insights about my administrative style areas that I can address to be a more productive administrator and resources and connections that will assist me in my role.

My mentor provided me with outstanding insights and strategies. I did not realize how "alone" I had been feeling. I appreciate the collegial support of all of the experienced staff. I would not have survived my first year without you.

It was helpful to hear the private and constructive criticism from an experienced mentor who, without reservation, helped me to reflect clearly. I would do the assessment again, given the opportunity.

It made me much more aware of involving my vision in daily communication. In balancing time vs. perfectionism, I have found that I can take care of managerial matters faster—leaving me more time for instructional leadership.

This program/opportunity is so very valuable to administrators, so much so that I continue to encourage my colleagues to take advantage of it. The mentor program is probably the most valuable part.

University Models

MODEL 6.1

University of California, Santa Cruz
Coaching Leaders to Attain Student Success (CLASS)
The New Teacher Center (NTC)

Gary Bloom, Associate Director
The New Teacher Center
725 Front Street, Suite 400, Santa Cruz, CA 95060
831-459-4323   gsbloom@ucsc.edu   www.newteachercenter.org

The following descriptions are mostly taken from brochures and materials published by The New Teacher Center, with their permission.

Urban/suburban/ rural school	Not applicable	**Grade levels of school**	Not applicable
Student population	Not applicable	**Per pupil expenditure**	Not applicable
Mentoring is/is not mandated for ongoing certification/ licensure	Mentoring is not mandated for the clear professional credential	**Mentoring program is/is not funded by the state**	No state funding
Unique feature of program	One-on-one coaching for two years	**Duration of program for new principals**	Two years
Mentors are full-time principals from same district / from another district **Retired principals**	Coaches are full-time or part-time coaches, from another or no school district Many coaches are recently retired principals	**Mentor selection criteria exist/do not exist** **Mentor matching process exists/does not exist**	Candidates are highly experienced administrators who possess a track record of success A selection process includes interviews, a coaching role play, and reference checks. Coaches are matched by program coordinator(s)
Mentors are trained/not trained for role **Mentors receive/do not receive ongoing support**	Coaches must have CLASS foundation training and participate in ongoing CLASSNet, which meets monthly for NTC coaches and four times for coaches not directly hired by NTC. Beginning in 2004, the NTC is able to credential new principals, and the coaches working with credential candidates have to be certified by the NTC.	**Mentors are/are not part of a team to support new principals**	This varies by school district. In districts where leadership coaching is established, there are clear systems of support for novice principals. This is a system for which the NTC advocates
Coaching is/is not a component	Coaching is the main component	**Daily/weekly/yearly expectations for mentor**	Coaching once every two weeks for first year and once every three weeks in second year. Intermediate contacts by home and e-mail are offered
Mentors evaluate/do not evaluate the new principals	Coaches do not evaluate	**Portfolio is required/ is not required**	Coaches seeking certification must complete a portfolio in the certification process
Mentor remuneration	Coaches are paid $3,000 per coachee	**Higher education affiliation**	University of California, Santa Cruz
Cost of program	$3,500 per coachee	**Funding**	Foundations
Years program in existence	Six years	**Full-time/part-time program coordinator/ program coordination is part of other role in system/ organization/state**	Full-time coordinator

STATE MANDATES

Is mentoring mandated for new principals?

No, although the state allows for a number of credential pathways, not all of which include a mentoring component.

Is mentoring part of certification or licensure?

The Coaching Leaders to Attain Student Success (CLASS) program is the only state-approved mentoring-based authorized pathway to the clear professional credential. The clear professional credential is the second stage of the California administrative services credential. First, administrators get a preliminary credential, typically by taking a college-based program. Five years after getting their first position, administrators must complete additional requirements for the clear credential, either through a program such as at the New Teacher Center (NTC) or through an institution of higher education.

Is funding provided by the state to support the mandate

No state funding is currently allocated for any professional credentialing program.

HISTORY

Why was the program started?

A large body of research demonstrates the critical importance of effective school site leadership. Our nation's schools are currently facing an unprecedented need for new school leaders and a critical shortage of qualified candidates. Our schools and our students will suffer if they are burdened with unprepared, unsupported leaders and with high administrative turnover.

The NTC at the University of California, Santa Cruz, is nationally recognized for its expertise in professional development and teacher induction. This research-based program has demonstrated its effectiveness in supporting site administrators in their first years of service.

GOALS

What is the goal of the program?

The goal of the program is to support site administrators in their first years of service. While the work of the NTC is consistent with the California Professional Standards for Educational Leaders (CPSEL) and the Interstate School Leaders Licensure Consortium (ISLLC), they place an emphasis upon the development of school leaders who

- Are committed to equity and to the role of education in a democracy
- Focus relentlessly upon student achievement
- Understand the power of collaboration
- Are teacher leaders and envision school administration as one teacher leadership role along a continuum of teacher professional growth
- Possess a leadership style that is inclusive and collaborative and are committed to building the leadership capacity of staff, students, and community
- Are learners and are committed to their own ongoing professional growth through collaborative processes and through cycles of action and reflection
- Support teachers and their professional development and build a community of practice that is focused upon student achievement

- Have expertise in a broad spectrum of areas, including instruction, adult learning, communication, assessment, supervision, organizational development, community engagement, and change processes
- Are fueled by a passion to make a difference; they see themselves as change agents and are relentless in the pursuit of their vision for students, school, and staff.

PROGRAM DESIGN

Who designed the mentor program?

This program was designed by NTC staff, based on their 16 years of experience working with beginning teachers and school leadership. The Stupski and Noyce Foundations contributed to the development of these teacher induction and administrative leadership development programs.

What are the components and recommended schedule of the program?

The key components of the program are as follows:

- First-year principals receive one-on-one coaching with an experienced coach once every two weeks.
- Second-year principals continue one-on-one coaching with an experienced coach once every three weeks.
- Coaches maintain weekly communication via telephone and e-mail.
- Mentoring includes observation of principals engaged in real work that will allow for targeted coaching, to include at a minimum
  - A teacher observation cycle
  - Facilitation of a staff or site council meeting
  - A case study of a teacher's professional development
  - A school culture analysis
- Coaches provide
  - Educational research
  - Professional development
  - School improvement resources
  - Organizational strategies
  - A 360-degree feedback process for the principal
- Coaches participate in a three-day foundational training.
- Networking sessions and workshops for principals take place four times each year. Workshops are tailored to the needs of each group and are designed to further the learning of the coaching group.

Are there any programs that complement the mentor program?

The NTC offers a New Administrator Institute, which is a series of nine seminars that focus on the knowledge and skills essential to site leadership and designed to complement the New Administrator Program. In addition, the NTC collaborates with a number of programs, both inside and outside of California, to design and deliver content-based seminars in support of principal development.

PROGRAM ADMINISTRATION

Who coordinates the program?

Gary Bloom is the associate director the NTC's Administrative Leadership Division. Ellen Moir is the executive director of the NTC.

Program coordination is managed by the NTC Administrative Leadership Development team.

How is information communicated to shareholders?

Information about the CLASS New Administrator Program (NAP) is communicated through flyers, brochures, e-mails, presentations, the Web, as well as through the Association of California School Administrators (ACSA) publications.

Who coordinates the integration of this program with other professional development opportunities or requirements in the school or district?

The NTC is committed to the implementation of focused and coherent professional development in its client districts. NTC program coordinators lead this process in client districts.

PARTICIPATION IN THE PROGRAM

Who is served?

First- and second-year principals, vice principals, and other novices are served by CLASS. Although the focus of CLASS is the novice site administrator, the program has also served central office and veteran site administrators.

Is the participation of new principals voluntary or mandatory?

Participation in CLASS is voluntary.

How long is the program?

CLASS is a two-year program. Occasionally, client districts request one-year coaching relations, which the NTC honors. Some principals have requested a third year in the program, and those requests are met as well.

WHO PROVIDES THE MENTORING AND INDUCTION?

What are the criteria for being a mentor?

A key expectation for the role of the coach in the NAP program is a track record of successful site-level leadership. The program looks for coaches who have served at the school site for more than five years, believing that significant tenure as a principal strengthens the coach's ability to support the novice principal. Candidates for coaching positions are screened through a multiphase process, which includes an interview, a coaching role play, and professional reference screening.

Are mentors full-time principals or retired principals?

CLASS coaches are either full-time administrators on loan to the university or retirees.

Are mentors from the same district as new principals?

In most cases, coaches are not from the same district as new principals. The CLASS model advocates for a coach who is outside the district of the novice administrator.

How are mentors selected?

Coaches submit a cover letter and resume with references and are interviewed by NTC staff. The interview includes a simulated coaching situation. References are carefully checked.

How are matches made between mentors and new principals?

The program coordinator matches the coach and the coachee, matching background and experience. Frequently the district will identify qualities that might best fit the novice administrator's needs and situation.

WHAT IS EXPECTED OF MENTORS?

What are the job responsibilities of mentors?

Coaches are expected to

- Do one-on-one coaching once every two weeks in the first year and once every three weeks in the second year
- Maintain weekly communication via telephone and e-mail
- Observe and do target coaching, to include at a minimum
  - A teacher observation cycle
  - Facilitation of a staff or site council meeting
  - A case study of a teacher's professional development
  - A school cultural analysis
  - A 360-degree feedback process with the principal

Is the relationship between the mentor and the new principal confidential?

Yes, the relationship is entirely confidential. Coaches keep the principal's supervisor apprised of the type of activities that are taking place. However, comments are never evaluative in nature.

Are observation and coaching requirements of mentors?

Yes, observation and coaching are requirements of coaches. Coaching takes place in real time—during the school day, in real work situations.

Do mentors formally evaluate new principals?

No, coaches do not formally evaluate new principals. Their role is as a confidential support to the novice administrator.

How much time are mentors expected to work with new principals (weekly, monthly, and for how long)?

Coaches work with new principals once every two weeks for the first year and once every three weeks the second year. Depending on the situation and the needs of the coachee, meetings are typically from one and one-half hours to three hours in duration. Occasionally, coaches will shadow the coachee for a half or full day.

When do mentors meet with the new principals?

Coaches meet with new principals during the school day. They are also available to observe evening meetings and other high-stakes events.

WHAT SUPPORTS ARE AVAILABLE FOR MENTORS?

Are mentors remunerated?

Coaches are paid as consultants and receive a set fee per client, as well as a mileage reimbursement.

Are mentors trained? If so, by whom?

CLASS is a three-day foundational training offered by NTC staff. The training focuses on the knowledge, skills, strategies, and tools critical for individuals who coach beginning and/or experienced principals. All coaches must participate in the CLASS training as well in the yearly coaching network—CLASSNet.

Key components of this training are as follows:

- Blended coaching strategies
- A variety of basic coaching skills
- A range of tools and resources for coaches and their coaches
- The importance of understanding emotional intelligence, mood, and dispositions
- The establishment of trust and rapport
- The initiation, maintenance, and strengthening of the coaching relationship
- Coaching that strengthens cultural proficiency
- Coaching that is used for systemic solutions
- Listening skills to empower the coaching relationship
- The importance of understanding and coaching through personal and situational bias
- Instructional, facilitative, and transformational coaching
- The importance of understanding the power of listening for assertions and assessments

CLASS training and support for the development of principal induction programs are offered by the NTC to interested districts and other agencies on a contract basis.

Is there professional development for mentors after the initial training? If so, who provides it?

The NTC offers CLASSNet, which is an ongoing series of professional development seminars designed to continue to build the coach's coaching expertise and practice. Participation in the network is mandatory for those coaches seeking coaching certification through the NTC. CLASSNet includes an online resource. CLASS coaches may be eligible for certification by the NTC and the ACSA as master coaches.

Do mentors meet regularly with other mentors? If so, how often and for how long?

The NTC coaching cadre meets monthly for three hours. Coaches working independently attend CLASSNet. CLASSNet meets four times a year for full-day sessions.

Is there any other ongoing support for mentors? If so, who provides it?

Coaches new to the center shadow veteran CLASS coaches and in turn are shadowed by a veteran coach. Ongoing support and consultation are offered to all coaches by veteran CLASS coaching staff.

Are any other resources available for mentors?

Coaches are invited to attend NTC seminars developed for school administrators.

Are mentors supervised? If so, by whom and how frequently?

Coaches are supervised by the program director via a process of shadowing and through the online interview process with the principal, coached for feedback on the coach. Coaches seeking certification complete a portfolio process, receive written feedback from coaches, and a coaching observation.

WHAT IS EXPECTED OF NEW PRINCIPALS REGARDING THEIR PARTICIPATION IN THE MENTORING PROGRAM?

How often do new principals meet with their mentors and for how long?

Principals meet with their coach once every two weeks the first year and once every three weeks the second year. Meetings between coaches and coachees are from one and one-half to three hours. Coaches also shadow coaches for longer periods of time, that is, a full or half day as the need arises.

Are there other people with whom the new principal meets for mentoring and support?

The program encourages districts to appoint an in-house mentor for novice administrators. The NTC provides networking sessions and workshops for principals that take place approximately three times each year. Workshops are tailored to the needs of each group. Most participants in the NAP typically attend the New Administrator Institute series as well.

Is formative assessment of new principals required? If so, when, how, and by whom?

A formative assessment process was developed and implemented in 2004 for clear credential candidates. This process may extend to the entire coaching program, but that process has not yet been determined.

Are new principals required to prepare a portfolio?

Candidates participating in the clear credential program complete an online portfolio as part of the CLASS credentialing program.

ARE ADDITIONAL SUPPORTS AVAILABLE FOR NEW PRINCIPALS?

Is any other professional development provided? If so, when and by whom?

The NTC offers a New Administrator Institute—a series of nine seminars focusing on the knowledge and skills essential to site leadership and designed to complement the NAP. The institute developed as a partnership between the NTC and the California School Leadership Academy at the Santa Clara County Office of Education.

Do new principals meet regularly with other new principals?

Principals attending the New Administrator Institute meet monthly with other novice administrators.

The NTC encourages participating districts to organize in district cohort support and induction to further support their novice administrators.

What resources are required for the mentoring program?

- Coach training: $475 for the three-day CLASS training
- New principal orientation: $800 per person or $650 per person if the district sends a team of more than two administrators to the New Administrator Institute. Districts pay $3,500 per year for CLASS model coaching
- Ongoing professional development for coaches and/or new principals: CLASSNet is $450 for the four yearly sessions
- Remuneration for coaches: Coaches receive $3,000 per coachee
- Project director's salary, or portion related to coaching: Has not been calculated

FUNDING

What are the funding sources?

With support from the Noyce and the Stupski Foundations, the NTC built this site administrator induction program.

CLASS coaching uses direct revenue to support the cost of full- and part-time coaches.

Who requests the funding?

The associate director and the NTC grant writer seek funding to support the work of CLASS, the NAP, and the New Administrator Institute.

EVALUATION OF THE PROGRAM

Is the program evaluated formatively? Summatively? Who does the evaluation?

The NTC Research Team does a yearly internal evaluation. All participants complete a survey in the fall and spring that assesses the impact of the coaching support on their leadership and retention as administrators.

Who sees the results?

The NTC Research Team and coaching staff review the results and identify areas for future research and program development. In addition, each CLASS coach receives evaluative feedback from participants for their analysis and planning. The CLASS coaching team uses the aggregated evaluation data for program assessment and planning.

RECRUITMENT, HIRING, AND RETENTION OF NEW STAFF

How many new principals are recruited and hired each year?

Not applicable.

Are there any data that correlate the mentoring program with the retention of new principals?

Research is underway to study the impact of the program on the retention of participants. Perceptual data collected in the yearly evaluation survey indicate that many participants credit their coach for their survival and their remaining on the job.

Are there any data that correlate the mentoring program with the performance of the new principals?

There is not any data at this time.

What are the indicators of program success?

A yearly survey of all coachees indicates overwhelming support for the coaching program. A common theme in the participant evaluation survey is the comment that without the coach, the participants would not have survived their first years on the job.

The following are comments from participants in CLASS:

Everything I needed, my advisor provided. If he couldn't provide it, he found a way to provide it through other sources.

There were times I felt very isolated and really alone . . . and it was nice to know that my advisor was right there.

I'm really happy with the advisors, the people spearheading this program . . . truly quite impressed with what they're doing, what they're trying to do, and how they're trying to develop things.

Other than being exhausted . . . I love my job. I love it! It felt like I make a difference. It's good to be asked that question, Why do you do what you do in this job, because yesterday I graduated a class of students, and it's right in front of you when you look at them!

MODEL 6.2

University of North Carolina
Leadership Program for New Principals

Alice Maniloff, Assistant Director
Center for School Leadership Development
University of North Carolina, Chapel Hill, NC 27517
919-962-1641   amanilof@northcarolina.edu

Urban/suburban/rural school	Not applicable	Grade levels of school	Not applicable
Student population	Not applicable	Per pupil expenditure	Not applicable
Mentoring is/is not mandated for ongoing certification/ licensure	Mentoring is not mandated	Mentoring program is/is not funded by the state	Mentoring is not funded
Unique feature of program	18-day program, ISLLC based	Duration of program for new principals	One year

Mentors are
Full-time principals
  from same district
  from another district
Retired principals
	Mentoring is not part of the program	Mentor selection criteria exist/do not exist
		
		Mentor matching process exists/does not exist
			Not applicable
			
			Not applicable

Mentors are trained/not trained for role Mentors receive/do not receive ongoing support	Not applicable Not applicable	Mentors are/are not part of a team to support new principals	Not applicable
Coaching is/is not a component	Coaching is not a component	Daily/weekly/yearly expectations for mentor	Not applicable
Mentors evaluate/do not evaluate the new principals	Not applicable	Portfolio is required/is not required	Portfolio is not required
Mentor remuneration	Not applicable	Higher education affiliation	University of North Carolina
Cost of program	$1,000 per participant	Funding	State legislature
Years program in existence	20 years	Full-time/part-time program coordinator/program coordination is part of another role in system/organization/ state	Program coordination is part of another role

Used with permission of Alice Maniloff, Assistant Director of The Center for School Leadership Development, University of North Carolina Leadership Program for New Principals.

STATE MANDATES

Is mentoring mandated for new principals?
No, mentoring is not mandated for new principals.

Is mentoring part of certification or licensure?
No, mentoring is not part of certification.

Is funding provided by the state to support the mandate?
No, the state doesn't fund mentoring.

HISTORY

Why was the program started?
The overall program was started 20 years ago by C. D. Spangler, who was then the chair of the North Carolina State Board of Education. He was a graduate of the Harvard Business School. He returned to Harvard every summer to an executive refresher course, and he wanted something like that for principals. He realized that principals were trained as teachers, not as managers or leaders. So the overall Principal Executive Program began as a leadership program for practicing principals. Twenty years ago, the program was 26 days long. It was the same program whether you were an elementary, middle, or high school administrator. It was heavily rooted in liberal arts. Since then, principals' time has become much more restricted, and so the programs have become differentiated as to need. Now there are separate programs for assistant principals, experienced high school principals, and new principals.

The New Principals Program is 18 days long, beginning in September and ending in March. There were 75 participants in 2004, up from 25 the previous year. The year 2005 marks the seventh year of this program. There are more new principals in the state, and the program is committed to not having a waiting list.

GOALS

What are the goals of the program?
The leadership program for new principals is designed to strengthen leadership behaviors and management skills.

PROGRAM DESIGN

Who designed the mentor program?
The faculty of the Leadership Program for New Principals designed the program, and it has been revised through the years.

What are the components and recommended schedule of the program?
The components of the program are as follows:

- There are six required two and one-half-day residential sessions. Participants work in a collaborative group of 75 as well as school-level breakout groups.
- The program is organized around the Interstate School Leaders Licensure Consortium (ISLLC) standards:

- The program starts with ISLLC Standard 3—management. New principals could get fired over management issues faster than anything else.
- The second session has to do with school culture and the political nature of the job.
- The third session is on instructional issues.
- The fourth session is on community and diversity.
- The fifth session is on ethics.
- The last session, which is actually ISLLC Standard 1, is vision. Principals can only get to vision after they've lived in the culture for a year.
- Some of the topics covered include the following:
  - Best practices in instructional leadership
  - Change management
  - Effective professional development standards
  - Personnel law and student legal issues
  - The use of school data to improve instruction
  - The development of capacity and leadership in teachers
  - The importance of school culture
- Instructors are nationally recognized experts as well as North Carolina leaders.
- "Expert" principals, some of whom have been through this program before, are included. They are not assigned as mentors; they are there to react to the keynotes. They also give some panel discussions on "how it really is." The hope is that by putting practicing, experienced principals in front of new principals, the new principals will think they can call upon the experienced ones presenting.

Are there any programs that complement the mentor program?

There is a program for schools receiving federal funds for whole-school improvement efforts, and that program has involved mentors. That is a fee-based program that is purchased by the school districts.

PROGRAM ADMINISTRATION

Who coordinates the program?

Alice Maniloff, assistant director of the Center for School Leadership Development at the University of North Carolina, coordinates the program.

How is information communicated to shareholders?

Information is communicated through

- A monthly Listserv to every principal in the state of North Carolina, where new programs are announced
- Letters to superintendents
- Word of mouth (this is the oldest, longest-standing principal training academy in the United States)

Who coordinates the integration of this program with other professional development opportunities or requirements in the school or district?

Not applicable.

PARTICIPATION IN THE PROGRAM

Who is served?
The program serves 75 new principals who have applied to be in it.

Is the participation of new principals voluntary or mandatory?
Some individual superintendents require their principals to attend this program. Typically, the program is voluntary.

How long is the program?
The program is one year long.

WHO PROVIDES THE MENTORING AND INDUCTION?

Not applicable. Mentors are not specifically part of the program.

WHAT IS EXPECTED OF MENTORS?

Not applicable.

WHAT SUPPORTS ARE AVAILABLE FOR MENTORS?

Not applicable.

WHAT IS EXPECTED OF NEW PRINCIPALS REGARDING THEIR PARTICIPATION IN THE MENTORING PROGRAM?

How often do new principals meet with their mentors and for how long?
Not applicable.

Are there other people with whom the new principal meets for mentoring and support?
The new principals may individually contact some of the experienced principals who presented during the sessions. Generally, the new principals tend to communicate with each other. They form support groups among themselves.

Is formative assessment of new principals required? If so, when, how, and by whom?
Formative assessment of new principals is anecdotal.

Are new principals required to prepare a portfolio?
No, portfolios are not required.

ARE ADDITIONAL SUPPORTS AVAILABLE FOR NEW PRINCIPALS?

Is any other professional development provided? If so, when and by whom?

Eighteen days is probably enough for new principals during their first year.

Do new principals meet regularly with other new principals?

New principals informally meet with each other.

What resources are required for the program?

The program costs $1,000 per participant.

FUNDING

What are the funding sources?

The state legislature funds the program.

Who requests the funding?

The program is a recurring budget item embedded in the state budget.

EVALUATION OF THE PROGRAM

Is the program evaluated formatively? Summatively? Who does the evaluation?

The program is formatively evaluated daily, after each session, and adjustments are made accordingly. Periodically, there are full-scale evaluations. The last one was done by Stephanie Hirsch of the National Staff Development Council (NSDC) in 2002.

Who sees the results?

An oversight committee of the state legislature sees the evaluations.

RECRUITMENT, HIRING, AND RETENTION OF NEW STAFF

How many new principals are recruited and hired each year?

Information about how many principals are recruited and hired is not available. It has been said, anecdotally, that assistant principals from the program are often hired for principalships. They think the New Principals Program gives them a leg up in hiring.

Are there any data that correlate the program with the retention of new principals?

No, there aren't any data that correlate the program with the retention of new principals.

Are there any data that correlate the program with the performance of the new principals?

There are anecdotal data and focus group data from the new principals; it is all self-reported. Superintendents are not given information about program participants' performance.

What are the indicators of program success?

The program tripled in 2004 from 25 to 75 participants. Feedback on the question about what was valuable to participants included the following:

The collaboration and expertise from other principals just like me. How wonderful to network and find support in other administrators. The sessions were outstanding; well-planned and appropriate topics.

Case study—working with a partner to create a division of labor in attacking the problem and then feeling our solution was not only cost saving but also creative. Networking with administrators outside of my district.

The opportunity to interact (inside and outside the sessions) with colleagues who have relevant experiences that I can learn from.

The most valuable experience that I had was in school finance. I learned information that I needed to help me operate efficiently.

I will use the tools I have been given to gather information to help me make decisions. I will also apply the techniques we learned in the power thinking session. Most of all I will not hesitate to call on others for help and/or advice.

I am going to set up a data day and incorporate data at *all* faculty meetings. I am going to review our financial procedures and set up regular times to conference with my treasurer.

I will use the power thinking to be a reflective practitioner to try to improve my own leadership qualities.

I will introduce the Socratic seminars to my staff for a change in thinking.

I will use my self-assessment results to help me be more effective in my instructional leadership. It was helpful to network with other principals and see different perspectives and realize that different strategies can work in similar situations.

I will use the data information to help students, teachers, and parents understand what they all need to do to help students show growth.

Better, more focused staff development concentrating more on instrumental strategies.

Collaborative
Models

MODEL 7.1

Arkansas Leadership Academy and Master Principal Program

Dr. Paula Cummins, Associate Director
Arkansas Leadership Academy
32323 Kanis Road, Paron, AR 72122
501-821-9917   pgcummins@aol.com

Dr. Beverly Elliott, Director
Arkansas Leadership Academy
University of Arkansas
346 North West Avenue, Room 300, Fayetteville, AR 72701
beverly@uark.edu

Urban/suburban/rural school	All	Grade levels of school	K–12
Student population	Not applicable	Per pupil expenditure	Not applicable
Mentoring is/is not mandated for ongoing certification/ licensure	Mentoring is mandated	Mentoring program is/is not funded by the state	Mentoring program is funded by the state
Unique feature of program	Forty-four partners developed program; performance assessments after each learning phase, needed before movement to learning phase; principals eligible for up to $34,000 per year bonus upon completion	Duration of program for principals	Minimum of three years, for principals with experience
Mentors are Full-time principals from same district from another district Retired principals	Performance coaches are educators who have appropriate knowledge, skills, and experience	Coach selection criteria exist/do not exist Coach matching process exists/does not exist	Performance coach selection criteria exist but are not fully formalized Performance coach matching process does exist
Mentors are trained/not trained for role Mentors receive/do not receive ongoing support	Performance coaches are trained Performance coaches do receive ongoing support	Mentors are/are not part of a team to support new principals	Coaches are part of a support team

(Continued)

MODEL 7.1 (Continued)

Mentoring is/is not a component	Performance coaching is a component	**Daily/weekly/yearly expectations for performance**	Weekly
Performance coaches evaluate/do not evaluate the new principals	Performance coaches do not evaluate	**Portfolio is required/is not required**	Portfolio is required
Mentor remuneration	Performance coaches are paid $1,000	**Higher education affiliation**	Thirteen Arkansas universities are partners in the Arkansas Leadership Academy
Cost of program	State funds Master Principal Program at $500,000 per year	**Funding**	State
Years program in existence	First year for Master Principal Program based on 13-year history of Arkansas Leadership Academy	**Full-time/part-time program coordinator/program coordination is part of another role in system/organization/state**	Full-time program coordinator

Used with permission of Paula Cummins, Associate Director, Arkansas Leadership Academy.

(See Chapter 4 for the Arkansas Beginning Administrator Induction Program for new administrators, which complements this program.)

STATE MANDATES

Is mentoring mandated for new principals?

Yes, mentoring is mandated for new principals. In 2000 the first group of administrators had performance-based programs in their university study. Since then, anyone who comes out of those programs is required to have a mentor.

Is mentoring part of certification or licensure?

Yes, mentoring is part of the certification requirements.

Is funding provided by the state to support the mandate?

Yes, the state provides funding for the program.

HISTORY

Why was the program started?

The Arkansas Leadership Academy was created by the legislature in 1991 to "raise the skill and knowledge base of principals, superintendents, board members, other administrators and teachers." The design of the academy was to involve stakeholders as partners and focus on system change by developing leadership throughout the system. The job of the Leadership Academy is to work with any educational leader who is trying to make a difference, regardless of the job title. Over the years, various programs have been developed out of the shareholder groups, including superintendents, school boards, principals, and teachers. There are 44 partners who represent all the educational stakeholders in the state.

In spring 2004, the Arkansas Legislative Assembly voted into law the newest program for the Arkansas Leadership Academy to design and administer. It is the Master Principal Program. The program is a three-phase process with performance assessment at the end of each phase. The guidelines for entry include three years of experience as a principal.

Earlier legislation mandated that first-year principals must have a mentor in that year. After two or more years, they may enter the Master Principal Program. The Master Principal Program is the extension of the Arkansas Beginning Administrator Induction Program in Chapter 4.

The 44 partners come together several times a year to help develop the strategic direction of the academy. The partners are: 4 (all) of the state agencies that work with education (the State Department of Education, Educational Television, Department of Workforce Education, Department of Higher Education); 13 deans of the Colleges of Education; 15 educational service center directors; 10 professional organizations (Arkansas School Board Association; Arkansas Educational Administrator Association; Arkansas Education Association; Arkansas Teacher Union; Arkansas Association of Supervision and Curriculum Development [ASCD]; Arkansas & the National Teachers of the Year; Arkansas North Central Association; Arkansas Rural Education Association; Arkansas School Public Relations Association; and Arkansas Parent Teachers Association); 2 business and industry: Wal-Mart Stores Inc. and Tyson Foods Inc. (which are both Arkansas companies). The partners meet several times a year to discuss strategies and align their organizations to support the needs of the school leaders of Arkansas.

The partners help develop the strategic direction of the academy services. The staff researches best practices and designs the professional development. The research and work with principals began in 1999.

GOALS

What are the goals of the Master Principal Program?

The goal is to heighten leadership effectiveness across the state. This was not mandated. Principals determine if this is the best professional development for them. It is based on an understanding that everyone can get better. Higher means leading at the master level, which includes being effective in turning around a school and having the ability to help others do the same thing.

PROGRAM DESIGN

Who designed the induction program?

A team of nine people from around the country researched what principals need to know and be able to do. The content of the Master Principal Program is the five performance areas:

1. Leading and managing change

2. Possessing deep knowledge about teaching and learning

3. Building and maintaining accountability systems

4. Creating and living the vision and mission (culture)

5. Building and maintaining collaborative relationships, both internally and externally

What are the components and recommended schedule of the program?

The Master Principal Program has three phases. Principals have the option to complete a performance assessment to apply for the next phase. The performance assessment includes a portfolio with narratives and artifacts to show evidence of progress on each of the five performance areas. There are also interviews with the principals and other shareholders of the school and site visits to the school. Independent scorers use a rubric to score each portfolio. Participants who score in proficient move to the next phase.

Phase 1 begins in July. It is a four-day event. Phase 1 principals meet three additional times over the year for three days each time. There are work assignments that the principals apply in their own schools between these quarterly sessions. Since the Master Principal Program is an expansion of the original Principal Institute, a number of principals have had the basic curriculum of Phase 3. Those principals can apply to move into Phase 2 by completing the portfolio requirements described above. Also, graduates of the performance-based university programs who have three years of experience as building-level principals can develop the portfolio described above and be selected into Phase 2.

The same portfolio process moves a principal into Phase 3 and into the designation of Master Principal. The legislature and the Arkansas Department of Education administer the bonuses that are linked to the Master Principal designation.

Are there any programs that complement the Leadership Academy?

Over 13 years, the academy has offered professional development to support system change. While there are institutes for superintendents and CEOs and teachers, the institutes that are most relevant to principals are the following:

The Team Institute

Teams of educators from school districts, universities, and coagencies learn and practice the language, processes, and tools for building high-performing teams. They also learn a process for strategic planning, using a model that can be a blueprint for solving any problem. This institute includes all leaders—parents, teachers, principals, community members, board members, superintendents, and university professors. Each team leaves the institute with a product as well as the skills and tools to engage others in a change process.

Each team is provided with a trained process coach. The process coaches, who volunteer their time to work with a team for a week, are trained. Many principals take this training and work as a process coach with a team from another district as a way to practice what they are learning before they do it in their own building. Teachers, superintendents, deans, and professional association representatives all work as process coaches.

Seminars

When a partner or district identifies a need for an innovation that will strengthen the mission of the academy partners and/or the system, the staff develops and provides the supports needed for professional development. These institutes vary in length, audience, and purpose. These seminars are not duplications of a service that another partner does. For example, the university trains principals. The new licensure program requires that new principals be mentored. The academy does not do mentoring for new principals. The Arkansas Department of Education does the professional development part of the Team Institute and handles the specifics of mentoring. Their goal is to get practicing administrators to support the new principals during their first year. Since those programs are in place, the academy's role is to provide continuous professional development for principals after mentoring.

PROGRAM ADMINISTRATION

Who coordinates the program?

The Arkansas Leadership Academy is a collaborative partnership housed at the University of Arkansas and operates with the following staff: director, associate director, Master Principal leader, and Teacher Institute leader.

How is information communicated to shareholders?

As a statewide collaborative partnership, the shareholder partners help develop the information and communicate within their organizations. Those organizations include parents (state PTA organization), universities, education service cooperatives, professional associations, governmental agencies (Department of Education), and business. The Arkansas Leadership Academy also has a newsletter and a Web site.

Graduates and current Master Principal Program participants are connected with a principal Listserv. Each principal at Phase 2 or Phase 3 of the Master Principal Program has a performance coach. Those performance coaches are members of the principal Listserv and have their own coach Listserv as one element of their community of practice.

Who coordinates the integration of this program with other professional development opportunities or requirements in the school or district?

As a collaborative organization, the Arkansas Leadership Academy has a goal to work collaboratively so that efforts are targeted and focused on appropriate professional development opportunities throughout the state that are aligned with the vision of the state and with the needs of the students, schools, districts, and staff.

PARTICIPATION IN THE PROGRAM

Who is served?

Full-time public school principals with three years of experience are eligible to participate in the Master Principal Program.

Is the participation of new principals voluntary or mandatory?

Participation is voluntary.

How long is the program?

Each of the three phases of the Master Principal Program is approximately one year in length. Principals can wait up to two years between each phase before submitting the performance assessment. Then the program may take from three to seven years to complete the coursework and prepare to sit for the Master Principal final assessment.

WHO PROVIDES THE MENTORING AND INDUCTION?

Mentoring is not part of the Master Principal Program. Mentoring is part of the Beginning Administrator Induction Program through the Arkansas Department of Education (see Chapter 4).

However, once principals have achieved acceptance into the Master Principal Program, they could help the state and others by mentoring new principals. These conversations are occurring with the state.

What is expected of mentors?

Not applicable.

What supports are available for mentors?

Not applicable.

What is expected of new principals regarding their participation in the mentoring program?

Not applicable.

ARE ADDITIONAL SUPPORTS AVAILABLE FOR NEW PRINCIPALS?

Is any other professional development provided? If so, when and by whom?

Not applicable.

Do new principals meet regularly with other new principals?

Not applicable.

What resources are required for the Master Principal Program?

The academy provides lodging, meals, resources, materials, facilitators, connections to national leaders, a Web site, a Listserv, trained performance coaches, and trained specialist coaches for Phases 2 and 3.

FUNDING

What are the funding sources?

The Arkansas Leadership Academy operates under the assumption that state money should not be spent in duplication of services. Therefore, the academy does not provide services offered by its partners, including the universities, educational cooperatives, and professional associations.

Both the Arkansas Leadership Academy and the Master Principal Program were created by legislation and hold line items in the state budget. In addition to state funding, partners provide other funding either through cash or in-kind services, facilities, or supplies.

Who requests the funding?

Funding requests are made each biennium to the Arkansas Department of Education and to the state legislature by academy staff and other academy partners.

EVALUATION OF THE PROGRAM

Is the program evaluated formatively? Summatively? Who does the evaluation?

The program evaluations and assessment range from participant reactions, to doctoral dissertations, to statewide studies conducted by both in-state and out-of-state agencies. There have been seven dissertations written on elements of the academy, and an additional three are in progress.

Although it is difficult to find existing measures to assess system change, there are indicators that system change is occurring that can be tied to academy work. In the Team and Principal Institute, for example, the academy strives to check for each level of Guskey's Five Levels of Professional Development Evaluation (1999). The five levels are participant reactions, participants' learning, organization support and change, participants' use of new knowledge and skills, and student learning outcomes.

Who sees the results?

Daily assessments are shared with all participants and addressed each day. End-of-program assessments are used to make changes in program agendas and activities. Statewide studies are analyzed by academy partners and are used to chart future direction and to share results with the public and with those who fund the academy. All evaluations, assessments, and studies are open for anyone to view.

RECRUITMENT, HIRING, AND RETENTION OF NEW STAFF

How many new principals are recruited and hired each year?

Not applicable.

Are there any data that correlate the mentoring program with the retention of new principals?

Not applicable.

Are there any data that correlating the mentoring program with the performance of the new principals?

Not applicable.

What are the indicators of program success?

The following are indicators of success:

- Change and alignment within the statewide system of education
- Change within the partner organizations
- Support for participants from partner organizations
- An increase in the level of principal leadership within the state
- Principals accepting responsibility for system change
- Dramatic improvement of student scores in low-performing schools
- Completion of the process by a large percentage of principals
- A small percentage of those principals that complete the process become principals in identified low-performing schools

MODEL 7.2

Educational Leadership Development Academy (ELDA)
Induction and Support Program
San Diego, CA

Melinda Martin, ELDA Program Facilitator
5998 Alcala Park, San Diego, CA 92110-2492
619-260-4181   melinda@sandiego.edu

Urban/suburban/ rural school	Urban	Grade levels of school	K–12
Student population	138,613	Per pupil expenditure	Ranges from $4,325 to $5,909
Mentoring is/is not mandated for ongoing certification/licensure	Mentoring is mandated	Mentoring program is/is not Funded by the state	Mentoring program is not funded by the state
Unique feature of program	New principals can earn next level of certification in this program; mentors meet with new principals three hours/ week; extensive training at university and coordination with district	Duration of program for new principals	Two years
Mentors are Full-time principals from same district from another district Retired principals	Mentors are full-time or recently retired principals from the district	Mentor selection criteria exist/do not exist Mentor matching process exists/does not exist	Mentor selection criteria do exist Mentor matching process does exist
Mentors are trained/not trained for role Mentors receive/do not receive ongoing support	Mentors are trained for the role Mentors receive ongoing support	Mentors are/are not part of a team to support new principals	Mentors are part of team that supports new principals
Coaching is/is not a component	Coaching is a component	Daily/weekly/yearly expectations for mentors	Mentors meet three hours/ week for two years
Mentors evaluate/do not evaluate the new principals	Mentors do not evaluate new principals	Portfolio is required/is not required	Videotape is required
Mentor remuneration	$3,000/semester	Higher education affiliation	University of San Diego
Cost of program	$702,500	Funding	Broad Foundation
Years program in existence	Two years	Full-time/part-time program coordinator/program coordination is part of another role in system/organization/state	Full-time program coordinator

STATE MANDATES

Is mentoring mandated for new principals?

Yes, mentoring is mandated for new principals.

Is mentoring part of certification or licensure?

Yes, it is required by the state for licensure.

Is funding provided by the state to support the mandate?

No, funding is not provided by the state for mentoring.

HISTORY

Why was the program started?

The Educational Leadership Development Academy (ELDA) was established in 2000 through a grant-funded partnership between the University of San Diego (USD) School of Education and the San Diego City Schools to identify, recruit, and prepare strong educators for the complex challenges of school site leadership. This Aspiring Leaders Program was initially created as a one-year, cohort-based preparation program combining university course work with a full-time internship that pairs each student with an experienced supervising principal who provides ongoing coaching and support. In 2002, the induction and support program was initiated to provide job-embedded mentoring and support for newly placed principals, vice principals, and secondary content specialists receiving their professional administrative services credential.

The program was the brainchild of the new superintendent, Alan Bersin, and the dean of the School of Education at the University of San Diego, Paula Cordeiro. They started their tenure in their positions on the same day. They went to lunch and discussed the need for building the capacity of principals. Many principals were retiring, and there was a need to build the capacity of the replacement principals. The new superintendent and the dean of the School of Education felt that principals should be instructional leaders, or lead learners in a community of learners. In order to do this, they need training as instructional leaders. The ELDA program was created in response to the growing shortage of high-quality, credentialed administrators available to lead the instructional reform initiated by Bersin in his *Blueprint for Student Success*.

The ELDA program started in 2000 with 10 teachers who were released from the classroom for a year. They were apprenticed to principals whom they worked alongside during the entire school year. They also took classes at the university. At the end of the year, 9 out of the 10 were appointed to administrative positions, having earned their preliminary credential through the ELDA program.

After the first year, it was decided to expand the program to provide an opportunity for new principals and vice principals to earn their professional credential, which they are required to do within the first five years of their employment as an administrator.

The first cohort of people in the program to get their professional administrative services credential had 25 participants. Fourteen had been in the preliminary program, and 11 had earned their preliminary credential from other universities.

GOALS

What are the goals of the program?

The *Blueprint for Student Success* envisioned the transformation of school administration from school management to instructional leadership.

The key goals of the program are to

- Assist new leaders to successfully fulfill their roles in schools
- Provide consistent and strong support for site administrators in their work to lead schools in improving teaching and learning
- Support experienced principals with meaningful opportunities to deepen their practice through mentoring relationships
- Support experienced administrators in deepening their knowledge and skill base

PROGRAM DESIGN

Who designed the mentor program?

Alan Bersin, the new superintendent, and Paula Cordeiro, the new dean of the School of Education, designed and began the program in 2000 for the teachers working toward their preliminary administrative services credential. Melinda Martin and Margaret Barber joined the program in 2001, and they and Elaine Fink developed the program for participants to earn their professional credential. Elaine Fink, from New York, helped design the program and became the ELDA executive director.

The program is framed by four central pillars:

1. Theory must be balanced and mediated through practice.

2. Students learn best through the development of field-based knowledge and skills, not just through the completion of activities removed from the domain of practice.

3. Consistent inquiry, reflection, and critical feedback are essential for continued growth and adult learning.

4. Effective administrators must develop a set of specific educational leadership skills (such as articulation of a leadership voice, or the capacity to articulate and reflect a set of beliefs through all aspects of one's work as site leader).

What are the components and recommended schedule of the program?

This is a two-year program for principals working toward their professional credential. The requirements include the following:

- Participants are provided a mentor for two years with whom they meet for a minimum of three hours each week.
- Participants take courses at the university for the second half of the first year and the entire second year, totaling 12 units. (ELDA prescribes the 12 units of courses the participants take. ELDA was designed to be aligned with the California Professional Standards for Educational Leaders [CPSEL], which are based on the Interstate School Leaders Licensure Consortium [ISLLC] standards).
- The principal or the mentor (their choice) logs the focus of the weekly meetings, which focus on instructional issues as well as operational issues.
- Participants must prepare and present a video at the end of their second year to demonstrate their achievement of the standards. The major focus is on Standards 1, 2, and 5, leadership and professional development. These videos are viewed by a panel and scored using a rubric. Candidates are provided critical feedback.

Are there any programs that complement the mentor program?

ELDA is working to develop a connection between the leadership course work and the monthly instructional conferences for principals and vice principals held at the San Diego Unified School District. These are full-day instructional conferences that are mandated for all principals in the school district. A goal is for the participants to be learning leadership skills through ELDA that are congruent with the principal instructional conferences offered by the district.

PROGRAM ADMINISTRATION

Who coordinates the program?

Melinda Martin, the ELDA program facilitator, coordinates the ELDA induction and support program.

How is information communicated to shareholders?

Information is communicated in a variety of ways:

- Annual newsletter
- Advisory board
- E-mail
- Minutes or reports of the Administrative Meeting Group, which meets six times a year, composed of the superintendent, the deputy superintendent, USD dean, and executive director of ELDA (this position is currently vacant)

Who coordinates the integration of this program with other professional development opportunities or requirements in the school or district?

The ELDA executive director, Ann Van Sickle, coordinates the integration of ELDA with other professional development opportunities in the district.

PARTICIPATION IN THE PROGRAM

Who is served?

Any principal or assistant principal, math or literacy administrator in the San Diego Unified School District who needs a professional credential may apply to participate in the program.

Is participation of new principals voluntary or mandatory?

Participation is voluntary. They apply to ELDA. If the district highly recommends that specific administrators participate in ELDA, they are given preference to be accepted.

How long is the program?

ELDA is a two-year program.

WHO PROVIDES THE MENTORING AND INDUCTION?

What are the criteria for being a mentor?

Mentors must be current or retired principals from the district with strong leadership skills, proven by their record of leading their own school to improvement.

Are mentors full-time principals or retired principals?

The mentors are full-time or retired principals. Full-time principals may mentor only one new principal. Retired principals may mentor several new principals.

Are mentors from the same district as new principals?

Yes, the mentors are in the same district as the new principals.

How are mentors selected?

Instructional leaders in the district who supervise the principals confer with the ELDA executive director regarding mentor selection.

How are matches made between mentors and new principals?

New principals are matched with mentors whose schools are similar to their own, such as low-performing schools in low socioeconomic areas, high-performing schools in high socioeconomic areas, schools with a high English language learner population, and schools with similar staff or student needs.

Since the goal is to improve teaching and learning, matches are made to support the different needs of new principals.

WHAT IS EXPECTED OF MENTORS?

What are the job responsibilities of mentors?

The job responsibilities of mentors are to

- Meet with their partners a minimum of three hours each week for the two years of the program
- Respond to the needs presented by the new principals
- Participate in seven to eight training meetings each year
- Keep a log of how much time is spent with the new principals and on what topics (the mentor and new principal may decide that the new principal will keep the log)
- Be available by phone or e-mail in emergencies
- Participate in instructional walk-through meetings of the new principal's school done by the ELDA executive director
- Assist with any topics or issues needed by the new principal
- Attend the first meeting of the first class with the new principal, to understand the requirements of the induction plan and final videotape
- Assist the new principal in preparing the videotape and making sure the elements of the rubric are addressed

Is the relationship between the mentor and the new principal confidential?

Yes, the relationship between the mentor and the new principal is confidential. However, either the mentor or the mentee may discuss concerns with the executive director.

Occasionally, new principals have asked for a different mentor because they don't feel that the mentor is meeting their needs, and in most cases this request has been accommodated by the ELDA staff.

Are observation and coaching requirements of mentors?

Yes, observation and coaching are required. The focus of the program is on adult learning; if the adults in the school are learning, the children will be learning too. Mentors observe new principals in teacher conferences or talking with a community group, for example. They debrief and give critical feedback to the mentee.

Do mentors formally evaluate new principals?

No, mentors do not evaluate new principals.

How much time are mentors expected to work with new principals?

Mentors meet with new principals for a minimum of three hours each week for two years. These mentoring sessions might consist of reviewing and analyzing student achievement data and developing appropriate strategic plans to improve schoolwide teaching, or they might include a mentor observing a principal's conversation with a teacher and then providing one-on-one feedback.

When do mentors meet with the new principals?

Mentors meet with their new principal partners at times that are mutually agreeable to them, including during school, after school, evenings, or weekends.

WHAT SUPPORTS ARE AVAILABLE FOR MENTORS?

The executive director, Ann Van Sickle, and the induction and support program coordinator, Katherine Casey, support mentors.

Are mentors remunerated?

Mentors are paid $3,000 each semester.

Are mentors trained? If so, by whom?

There is a three-hour orientation before mentors begin that is offered by the executive director. Then there are training sessions monthly during the school year. The training sessions provide opportunities for the mentors to improve their coaching and self-reflecting skills. There is an emphasis on strategies for improving adult learning. The training and support of mentors is an ongoing part of the academy's work. Most of the mentors who coach the induction and support candidates have not themselves participated in the ELDA program. As a result, it has been necessary to communicate a consistent and clear understanding of their roles and responsibilities. The ELDA monthly training sessions include discussions of mentoring fundamentals, collaborative work on helping the candidates develop their induction plans, and general problem solving.

Is there professional development for mentors after the initial training? If so, who provides it?

The executive director holds monthly training meetings with the mentors. Also, mentors may attend the principals' instructional conferences offered each month by the district. If they choose to attend, they attend without cost, as the district's guests.

Do mentors meet regularly with other mentors? If so, how often and for how long?

Mentors may meet with each other at their own initiation; no meetings of mentors are scheduled. However, the monthly meetings provide an opportunity for mentors to network and discuss instructional leadership issues.

Is there any other ongoing support for mentors? If so, who provides it?

Mentors may attend the instructional conferences for principals that are offered each month by the district. If they choose to attend, they attend without cost, as the district's guests.

Are any other resources available for mentors?

ELDA purchases many books on coaching and leadership. The executive director conducts study groups with the mentors, using some of these books.

Are mentors supervised? If so, by whom and how frequently?

The mentors are not supervised. If they are currently principals, instructional specialists supervise them in their role as principal.

WHAT IS EXPECTED OF NEW PRINCIPALS REGARDING THEIR PARTICIPATION IN THE MENTORING PROGRAM?

As participants in the ELDA induction and support program, new principals

- Attend and participate in classes
- Write an induction plan
- Meet with their mentors a minimum of three hours a week
- Attend any meetings that are called
- Prepare and present their culminating videotape at the end of the second year
- Maintain a B average in all course work.

How often do new principals meet with their mentors and for how long?

Mentees meet with their mentors for a minimum of three hours each week for the entire two-year program.

Are there other people with whom the new principal meets for mentoring and support?

New principals meet with instructional leaders. They participate in mandatory districtwide study groups with other new principals approximately every six weeks after school.

Is formative assessment of new principals required? If so, when, how, and by whom?

Deep ongoing and crucial assessment runs through the program as a vehicle for fostering self-reflection and growth and for tracking individual and collective progress. Program participants are tracked and monitored from their first observation during the selection process through their culminating video assessment. Relying on data collected during site visits, formal and informal assessment from course instructors, and performance data on seminal course and program projects, the program administration is able to identify and correct weaknesses early on in the course of the participants' involvement and support participants in reflecting on and correcting their own deficiencies.

Assessment is not a formal requirement of mentoring. It often happens at the new principals' initiation. For example, candidates may videotape themselves, perhaps presenting to the staff, and then the mentor and the candidate view the videotape and look for key elements (leadership voice, belief system, etc.).

Are new principals required to prepare a portfolio?

Candidates are required to write an induction plan. The mentoring relationship and the course work are both guided by the development of the participants' induction plan. The induction plan is the framing document for induction and supports candidates' work with their mentors. When determining the focus of the induction plan, candidates begin by considering the focus of their work plan, since everything that happens at a school site should be in the service of accomplishing the goals of the work plan (as required by the district for all administrators). The induction plan serves to guide the work of the mentors and candidates, which focuses on improving the use of leadership skills to accomplish the goals articulated in the induction plan. Candidates and their mentors usually work on a specific aspect of the work plan, so candidates receive intensive support to improve their leadership skills.

The culminating project of the induction and support program is a comparative analysis and reflection of a baseline and final video. At the start of the program, participants videotape themselves in a leadership situation and write a reflection of their leadership ability by analyzing the clarity of purpose, leadership voice, justification, teachable point of view, evidence of accomplishment, and barriers to learning. At the end of the program, participants again videotape themselves and write another reflection that compares their baseline video to their culminating video, identifying the area of growth relationship to instructional leadership and also identifying areas of weakness and proposed next steps and resources to remedy those deficits.

ARE ADDITIONAL SUPPORTS AVAILABLE FOR NEW PRINCIPALS?

New principals can also take courses at reduced tuition, paying about $1,800 a year instead of $850 a unit. Nine units in the second tier can be applied toward a doctorate; 10 units can be applied toward a master's degree, though most principals already have a master's degree.

Is any other professional development provided? If so, when and by whom?

New principals may choose to participate in offerings of the university on specific topics.

Do new principals meet regularly with other new principals?

Yes, new principals meet informally with other new principals.

What resources are required for the mentoring program?

Tuition for students (the grant pays for 70 percent and students pay 30 percent): $700,000
Training mentor principals: $2,500

FUNDING

What are the funding sources?

Eli Broad, of the Broad Foundation, is very interested in improving teaching and learning by working with leadership programs and school boards.

The Broad Foundation provided a $3 million grant over the course of three years. A renewal grant was made for $2.7 million for 2004–2005; part of this allocation is for the Aspiring Leaders program, which is for teachers who are getting their preliminary credential.

Who requests the funding?

The ELDA staff and school district personnel write a business plan requesting the funding from the Broad Foundation.

EVALUATION OF THE PROGRAM

Is the program evaluated formatively? Summatively?

The instructional leaders rated their ELDA principals or vice principals as "good" or "excellent" across a range of domains of leadership ability. They described 100 percent of their ELDA principals or vice principals as "good" or "excellent" in the following domains:

- Development of a belief system reflected in voice and actions (30 percent good, 70 percent excellent)
- Ability to design an organization around adult learning (80 percent good, 20 percent excellent)
- Modeling a code of personal ethics and development of professional leadership capacity (60 percent good, 40 percent excellent)
- Management of the organization to support a safe, efficient, and effective learning outcome (80 percent good, 20 percent excellent)

The program views the data as suggesting that the program has been effective in targeting these areas for development.

Who sees the results?

The Broad Foundation, the district administrators, ELDA staff, and participants in the program see the data. Preliminary data showed that students in schools with principals who participate in ELDA perform better in five out of seven of the subtests of the California Standards tests than do the students in schools with principals who do not participate in ELDA.

RECRUITMENT, HIRING, AND RETENTION OF NEW STAFF

How many new principals are recruited and hired each year?

Table 3.1   Past and projected district leadership vacancies in 2001–2006

School Year	Principal	Vice Principal	Principal (Projected)	Vice Principal (Projected)
2001–2002	30	55	24	42
2002–2003	69	52	30	40
2003–2004	27	55	20	33
2004–2005			15	27
2005–2006			10	15

Evidently, there were many more vacancies than had been projected. The projections did not anticipate the severe state and local budget constraints that resulted in 2003 in an offer of early retirement to San Diego's certificated personnel, increasing significantly the number of senior principals and vice principals who elected to retire.

In 2002–2003, many principals retired because there was a retirement incentive offered by the district. Now there are many young administrators who hold principal or vice principal positions.

Are there any data that correlate the mentoring program with the retention of new principals?

Ninety-eight percent of the participants have stayed in their positions.

Are there any data that correlate the mentoring program with the performance of the new principals?

In addition to the data about student scores on the California Standards subtests, there are soft data about satisfaction with the program.

What are the indicators of program success?

The district hires ELDA graduates as soon as they complete the Aspiring Leaders program. ELDA graduates are seen as strong, effective instructional leaders.

People's feelings, as represented in the following anecdotal comments, are also an indicator of success:

ELDA was a lifesaver. Without this program I wouldn't have made it.

Many people call and visit because they want to replicate the model.

ELDA invites readers to come visit the program and some of their schools.

MODEL 7.3

Independence (Missouri) Comprehensive Leadership Model

Dr. Patricia Schumacher, Associate Superintendent
218 North Pleasant Street, Independence, MO 64050
816-521-2700   pschumacher@indep.k12.mo.us

Urban/suburban/rural school	Suburban	Grade levels of school	Pre-K–12
Student population	11,200	Per pupil expenditure	$6,500
Mentoring is/is not mandated for ongoing certification/licensure	Mentoring is mandated	Mentoring program is/is not funded by the state	Mentoring is not funded
Unique feature of program	Administrators may earn a doctorate in educational leadership through the University of Missouri, and courses are all offered in Independence. In addition, the course work is related to the district and school program improvement goals and is tied to student achievement	Duration of program for new principals	The doctoral program offered to new principals, as well as all other district administrators, is a three-year program
Mentors are **Full-time principals** from same district from another district **Retired principals**	Mentors are full-time principals/district administrators from within the district	Mentor selection criteria exist/do not exist Mentor matching process exists/does not exist	Mentor selection criteria does exist Mentor matching is based on school level
Mentors are trained/not trained for role Mentors receive/do not receive ongoing support	Mentors are trained Mentors receive ongoing support	Mentors are/are not part of a team to support new principals	Mentors are part of a team of support for new principals
Coaching is/is not a component	Coaching is a component	Daily/weekly/yearly expectations for mentors	Minimum of four times a month meetings
Mentors evaluate/do not evaluate the new principals	Principals do not evaluate other principals. The associate superintendent, who sometimes mentors, evaluates all principals	Portfolio is required/is not required	Portfolio is required
Mentor remuneration	No additional compensation to district administrators for mentoring	Higher education affiliation	University of Missouri
Cost of program	$45,000	Funding	School budget and SAELP Grant
Years program in existence	Two years	Full-time/part-time program coordinator/ program coordination is part of another role in system/organization/state	Coordination is part of another role in the system

Used with permission of Patrica Schumacher, Associate Superintendent, Independence Schools.

STATE MANDATES

Is mentoring mandated for new principals?
No, mentoring is not mandated for new principals.

Is mentoring part of certification or licensure?
No, it is not part of certification or licensure.

Is funding provided by the state to support the mandate?
No, mentoring is not funded.

HISTORY

Why was the program started?
The program was created to enhance the leadership skills of brand-new and veteran principals. Existing principals report that they have a need to grow, that they want professional development.

GOALS

What is the goal of the program?
The goal of the program is to enhance instructional leadership, which has a positive impact on student performance. We know that the key to student performance is the quality of the instructor in the classroom, and it is the principal as the instructional leader who helps define what that quality instruction looks like in a classroom.

PROGRAM DESIGN

Who designed the mentor program?
Dick Andrews, dean of the College of Education, and Patricia Schumacher, associate superintendent of schools, collaborated to design the program.

What are the components and recommended schedule of the program?
The components of the program are as follows:

- The EdD program in educational leadership is offered in Independence, Missouri, only to Independence principals. Independence is 120 miles away from the University of Missouri.
- The EdD professors collaborate with the superintendent and associate superintendent in designing the course work, which is all relevant to the individual school improvement plans (SIPs) of the participating principals. The SIPs align to the district's comprehensive school improvement programs (CSIPs).
- The entire EdD program is related to students' improvement. Everything done in the school district is relevant to student improvement, as stipulated in No Child Left Behind (NCLB).
- This is the first doctorate program that is directly related to student improvement. Whether this program is replicated depends on the student improvement results.
- A requirement for the course work is that the principals have to teach the course work to teachers in the district who are interested in getting a master's degree in educational leadership.

- The program began in 2003 and the first cohort will finish in 2006.
- Principals meet year long, on a university schedule, in Independence. Each semester, the principals take two courses as well as teach one semester of a course for the master's level program.
- The superintendent and the associate superintendent teach a course, thereby keeping the program relevant to the district's mission and focus on student improvement.

Are there any programs that complement the mentor program?

Yes, the State Action for Education Leadership Project (SAELP) complements the program. It is funded by the state Department of Education based on a competitive grant, which is used to develop the leadership potential of a person within the district. That person job-shadows a master-level principal for a summer and an entire school year.

PROGRAM ADMINISTRATION

Who coordinates the program?

The associate superintendent of schools and the department chair of the Educational Leadership Policy Analysis Department jointly coordinate the program.

How is information communicated to shareholders?

Information is communicated through e-mail to the principals in the program. It is a two-way information stream via the Independence school system and the university.

Who coordinates the integration of this program with other professional development opportunities or requirements in the school or district?

The associate superintendent and the district professional development director coordinate the integration of this program with other professional development in the district.

PARTICIPATION IN THE PROGRAM

Who is served?

Principals and district-level administration in the Independence schools who are interested in furthering their degrees and focusing on improving student performance are in the program.

Is the participation of new principals voluntary or mandatory?

Participation is voluntary now. If it becomes clear that student performance is enhanced, a version of the program may become mandatory.

How long is the program?

The program lasts for three years.

WHO PROVIDES THE MENTORING AND INDUCTION?

What are the criteria for being a mentor?

Mentors of new principals are master principals or district administrators who demonstrate quality instructional leadership skills.

Are mentors full-time principals or retired principals?

The mentors are full-time principals and district administrators.

Are mentors from the same district as new principals?

The mentors are from the same district as new principals.

How are mentors selected?

The associate superintendent and the district professional development director choose the mentors based on their instructional leadership skills as evidenced in their job performance.

How are matches made between mentors and new principals?

The matches are made based on division level (e.g., elementary, middle, and high school).

WHAT IS EXPECTED OF MENTORS?

What are the job responsibilities of mentors?

Mentors are expected to offer support and guidance to new principals in areas of instructional leadership.

Is the relationship between the mentor and the new principal confidential?

The relationship is confidential.

Are observation and coaching requirements of mentors?

Observation and coaching are requirements of mentors. The associate superintendent and/or the mentors do walk-throughs in the building with the new principals. There are a prescribed set of "look fors," and there is coaching before and after the walk-through.

Do mentors formally evaluate new principals?

The associate superintendent does the principals' evaluations and is also sometimes a mentor.

How much time are mentors expected to work with new principals (weekly, monthly, and for how long)?

The minimum amount of time mentors work with new principals is four hours a month.

When do mentors meet with the new principals?

Mentors may meet during the day at the new principals' schools. There are also professional development sessions and administrator meetings of all administrators in the district, each of which takes place each month. There is also a three-day summer retreat for all administrators, which is the first time that new principals begin to interact with the other administrators.

WHAT SUPPORTS ARE AVAILABLE FOR MENTORS?

Are mentors remunerated?

Mentors are part of the existing staff, so they do not receive additional compensation.

Are mentors trained? If so, by whom?

Administrators who mentor new principals work with the associate superintendent, who does sessions for mentors both for content and support.

Is there professional development for mentors after the initial training? If so, who provides it?

The associate superintendent and the district professional development director provide professional development as needed.

Do mentors meet regularly with other mentors? If so, how often and for how long?

No regular meetings are scheduled.

Is there any other ongoing support for mentors? If so, who provides it?

Whatever support is needed for mentors is provided.

Are any other resources available for mentors?

No, there aren't any other resources for mentors.

Are mentors supervised? If so, by whom and how frequently?

Yes, the district professional development director supervises the associate superintendent and the mentors on an ongoing basis.

WHAT IS EXPECTED OF NEW PRINCIPALS REGARDING THEIR PARTICIPATION IN THE MENTORING PROGRAM?

How often do new principals meet with their mentors and for how long?

New principals meet with their mentors a minimum of once a month, all year long. They meet more extensively in the beginning of the year.

Are there other people with whom the new principal meets for mentoring and support?

District administrators, including the human resources director, the assistant superintendent of curriculum instruction and assessment, and the assistant superintendent in charge of technology meet with the new principals. Master-level principals (those who display exceptional leadership skills) also meet with new principals.

The teaching and learning coaches are a tremendous support to new principals. These coaches are released full time from the classroom to work with teachers and administrators, especially the new principals, on curriculum and instruction and assessment.

Is formative assessment of new principals required? If so, when, how, and by whom?

The associate superintendent does a formative and summative assessment of the new principals beginning in October and through the end of January. The recommendation of hiring is determined on February 1.

Are new principals required to prepare a portfolio?

Yes, each principal prepares a portfolio to share with the associate superintendent in February after they have their summative conference in January.

ARE ADDITIONAL SUPPORTS AVAILABLE FOR NEW PRINCIPALS?

Is any other professional development provided? If so, when and by whom?

New principals meet with other principals and district administrators a minimum of twice a month.

Do new principals meet regularly with other new principals?

Yes, new principals meet with each other periodically when the associate superintendent and the district professional development director arrange a meeting.

What resources are required for the mentoring program?

The program costs approximately $45,000 for professional development.

FUNDING

What are the funding sources?

The program is funded from the district professional development budget and the SAELP grant.

Who requests the funding?

The associate superintendent and the district professional development director request the funds.

EVALUATION OF THE PROGRAM

Is the program evaluated formatively? Summatively? Who does the evaluation?

The University of Missouri evaluates the program.

Who sees the results?

The university and the Independence School District see the results.

RECRUITMENT, HIRING, AND RETENTION OF NEW STAFF

How many new principals are recruited and hired each year?

Two new principals are hired, on average, each year.

Are there any data that correlate the mentoring program with the retention of new principals?

There has been a high retention of new principals for several reasons, including the support provided for them as well as the generous salary scale of the district. Not one principal has voluntarily left the district in the last five years, outside of retirement.

Are there any data that correlate the mentoring program with the performance of the new principals?

Data are being collected as student academic success in each of the schools is monitored.

What are the indicators of program success?

Indicators of program success are an increase in student performance and the retention of new principals. Another indicator is the number of applicants for principalships in Independence.

MODEL 7.4

The New York City Leadership Academy's Principal Mentoring Program in Collaboration With New Visions for Public Schools

Arthur Foresta, Codirector
Principal Mentoring Program
New Visions for Public Schools
320 West 13th Street, New York, NY 10014
646-486-8142   aforesta@newvisions.org

Lili Brown, Vice President External Affairs
New Visions for Public Schools
320 West 13th Street, New York, NY 10014
646-486-8131   lbrown@newvisions.org

Urban/suburban/rural school	Urban	Grade levels of school	Pre-K–12
Student Population	1.1 million	Per pupil expenditure	$10,593
Mentoring is/is not mandated for ongoing certification/licensure	Mentoring is not mandated for licensure, it is mandated in NYC public schools	Mentoring program is/is not funded by the state	Mentoring is not funded by the state
Unique feature of program	Consistent program for new principals across all of the NYC public schools	Duration of program for new principals	One to two years
Mentors are full-time principals from same district from another district Retired principals	Mentors are 160 full-time or recently retired principals from the same district	Mentor selection criteria exist/do not exist Mentor matching process exists/does not exist	Selection criteria do exist Matching process does exists
Mentors are trained/not trained for role Mentors receive/do not receive ongoing support	Mentors are trained Mentors receive ongoing support	Mentors are/are not part of a team to support new principals	Mentors are part of a team of support
Coaching is/is not a component	Coaching is a component	Daily/weekly/yearly expectations for mentor	Full-time principals meet three times a month with new principals; retired principals meet a total of 24 half days with each new principal
Mentors evaluate/do not evaluate the new principals Mentor remuneration	Mentors do formative assessment; they do not evaluate $2,500–$3,000 per semester	Portfolio is required/is not required Higher education affiliation	Portfolio is recommended, but not required None
Cost of program	$1.7 million (to support and mentor 130 first-year principals and 46 second-year principals)	Funding	Private sources
Years program in existence	Four years	Full-time/part-time program coordinator/program coordination is part of other role in system/organization/state	Full-time program coordination

STATE MANDATES

Is mentoring mandated for new principals?

Mentoring is not mandated in the state of New York. However, it is mandated for all first-year principals in the New York City public schools.

Is mentoring part of certification or licensure?

Mentoring is not part of certification or licensure.

Is funding provided by the state to support the mandate?

The program is fully funded through private sources.

HISTORY

Why was the program started?

The New Visions for Public Schools (NVPS) principal mentoring program was created in 2000 to support new principals at several of the 35 small schools that New Visions created in the 1990s that were transitioning from their founding principals. At first, the program supported five principals. In 2001, NVPS expanded the program at the request of the New York City Board of Education to respond to the anticipated retirement over a five-year period of more than 50 percent of New York City's existing principals. Since 2001, NVPS has mentored a total of over 500 new principals.

NVPS, originally called the Fund for New York City Public Education, was founded in 1989 to mobilize private sector support for lasting improvements in the city's public schools. NVPS is a private nonprofit entity and is independent of the New York City Department of Education. NVPS is dedicated to improving the quality of education that children receive in New York City's public schools and works in partnership with the Department of Education to ensure that all students have access to effective schools that enable them to realize their full potential. The NYC DOE chancellor sits on the board of NVPS.

In 2003, Chancellor Joel Klein created the Leadership Academy, a special initiative to recruit, train, and support principals, give them the skills to lead change in their school, and focus their efforts on improving student achievement. The Leadership Academy is designed to support principals at different stages of their development. There are three programmatic strands: (1) the Aspiring Principals program, which recruits, selects, and develops principal candidates through a rigorous 15-month training and school-based residency program, (2) the New Principal On-Boarding program, which provides mentoring to first-year principals, and (3) the Principal Leadership Development program, which provides incumbent principals with periodic training sessions.

From the onset, NVPS reached out to the academy as a supportive collaborating partner. Since 2003, NVPS has worked closely with the academy, taking primary responsibility for providing on-site mentoring for first-year principals by retired principals.

GOALS

What is the goal of the program?

The main goal of the NVPS is to bring a consistent level of quality mentoring to new principals across the system. Over the years, new principals have received different mentoring services, in different configurations, of varying quality. In some schools, there wasn't any mentoring. Some new principals received support from several different groups, and the support was usually not coordinated. For example, a regional superintendent and a chancellor would mandate different trainings that weren't coordinated with each other. Principals often felt that they were pulled out of their schools too often and were not getting support based on their needs. In contrast, NVPS designed its mentoring programs to give new principals the support they need in their schools, when they need it, based on the knowledge that adult learners use learning best when it is given when they need it.

In fall 2003, the Leadership Academy asked NVPS to take responsibility for mentoring 130 new principals, using NVPS retired principals as mentors. The academy took responsibility for developing the leadership capacity of the remaining new principals, assigning each of them a sitting principal as a mentor. The goal for the year was to align the training, tools, and protocols of the principal mentoring program to those of the Leadership Academy. After a year of running parallel mentoring models, the Leadership Academy merged the two approaches under a single banner: The New York City Leadership Academy's Principal Mentoring Program in Collaboration with New Visions for Public Schools. The unified model brings opportunities to achieve consistency of mentoring standards centrally and across regions.

PROGRAM DESIGN

Who designed the mentor program?

Arthur Foresta, codirector of the principal mentoring program, designed the mentoring program based upon available research on induction programs across the nation.

In 2002, NVPS, at the request of then Chancellor Harold Levy, enlisted excellent retired principals who had expertise and knowledge of the system to provide mentoring support to 75 new principals. Of the 90 principals interviewed, NVPS selected 16 to serve as mentors. As of 2004, the program had grown to over 50 retired principals and over 100 full-time principals who provide mentoring to over 380 first-year principals.

What are the components and recommended schedule of the program?

The principal mentoring program provides a two-year continuum of intensive training to newly hired principals. In 250 schools across New York City, NVPS's mentors provide on-site school-specific leadership training targeted to meet the individual needs of each of their new principals. Originally, mentors also facilitated structured network meetings, where their cohorts of principals studied research, conducted focused walk-throughs, and shared practices. This practice has now been assumed by the Leadership Academy as part of its new principals' training program. The goal of the program is to develop new principals as instructional and transformational leaders and sustain their professional growth.

The program design is based on the Interstate School Leaders Licensure Consortium (ISLLC) standards and 32 identifiable behaviors related to those standards. The responsibilities for mentoring new principals are shared by the Leadership Academy and NVPS, resulting in two support structures that are aligned. NVPS implements the mentoring model using 55 retired principals as mentors; the Leadership Academy coordinates over 100 active principals who mentor new principals.

The superintendents of each of the 12 regions within New York City choose which model they want. Since the system has limited funds, there needs to be a differentiated approach to mentoring. There needs to be the same operating philosophy; mentor development and the level of interaction need to be explicitly stated. A superintendent might select a sitting principal because the superintendent has a relationship with that principal or because it is less expensive to do it that way. Superintendents generally pick the retired principal model for their most challenging schools or for new principals with the greatest need. NVPS has created a series of tools and protocols, in collaboration with the Leadership Academy, to define expectations for all parties. These tools include: *Expectations of the Key Players of the Mentoring Program*, the *Mentoring Report*, and Mentor Profiles. Sitting principal mentors and retired mentors undergo training together. NVPS will have an important role in designing that training. Trainings include a two-day Mentor Summer Institute and six half days during the year.

The components of the NVPS program involving retired principals include the following:

- Recruitment and selection of mentors.
- Guidance of the regions in the matching of mentors and new principals by providing Mentor Profiles on each mentor and consultation.
- Assignment of up to six mentees to each mentor.
- A calendar with mentoring beginning in August, when the new principals meet their mentors and discuss the challenges of the school.
- The confidential nature of mentoring, which is not part of the supervisory structure. When the new principals sit with their instructional superintendents in August, the mentors also sit in on those meetings. In so doing, the mentors hear the expectations of the region, articulated by the instructional superintendents rather than only through the lenses of the new principals. Then the mentors are better able to help the new principals deal with the expectations of their supervisors.
- NVPS and Leadership Academy staff field visits in schools to assess the effectiveness of the mentoring relationship, both for retired principal mentors and sitting principal mentors. They use the standards-based documents to assess how the mentees are doing and whether they have any concerns or issues about the relationship; they also meet with mentors to assess their observations and their developmental needs. The field visits help shape and refine the technical assistance provided for mentors and new principals. They are an opportunity for mentors to ask for professional development. For example, retired principals requested training on the system's mandated Balanced Literacy Curriculum, since they had varying degrees of experience with that particular program. Mentor trainings include both retired and sitting principal mentors, allowing for a rich exchange of experience.

Are there any programs that complement the mentor program?

No, there aren't other programs that complement the mentor program. The goal is to provide consistency in the support for all new principals.

PROGRAM ADMINISTRATION

Who coordinates the program?

Arthur Foresta and Barbara Ghyll coordinate the program. The primary collaborator at the Leadership Academy is Neil Kreinik.

How is information communicated to shareholders?

Information is communicated through the common channels of the school system, including e-mail, telephone, and trainings as well as through the *Mentoring Report*.

Who coordinates the integration of this program with other professional development opportunities or requirements in the school or district?

The NYC DOE requested that NVPS work to coordinate an integrated model so that all new principals receive support that is consistent throughout the school system.

Collaboration between the Leadership Academy and NVPS is the goal. Accordingly, the mentoring component of the Leadership Academy is now called the Leadership Academy's Mentoring Program in Collaboration with New Visions for Public Schools. The development of the Leadership Academy is seen by NVPS as an enormous opportunity to take their mentoring principals model to scale.

PARTICIPATION IN THE PROGRAM

Who is served?

All new principals in the New York City schools are served by the Leadership Academy.

Is the participation of new principals voluntary or mandatory?

Participation in both the leadership training and mentoring of the Leadership Academy is mandatory.

How long is the program?

The program supports all new principals throughout their first year. At the discretion of the superintendent, there may be continued mentoring in the second year. This would involve a reduced number of on-site visits, e-mail, and telephone supports.

WHO PROVIDES THE MENTORING AND INDUCTION?

What are the criteria for being a mentor?

The following guidelines were created to assist regional leadership in recruitment of experienced principals, active or retired, to mentor new principals.

- Instructional leaders: They are knowledgeable about curriculum and instruction and can articulate what they do as instructional leaders.
- Student achievement: A longitudinal analysis of school data demonstrates improved student achievement under their leadership.
- Track record: They are known by their colleagues as being effective school leaders who have demonstrated a willingness to collaborate and to develop leadership in others.
- Passionate: They are enthusiastic about their field and about serving as a mentor to a new principal.
- Change agents: They are change agents who understand the theory and strategies of change.
- Human relations: They demonstrate strong human relations skills by listening actively, and being respectful, patient, sensitive, and supportive.
- Teacher and learner: They see mentoring as an opportunity to transfer their expertise to and also learn from their mentees.
- Guide: They can articulate how they would help their mentees find their own way with mentor guidance and support.
- Mover: They see their role at times to move their mentees to areas of challenge and discomfort in order to foster growth.
- Active: They see mentoring as an active role shadowing the mentees in all aspects of school leadership so that shared experiences can be reflected upon together.
- Strategic: They employ a variety of teaching strategies to transfer expertise, including modeling, role playing, questioning, prodding, direct instruction, and text study.
- Accessible: They are available and responsive to their mentees by visits, phone calls, and e-mail.
- Resourceful: They provide their mentees with sample documents, memos, letters, checklists, and articles when relevant.

Are mentors full-time principals or retired principals?

There are two options. Mentors may be retired principals or active principals. The program is different depending on the option chosen by the instructional superintendent for each new principal.

Are mentors from the same district as new principals?

Mentors are all from the New York City public schools, which are divided into twelve regions. Sitting principal mentors are assigned to new principals within their region, while retired mentors often cross regions.

How are mentors selected?

Retired mentors go through a rigorous selection process, including an application with essay questions, a review of their last Annual School Report, reference checks, and an interview that includes role plays. Superintendents are guided by selection criteria when determining which of their full-time principals would make good mentors.

How are matches made between mentors and new principals?

Regional superintendents are provided with detailed Mentor Profiles on each retired mentor and are already well acquainted with sitting principal mentors. The superintendent matches mentors to new principals.

WHAT IS EXPECTED OF MENTORS?

What are the job responsibilities of the mentor?

Mentors are expected to

- Work with the mentee to develop a trusting relationship
- Gather and analyze information about the mentee and the school, including the principals' self-assessment, conversations with the mentee, Principal Performance Review (PPR) (voluntary), the Annual School Report, the Comprehensive Education Plan (CEP), and recent student achievement data
- Employ techniques such as questioning, active listening, scripting observations, role play, shared resources, joint problem solving, shadowing, research study, modeling, and when appropriate, direct instruction to develop the leadership capacities of the principal
- Participate in a three-way discussion with the mentee and the local instructional superintendent (LIS) to ensure that there is alignment with the region's goals and expectations for the school and the principal
- Protect the confidentiality and trust of the mentor-mentee relationship
- Create with the mentee a plan for professional growth as school leader, most likely in the form of the PPR, which establishes goals and defines actions that build on strengths and address areas in need of development
- Collaborate with the mentee in the development of nonevaluative descriptions of the mentoring work in the form of periodic *Mentoring Reports* prepared by the mentor and approved by both before they are forwarded to the Leadership Academy and region
- Prepare a pre- and postassessment of new principals. The assessments are based on the 32 performance indicators of the ISLLC standards. The mentor combines the ISLLC assessment with observations and the results of a principal's self-assessment to
  - Help the new principal prepare the Principal Performance Review with the instructional superintendent and mentor. The preassessments are done in October and help define the individual growth plans of each new principal. This plan becomes part of the supervisory process and the basis for observations by the instructional superintendent
  - Keep the mentor and new principal focused on how the mentor provides support of the new principal. Mentoring is not only situational leadership. It is also trying to get new

principals to create a vision of leadership and their school based on other aspects of the standards as well. Transformational leadership is a goal of the growth plan and mentoring
- A postassessment is completed in May to measure the new principals' growth. Mentors prepare a total of three reports, in nonevaluative language, about what is happening in the mentoring relationship. These reports go to the instructional superintendents and the Leadership Academy, so that what is happening in the mentoring relationship is aligned with the supervisory expectations. Principals arrange a three-way meeting with their supervisors and mentors to make sure there is alignment of support. Mentors make sure the mentoring relationships are confidential and are aligned with and supportive of the region's goals

- Alert the Leadership Academy if the match with the mentee seems not to be working
- Complete the administrative responsibility of the mentoring program in a timely fashion
- Complete, for program development purposes only, an anonymous pre- and postassessment of program quality and mentee's professional growth

Is the relationship between the mentor and the new principal confidential?

Yes, the relationship between the mentors and new principals is confidential.

Are observation and coaching requirements of mentors?

Yes, mentors are required to do observations and coaching. The mentor shadows the principal in all leadership activities.

Do mentors formally evaluate new principals?

No, mentors do not formally evaluate new principals. However, mentors assist in the evaluation of the program. Mentors complete pre- and postassessments about the new principals. The goal of the preassessment is to provide new principals with baseline information as they develop their growth plans with their instructional superintendent supervisors. Pre- and postassessment data are coded and anonymous, and the data are reported as an aggregate.

How much time are mentors expected to work with new principals (weekly, monthly, and for how long)?

Mentors are expected to

- Make face-to-face contact several times a month. If the mentor is an active principal of a school, the mentor makes two visits each month for not less than two and one-half hours in addition to an afterschool meeting each month. Retired principal mentor visits can be for either a full or half day, with the frequency determined by the regional liaison
- Have the equivalent of 12 full-day visits (half days, 24 times) allocated for each new principal There is a reserve of mentor days that can be drawn upon to provide extra mentoring to a principal facing extraordinary challenges
- Invite the mentee to the school of the sitting principal mentor once a month to observe school practices, special events, and most important, the mentor actively engaged in leading a school
- Join the mentee at regional and network principals' meetings
- Extend the communication beyond face-to-face meetings through telephone and e-mail
- Participate in all mentor development sessions provided by the Leadership Academy and NVPS

When do mentors meet with the new principals?

Mentors meet with new principals in their schools, at network and regional principals' meetings, and at training sessions.

WHAT SUPPORTS ARE AVAILABLE FOR MENTORS?

Are mentors remunerated?

Sitting principal mentors receive $2,500 per semester. Retired mentors receive $3,000 per mentee per semester.

Are mentors trained? If so, by whom?

Mentors are trained by NVPS and the Leadership Academy prior to beginning their mentoring and throughout the school year.

As the program expands, NVPS is training veteran mentors to become lead mentors who will help plan and deliver the mentor training and provide follow-up support to less experienced mentors.

Is there professional development for mentors after the initial training? If so, who provides it?

NVPS and the Leadership Academy provide professional development for mentors throughout the school year.

Do mentors meet regularly with other mentors? If so, how often and for how long?

Mentors meet regularly with other mentors during the ongoing training they receive. The training includes problem solving about real case studies that mentors present to each other, the development of specific coaching skills, group study of professional literature, and a current aspect of principal training that has mentoring implications.

Is there any other ongoing support for mentors? If so, who provides it?

Mentors are notified about and encouraged to attend lectures and local conferences on leadership.

Are any other resources available for mentors?

NVPS is currently preparing a tool kit that is a compendium of materials developed by mentors throughout the years. Materials include samples of letters, forms, and memos that can be offered to mentees as models when needed. This tool kit was piloted in 2004.

Are mentors supervised? If so, by whom and how frequently?

Mentors are supervised regularly in the field by the program coordinators of NVPS and the Leadership Academy.

WHAT IS EXPECTED OF NEW PRINCIPALS REGARDING THEIR PARTICIPATION IN THE MENTORING PROGRAM?

How often do new principals meet with their mentors and for how long?

Mentees are expected to

- Welcome face-to-face contact several times a month. If the mentor is an active principal of a school, the mentor makes two visits each month for not less than two and one-half hours in addition to an afterschool meeting each month. Retired principal mentor visits can be for either a full or half day, with the frequency determined by the regional liaison
- Visit the mentor's school once a month to observe school practices, special events, and most important, the mentor actively engaged in leading a school

- Arrange for the mentor to join them at regional and network principals' meetings
- Extend the communication beyond face-to-face meetings through telephone and e-mail

Are there other people with whom the new principal meets for mentoring and support?

Yes, the new principal meets with the LIS to prepare for the PPR and in a three-way meeting with the LIS and the mentor to ensure that there is alignment in the assessment of the current school status, the goals of the principal, and the work ahead. Each LIS has 10 to 12 schools and makes regular site visits. They meet with their cohort of principals monthly for professional development.

Is formative assessment of new principals required? If so, when, how, and by whom?

Yes, the mentor conducts a preassessment of the new principal, using the National Association of Secondary School Principals (NASSP) instrument, to help the new principal create a professional growth plan. The mentor also maintains a private log of each mentee's development.

Are new principals required to prepare a portfolio?

Although not required, principals are encouraged by their mentor to maintain a portfolio. Principals often accept the suggestion, because when they are being reviewed and evaluated by their supervisor, the portfolio becomes evidence of the work they have done.

ARE ADDITIONAL SUPPORTS AVAILABLE FOR NEW PRINCIPALS?

Is any other professional development provided? If so, when and by whom?

The New York City Leadership Academy's Principal Mentoring Program in Collaboration with New Visions for Public Schools is extensive and designed to bring consistent support to all new principals.

Do new principals meet regularly with other new principals?

Each LIS has 10 to 12 schools and makes regular site visits. They meet with their cohort of principals monthly for professional development.

What resources are required for the mentoring program?

To mentor 130 first-year principals and 46 second-year principals in 2003–2004, the total cost was $1.7 million.

FUNDING

What are the funding sources?

Since 2004, the Leadership Academy has been engaged in raising $75 million; it is a private initiative. Part of that money provides remuneration for all mentors, sitting and retired. The chancellor and the mayor are making a huge commitment to this endeavor.

NVPS raises funds from five to six private foundations to cover the organization's principal mentorship program expenses. The Leadership Academy funds the salaries of the retired principal mentors.

Who requests the funding?

The Leadership Academy and NVPS each have their private funding sources.

EVALUATION OF THE PROGRAM

Is the program evaluated formatively? Summatively? Who does the evaluation?

NVPS tracks the disposition of the principals mentored in order to compile retention data. Also, the Graduate Center of the City University of New York, Dr. Burt Flugman, principal investigator, conducts a formal assessment of the mentoring program. The evaluation includes the growth of principals in leadership skills and the satisfaction of mentees and mentors.

Who sees the results?

The U.S. DOE, the NYC DOE, the Leadership Academy, NVPS, funders, and other interested parties see the evaluation results.

RECRUITMENT, HIRING, AND RETENTION OF NEW STAFF

How many new principals are recruited and hired each year?

During 2000–2003, the school system replaced 80 percent of the existing principals. In 2004, over 380 new principals were recruited, about 280 the year before, and over 200 in each of the preceding two years. That's over 1,000 principals over the past four years. During the same four-year period, NVPS mentored over 500 principals, nearly half the number of new principals. Full-time principals mentored the other half of the new principals.

Are there any data that correlate the mentoring program with the retention of new principals?

Over the first three years of the NVPS program, over 96 percent of the principals mentored were retained.

Are there any data that correlate the mentoring program with the performance of the new principals?

The formal evaluation conducted by Dr. Flugman concluded that there is a correlation between mentoring and the improved leadership skills of principals served that is statistically significant.

What are the indicators of program success?

- The demand for NVPS mentors has more than tripled in the last three years.
- Over 96 percent of the principals served by NVPS mentors have been retained.
- There is a statistically significant link between improved principal leadership skills and mentoring.
- On anonymous surveys, principals consistently report high levels of satisfaction with the mentoring program.
- On anonymous surveys, mentors consistently report high levels of satisfaction with the mentoring program.

MODEL 7.5

Principals' Leadership Academy of Nashville

Pearl G. Sims, Vanderbilt University
Department of Leadership, Policy and Organizations
Box 514, Peabody College, Nashville, TN 37203
615-343-697   Pearl.g.sims@vanderbilt.edu

Urban/suburban/rural school	Not applicable	Grade levels of school	Not applicable
Student population	Not applicable	Per pupil expenditure	Not applicable
Mentoring is/is not mandated for ongoing certification/ licensure	Mentoring is mandated	Mentoring program is/is not funded by the state	Not funded
Unique feature of program	Learning pairs, with coach and business member	Duration of program for new principals	One year
Mentors are Full-time principals from same district from another district Retired principals	Coaches are full-time principals from the same district	Mentor selection criteria exist/do not exist Mentor matching process exists/does not exist	Coach selection criteria do exist Coach matching process does exist
Mentors are trained/not trained for role Mentors receive/do not receive ongoing support	Coaches are not trained Coaches receive ongoing support from director	Mentors are/are not part of a team to support new principals	Coaches are part of a team to support the new principals
Mentoring is/is not a component	Coaching is a component	Daily/weekly/yearly expectations for mentor	Twice monthly meetings and phone calls as needed
Mentors evaluate/do not evaluate the new principals	Coaches do not evaluate	Portfolio is required/ is not required	Portfolio is not required
Mentor remuneration	$5,000	Higher education affiliation	Vanderbilt University
Cost of program	$176,500	Funding	District, university, Nashville Public Education Foundation, and other local charitable organizations
Years program in existence	Four years	Full-time/part-time program coordinator/program coordination is part of another role in system/organization/ state	Program coordination is part of another role in the university

STATE MANDATES

Is mentoring mandated for new principals?
No, mentoring is not mandated for new principals.

Is mentoring part of certification or licensure?
Mentoring is part of the requirements for new principals to move from the Beginning Administrators License to the Professional Administrators License.

Is funding provided by the state to support the mandate?
No, there is no funding for mentoring.

HISTORY

Why was the program started?
The program was started in 2000 at the request of administrators in the Nashville School District when they realized that 57 percent of their principals would be eligible for retirement within five years. They wanted to prepare a pipeline for people who could or would assume leadership of the schools. The Nashville Public Education Foundation was interested in getting involved in the school in a deeper way to impact the leadership of the schools. The director of the schools and the president of the Nashville Education Foundation worked with Camilla Benbow, then dean at Vanderbilt University.

GOALS

What is the goal of the program?
The goal of the program is to increase the number of people who are capable of taking the reins of leadership in the Nashville Public Schools. The specific goal is to prepare 25 leaders each year for five years.

PROGRAM DESIGN

Who designed the mentor program?
A group of people designed the program. To impact the schools, it would take the perspectives of many people: the school leaders themselves (the superintendent suggested five of his best principals, based on student achievement in their schools and parent satisfaction), some faculty from the Peabody School of Education at Vanderbilt University, and three community leaders. The program is built on three legs: the wisdom of practitioners, the intellectual capital of the university, and the practical knowledge of the business community.

What are the components and recommended schedule of the program?
The program includes

- A two-week intensive program in the summer, from 8:30 a.m. to 4:30 p.m. where participants get an overview of the program and start working with their school's data
- Wednesday evening meetings, once a month, from 4:00 to 9:00 p.m., including dinner
- Saturday meetings, once a month, from 9:00 a.m. to 3:00 p.m., with individualized help sessions from 3:00 to 5:00 p.m.

The components of the program are as follows:

- Each year there is a cohort of 25 new or aspiring principals. They are divided into teams of four, consisting of two learning pairs. Each team has a coach principal who has been identified by the school district and approved by the design team as somebody who is well versed in administration and is a business leader. The coach and the business leader each sit at the ends of the tables.
- Teams participate in challenge-based learning. The challenges are technologized. Everyone has a laptop that is provided by the school district and updated every other year. Every participant is given a digital camera at the holiday season and a PDA when they graduate. They use the PDAs to record each other's addresses and telephone numbers.
- Each session starts with a problem. Principal Edwards, a fictionalized character, is confronted by real-life problems. Principal Edwards is a teachable agent. Participants find that it is easier to talk about a fictionalized agent than about themselves. He is put through everything imaginable.

Are there any programs that complement the mentor program?

Not applicable.

PROGRAM ADMINISTRATION

Who coordinates the program?

Dr. Pearl G. Sims is the director of the Leadership Development Center. The Principals' Leadership Academy of Nashville is offered through the Leadership Development Center.

How is information communicated to shareholders?

This program counts for 24 of the 60 credits that principals need to have every five years for certification. The Tennessee Academy for School Leaders, later known as the Principals' Leadership Academy of Nashville, was mandated by the state legislature to support principals to keep their state license. Principals may also sign up for additional support through the state. Information is communicated in-house through Prometheus. Everything about the course is posted, including the syllabus. There are many group e-mails, in different configurations. Since school district administrators are part of the design team, they can help their systems coordinate their professional development opportunities and requirements with what is offered through the Leadership Development Center.

Who coordinates the integration of this program with other professional development opportunities or requirements in the school or district?

Not applicable.

PARTICIPATION IN THE PROGRAM

Who is served?

The program serves 25 licensed school administrators who are not yet practicing (assistant principals and classroom teachers) and new principals whose names were submitted by their superintendents. There is an application process that includes the use of technology, an assessment of their writing skills, and interviews with applicants by the design team.

Is participation of new principals voluntary or mandatory?

Participation in the program is voluntary.

How long is the program?

The program lasts one year.

WHO PROVIDES THE MENTORING AND INDUCTION?

What are the criteria for being a mentor?

In this program, the role is not mentor, it is coach. The term *mentoring*, in this environment, leaves a sense that the mentor knows something that another person needs. This program is trying to be more reciprocal, less hierarchical.

The criteria for being a coach are as follows:

- An experienced building leader. Coaches are practicing administrators. By being current, they can help with the day-to-day needs of the participants. Those kinds of questions can be offered outside class time.
- Someone who knows how to learn, considers her- or himself a learner, and models learning. It is not optimal to recruit people who will come to tell what they know so that other people will get it right. That will be a barrier to real learning.

Are coaches full-time principals or retired principals?

Coaches are full-time principals.

Are coaches from the same district as new principals?

All the coaches are from the same district as the new or aspiring principals.

How are coaches selected?

The design team matches coaches with the new principals.

How are matches made between coaches and new principals?

Participants are involved in all kinds of situations in the summer institute. A statistical software package arranges the seating so that the participants are seated with someone different every day for the 10 days. The participants are assessed through the Myers-Briggs Type Indicator, a listening assessment, and a team assessment. Dr. Ron Elsdon, a consultant from Drake, Beam, Morrin (DBM) Inc., administers and analyzes everything to balance the teams with different personalities and to create very diverse teams.

WHAT IS EXPECTED OF COACHES?

What are the job responsibilities of coaches?

The responsibilities of the coaches are to

- Assist in the summer institute, possibly as table helpers
- Observe and take notes on new classes
- Participate in Wednesday and Saturday meetings
- Speak on the phone with participants outside of class meetings
- Be available to the new or aspiring leaders on the day-to-day things that are not covered in class

- Ensure that participants are working on the final project, which is a culmination of assignments throughout the year
- Make sure that their table is progressing through each module of learning
- Model the willingness to make mistakes. The biggest mistake of new leadership is the unwillingness to be vulnerable and admit, "I don't know this."

Is the relationship between the coach and the new principal confidential?

Yes, the relationship is confidential within the learning teams. At the end of the year, the director of the Leadership Development Center reviews the end-of-the-year projects and the pre- and posttest results and may share these with superintendents about their individual staff members.

Is observation a requirement of coaches?

Observation of participants in their school settings is not a requirement of coaching. Observation in their learning pairs is part of coaching.

Do coaches formally evaluate new principals?

No, coaches do not formally evaluate new or aspiring principals.

How much time are coaches expected to work with new principals (weekly, monthly, and for how long)?

Coaches are expected to work with the learning pairs at the monthly Wednesday and Saturday sessions, as well as be available by phone in between.

When do coaches meet with the new principals?

Coaches meet with the new or aspiring principals at the Wednesday and Saturday sessions.

WHAT SUPPORTS ARE AVAILABLE FOR COACHES?

Are coaches remunerated?

Coaches earn a stipend of $5,000 per year. The money comes from the Nashville Public Education Foundation, not from the school, so it is not a union issue.

Are coaches trained? If so, by whom?

The training of coaches is done through conversations about the terms and expectations of their roles. The coaches are identified because they run successful schools and the districts approve them. Many of them are known to program staff.

They are also observed during the summer institute to make sure they can develop leaders.

Is there professional development for coaches after the initial training? If so, who provides it?

No, there isn't formal professional development for the coaches after the initial discussion. If there are six thoughtful people at a table, chances are that something good is going to happen.

Do coaches meet regularly with other coaches? If so, how often and for how long?

Yes, coaches meet quite often with each other. They also meet with an executive coach during the summer to make sure that they understand what coaching is. This gives them a format to pull their tables together. They establish norms of the tables, not just norms of the academy. The director of the

Leadership Development Center meets with the coaches twice during the year. They use the executive coaching model that came from DBM.

Is there any other ongoing support for coaches? If so, who provides it?

Coaches come to the director of the Leadership Development Center if there are issues.

Are there any other resources available for coaches?

No, there aren't any other resources for coaches.

Are coaches supervised? If so, by whom and how frequently?

The director of the Leadership Development Center informally supervises the coaches during the Wednesday and Saturday meetings to make sure they are making progress toward the end-of-the-year projects.

WHAT IS EXPECTED OF NEW PRINCIPALS REGARDING THEIR PARTICIPATION IN THE MENTORING PROGRAM?

How often do new principals meet with their coaches and for how long?

New principals meet with their coaches in the summer institute and at the Wednesday and Saturday meetings. They also speak by telephone. Sometimes they spend time shadowing the coach.

Are there other people with whom the new principal meets for mentoring and support?

New principals may also meet with the business leader at their table.

Is formative assessment of new principals required? If so, when, how, and by whom?

The new principals are formatively assessed through faculty feedback and monitoring of their progress during the projects that are done in the program.

Are new principals required to prepare a portfolio?

The end-of-the-year project gets submitted to the district superintendent. This project requires participants to find one thing in their schools, through examining lots of sources of school data, they think will significantly improve student performance. They spend the first part of the year identifying the problem. In the second part of the year, they develop a strategy for implementation. They share their projects with each other, and all the projects are distributed on CD-ROMs. These are becoming part of a technology library they have created. They are really pulling for each other.

ARE ADDITIONAL SUPPORTS AVAILABLE FOR NEW PRINCIPALS?

Is any other professional development provided? If so, when and by whom?

The principals have access to the Tennessee Academy of School Leaders (TASL) which has a wide menu of choices.

Do new principals meet regularly with other new principals?

In addition to the Wednesday and Saturday meetings, new principals meet with their learning pairs. This helps reduce the isolation they may be feeling.

There is an intense focus on the learning pairs. The pairs go into each other's schools twice a year to watch the interaction. Over the long term, a system of learners is developing.

What resources are required for this program?

It costs $176,500 per year to run this program, broken down into the following categories:

- Salaries for Vanderbilt faculty and staff (prorated to the time working on the project): $93,000
- Honorariums for coaches: $30,000
- Administration and analysis of the assessments: $10,000
- Software for computers, printing of class readings and materials: $22,000
- Technology purchases: $16,000
- Miscellaneous expenses: $5,500

FUNDING

What are the funding sources?

The program is funded in thirds by the school districts, the university, and the Public Education Foundation. The school districts pay a little more because they equip the computer lab.

Who requests the funding?

The design team oversees the funding.

EVALUATION OF THE PROGRAM

Is the program evaluated formatively? Summatively? Who does the evaluation?

There are formative and summative evaluations, which consist of

- Pre- and postevaluations of the new or aspiring principals using Interstate School Leaders Licensure Consortium (ISLLC) standards
- End-of-the-year project, which is a formative assessment during the year and summative at the end to see if they met the goals

Who sees the results?

The design team, dean, school director, and president of the National Education Foundation see the results.

Individual participant progress is reported to the school superintendents. Pre- and posttest results and the end-of-the-year project are shared with the superintendents.

RECRUITMENT, HIRING, AND RETENTION OF NEW STAFF

How many new principals are recruited and hired each year?

Ninety-six percent of the graduates from this program have some type of administrative position: assistant principal, principal, or administrator in the central office.

Are there any data that correlate the mentoring program with the retention of new principals?

There are no such data.

Are there any data that correlate the mentoring program with the performance of the new principals?

Such data are not available.

What are the indicators of program success?

There is an end-of-the-year survey to find out what the parties like, what they dislike, and what was the most meaningful experience for them. They are always so complimentary of the fact that they didn't know that they would grow to love and respect each other as much as they did.

Five of the class members came as ambassadors to request an alumni association, composed of past participants, to continue to learn from each other. The school district funded the newly formed alumni association with $20,000. Retired principals are coaches with the alumni association.

Dr. Pearl Sims, the director of the Leadership Development Center, reflects, "My life is different from getting to know these principals—people who convince me to the core of their intense love of education and their intense love of teaching. They remind me of why the university sits in the backyard of our school district."

PART III

Now What?

Planning/Enhancing Your Program

"In the midst of a massive demographic exodus in school leadership, new candidates for leadership who care about leading, want to lead, and feel able to lead in current circumstances are as rare as mosquitoes in the snow."

— A. Hargreaves (Foreword to Crowther, Kaagan, Ferguson, & Hann 2002)

The goal is to make sure that those who care about leading and want to lead are supported and able to lead. You have read about programs throughout the United States that mentor and/or induct new school principals. Some have focused on the mentoring or coaching as the key support for new principals. Others have focused on building skills and a deeper understanding of topics and issues that principals need to know in order to do their work.

Many of these programs are relatively new. The coordinators of the programs have begun collecting data about program effectiveness in terms of participant satisfaction. In the future, they may all be able to evaluate their programs based on principals' performance and retention in the profession, as well as student achievement. Therefore, for now you need to think about which models or ideas are relevant to your context.

Think first about what is best for new principals, without yet deciding that the programs are too expensive. There may be creative ways to fund and/or staff your offerings. For example, often there are funds already designated for professional development that could be used in different ways. Let your thinking initially be about supporting the entry and successful tenure of new principals. Enlist district and community resources to collaborate with you and learn from others in your state and throughout the country who endeavor to thoughtfully and successfully induct their new principals.

REALITIES, BELIEFS, AND GOALS FOR INDUCTING AND MENTORING NEW PRINCIPALS

The questions in the following figure are designed to help you clarify your beliefs about supporting new principals. You need to consider these beliefs within the realities of your organization as you consider planning or enhancing your program.

STATE ACTION FOR EDUCATION LEADERSHIP PROJECT

Progress is being made on inducting and supporting school leaders toward the goal of improved student performance. The State Action for Education Leadership Project (SAELP) is a partnership of five national organizations: the Council of Chief State School Officers, the Education Commission of the States, the National Association of State Boards of Education, the National Conference of State Legislatures, and the National Governors Association.

The project's stated goals and objectives for state action are the following:

> SAELP will assist decision makers, particularly governors, state legislators, state boards of education, and chief state school officers, in redesigning their state policies, laws, and practices to strengthen the leadership of superintendents, principals, and school leaders toward the objectives of improved student performance.

- States will establish an overall vision and expectation for the practice of educational leadership focused on improved teaching and learning at the district and school level throughout the state.

(Text continues on p. 235)

Figure 8.1   Realities, Beliefs, and Goals for Inducting New Principals

State Requirements
In your state,

1. Do certification requirements for new principals require mentoring?
2. Are there any requirements about districts providing induction for new principals?

Beliefs About Induction

1. Do you think new principals should be inducted into your district/state/organization?
2. Are you willing to make induction a priority for your district/state/organization?
3. What components of induction do you think are essential?
   a. Orientation and Entry Planning
      By superintendent, district, and building administrators, outgoing principal
      By parent groups, school board, and other town/city officials
      By organization leadership and staff
   b. Needs assessment based on ELSI (see Resource E) or ISLLC standards
   c. Professional development plan based on needs assessment
   d. Mentoring
   e. Skill building
   f. Portfolios
   g. Beginner principal support groups
   h. Network of experienced principals
   i. Meetings with district/state/organization administrators
   j. School visitations
   k. Principal shadowing
   l. Study groups
   m. Courses
   n. Other
4. How many years are optimal for an induction program?

Beliefs About Mentoring

1. Do you think mentoring is a key component of induction for new principals?
2. Should mentors be from within or outside the districts of the new principals? What are the advantages and drawbacks of each?
3. Do you think retired administrators would be good mentors?
4. What training and ongoing support is essential for mentors?
5. Do you think new principals should have a voice in selecting their mentors?
6. Do you think mentoring should include cognitive coaching as well as technical coaching?
7. Should the relationship between mentors and new principals be nonevaluative and confidential?

(Continued)

Figure 8.1 (Continued)

Principalship Vacancies

1. How many new principals do you typically hire each year?

2. Do you anticipate the number of vacancies changing? If so, in what way?

Applicant Pool for Principalships

1. Are you experiencing or do you expect to experience a shortage of applicants?

2. Has the number of applicants from within the district/state/organization changed?

3. Would these factors affect the emphasis of your induction program? If so, how?

Resources

1. Do you have enough new principals in your district/state/organization each year to warrant creating an induction program for them?

2. Would you consider participation in a regional program?

3. Can you envision your organization funding the creation/enhancement of an induction program?

4. Does your state Department of Education provide funding to support new administrators in their districts?

5. Does your state Department of Education offer programs to support new administrators?

6. Are you near a university that offers courses or programs for new administrators?

7. Do the administrative professional organizations in your state offer support programs for new principals?

8. Are there nonprofit organizations that offer programs to support new principals?

9. Are there local education foundations or businesses that might partner with you to support new principals?

Program Planning

1. What constituencies should you involve in planning/implementing an induction program?

2. Are there key people within your organization who will promote and enhance an induction program?

3. Are there people outside your organization who might join to plan/implement an induction program?

Evaluation

1. Do you think that program assessment should be considered during the design process of your program?

2. What data would you want collected, and what evaluation methods do you think would be appropriate? For example, do you want to know about program impact on principal performance, principal satisfaction with their role, principal retention, student achievement?

3. How will ongoing evaluation be used for program improvement?

- States will design and enact laws that establish the terms and conditions of practice as principal and superintendent, including criteria for licensure of individuals and accreditation of postsecondary programs that prepare education leaders.
- States will enact laws that establish governance, structures, and roles and responsibilities of education leaders, including local boards of education, school councils, etc.
- States will design an infrastructure that will connect education leaders to other areas of public and private endeavor, including business, research institutes, community-based organizations, etc.
- States will design and implement legislative and/or administrative policies that are informed by local schools and districts, especially those in high poverty areas.
- States will support demonstration districts where new policies are transformed into practice.

There are 15 state participants in SAELP. They are Connecticut, Delaware, Georgia, Illinois, Indiana, Iowa, Kentucky, Massachusetts, Missouri, Montana, New Jersey, Oregon, Rhode Island, Vermont, and Virginia. Each SAELP state receives a total amount of $250,000 to bring about policy change and strengthen education leadership. In addition, the Wallace Reader's Digest Fund's district initiative, Leadership for Educational Achievement in Districts (LEAD), has awarded one-year grants ranging from $527,000 to $1.34 million to 10 high-need districts located within the SAELP states. The grants are renewable annually for up to a total of $5 million over five years, provided the district demonstrates significant progress toward achieving its goals (see SAELP on the Council of Chief State School Officers Web site at www.ccsso.org/saelp).

Educational leadership is clearly a priority of these organizations, and by working together they will be effecting change that is far greater than could be achieved individually.

REDEFINING SCHOOL LEADERSHIP

Many acknowledge that the principalship is a role that is almost too difficult to perform to the standards identified. There are some who do the job admirably, and there is a lot to learn from their practice. In addition, I believe our country needs to examine its expectations and change the nature of school leadership. Our immediate attention is on what is currently happening and how you can support new principals today. In addition, we must redefine the principalship so that it is a doable job that educational leaders will aspire to perform.

Here are three ways to rethink school leadership that accommodate the changing nature of schools and the increased demands of society for school effectiveness:

1. *Job sharing*. School districts are experimenting with different ways to structure school leadership. Some schools are experimenting with having two administrators: one is in charge of the logistic management issues and the other is focused on instruction. Of course, there is overlap, and both principals work closely to ensure that the school is an optimal learning environment.

2. *Enhance leadership capacity of others*. Lambert (1998), in her work to understand and promote leadership capacity, posits: "Leading is a shared endeavor, the foundation for the democratization of schools. School change is a collective endeavor; therefore, people do this most effectively in the presence of others. The learning journey must be shared; otherwise, shared purpose and action are never achieved" (p. 9).

3. *Parallel leadership*. Crowther, Kaagan, Ferguson, and Hann (2002) define the role of the principal in nurturing what they call parallel leadership. The principal
    - Communicates a clear strategic intent
    - Incorporates the aspirations and views of others
    - Poses difficult-to-answer questions

– Makes space for individual innovations
– Knows when to step back
– Creates opportunities from perceived difficulties
– Builds upon achievement to create a culture of success.

> We need to redefine the principalship so that educators will want to use their leadership skills in this important role.

These ways of thinking expand the leadership role to include others in this important work. Do any of them advocate the abolishment of the role? Of course not. Principals play an essential leadership role in our schools.

If our society could expand its vision of leadership to include more of the constituents in meaningful roles, perhaps some of our principals would stop counting the days until they could retire and they would regain their enthusiasm for school leadership. It might also afford practicing principals opportunities to pursue related interests without having to leave the principalship.

REFLECTION

When I was a school principal, I spent many hours meeting with prospective homeowners who wanted to interview me before deciding to purchase a home in our school district. Sometimes I felt as though the realtors should share their commissions with me, because these meetings were keeping me from doing some of the many other things that were crying out for my attention. Yet I felt a kinship with those parents, so eager to pick a school community that would nurture their children. I had felt the same way when my firstborn was about to enter school. I wanted a sense of the principal who would oversee the school community into which my son would be entering. I wanted to know that the principal was a caring, thoughtful person who had the leadership skills to ensure that my son, and later daughter, would feel valued as a member of the school community, excited about learning, and safe enough to take risks to grow.

Eleven years after beginning my third principalship, I decided to work in education in other capacities, and I informed the school community that I would be leaving before the next school year began. The reactions to my departure were numerous. One made the biggest impression on me. Several parents were crying as they said to me, "We bought our houses because of you, and we wanted our children to be at this school under your leadership." The reason parents choose schools for their children are varied. They may be looking at higher test scores, safe physical environments, well-funded programs and classrooms, and/or a school environment that celebrates the diversity of the students and adults. Was I the only person who could shepherd their children through school? Certainly not. And though I was leaving, the many teachers and staff who had more frequent interactions with their children were remaining. Yet for these parents, there had been a sense of security in knowing that I was the principal.

When principals leave their positions, there is a period of adjustment for students, their families, and the staff as they await the appointment of their new principal. It is likely that many of the principals filling the positions will be new to the position, as well as possibly new to the community. It is imperative that we support new principals through induction programs that help them heighten their performance and enhance their entry into the school community and profession. There are successful mentoring and induction programs throughout the United States. Many more are needed. Join in.

Resource A

Model Description Template

State Mandates

- Is mentoring mandated for new principals?
- Is mentoring part of certification or licensure?
- Is funding provided by the state to support the mandate?

History

- Why was the program started?

Goals

- What are the goals of the program?

Program Design

- Who designed the mentor program?
- What are the components and recommended schedule of the program?
- Are there any programs that complement the mentor program?

Program Administration

- Who coordinates the program?
- How is information communicated to shareholders?

- Who coordinates the integration of this program with other professional development opportunities or requirements in the school or district?

Participation in the Program

- Who is served?
- Is participation of new principals voluntary or mandatory?
- How long is the program?

Who Provides the Mentoring/Induction?

- What are the criteria for being a mentor?
- Are mentors full-time principals or retired principals?
- Are mentors from the same district as new principals?
- How are mentors selected?
- How are matches made between mentors and new principals?

What Is Expected of Mentors?

- What are the job responsibilities of the mentor?
- Is the relationship between the mentor and the new principal confidential?
- Are observation and coaching requirements of mentors?
- Do mentors formally evaluate new principals?
- How much time are mentors expected to work with new principals (weekly, monthly, and for how long)?
- When do mentors meet with the new principals?

What Supports Are Available for Mentors?

- Are mentors remunerated?
- Are mentors trained? If so, by whom?
- Is there professional development for mentors after the initial training? If so, who provides it?
- Do mentors meet regularly with other mentors? If so, how often and for how long?
- Is there any other ongoing support for mentors? If so, who provides it?
- Are any other resources available for mentors?
- Are mentors supervised? If so, by whom and how frequently?

What Is Expected of New Principals Regarding Their Participation in the Mentoring Program?

- How often do new principals meet with their mentors and for how long?
- Are there other people with whom the new principal meets for mentoring and support?
- Is formative assessment of new principals required? If so, when, how, and by whom?
- Are new principals required to prepare a portfolio?

Are Additional Supports Available for New Principals?

- Is any other professional development provided? If so, when and by whom?
- Do new principals meet regularly with other new principals?

What Resources Are Required for the Mentoring Program?

- Mentor training
- New principal orientation
- Ongoing professional development for mentors and/or new principals
- Food for conferences and meetings
- Materials
- Remuneration for mentors
- Project director's salary, or portion related to mentoring
- Hardware/audiovisual equipment

Funding

- What are the funding sources?
- Who requests the funding?

Evaluation of the Program

- Is the program evaluated formatively? Summatively? Who does the evaluation?
- Who sees the results?

Recruitment, Hiring, and Retention of New Staff

- How many new principals are recruited and hired each year?
- Are there any data that correlate the mentoring program with the retention of new principals?
- Are there any data that correlate the mentoring program with the performance of the new principals?
- What are the indicators of program success?

Resource B

Chart Template

Urban/suburban/rural school		Grade levels of school	
Student population		Per pupil expenditure	
Mentoring is/is not mandated for ongoing certification/licensure		Mentoring program is/is not funded by the state	
Unique feature of program		Duration of program for new principals	

Mentors are
  Full-time principals
    from same district
    from another district
  Retired principals
		Mentor selection criteria
		  exist/do not exist
		Mentor matching process
		  exists/does not exist	

Mentors are trained/not trained for role Mentor receive/do not receive ongoing support		Mentors are/are not part of a team to support new principals	
Coaching is/is not a component		Daily/weekly/yearly expectations for mentor	
Mentors evaluate/do not evaluate the new principals		Portfolio is required/is not required	
Mentor remuneration		Higher education affiliation	
Cost of program		Funding	
Years program in existence		Full-time/part-time program coordinator program coordination is part of another role in system/ organization/state	

Resource C

District	Urban, Suburban, Rural	Student Population	Grades	Per Pupil Expenditure
Albuquerque, NM	Urban, suburban, and rural	83,000	PreK–12	$5,713
Bridgeport, CT	Urban	23,000	PreK–12	$8,617
Cooperative Education Services, CT	Urban, suburban, and rural	Not applicable	PreK–12	Not applicable
Chicago, IL	Urban	43,419	K–12	$8,482
Sheridan, CO	Rural and urban	1,861	PreK–12	$6,718
Wake, NC	Urban and suburban	114,000	PreK–12	$6,700
Independence, MO	Suburban	11,200	PreK–12	$6,500
New York City, NY	Urban	1.1 million	PreK–12	$10,593
San Diego, CA	Urban	138,613	K–12	$4,325-$5,909

Resource C2   Models in States That Mandate Mentoring, Internship, or Induction

State	Mentoring Is Mandated	Internship Is Mandated	Induction Is Mandated	State Funding for Mentoring
Arkansas	Yes			Yes
California	Yes			
Colorado			Yes	No
Indiana	Yes			Yes
Massachusetts	Yes			No
Mississippi	No			Sometimes
New Jersey	Yes			No
Ohio	Yes			Yes
Tennessee	Yes			No
Texas	Yes			No

Models That Are in States That Do Not Mandate Mentoring or Induction

Connecticut

Illinois

Missouri

New Mexico

New York

North Carolina

Washington

Resource C3   Duration of Mentoring or Induction Program

Context	Model	1 Year	2 Years	3 Years
District and Regional	Albuquerque, NM Extra Support for Principals (ESP)	*		
	Bridgeport, CT New Administrator Induction Program		*	
	Cooperative Educational Services (CES), CT New Administrator Induction Program		*	
	Chicago Public Schools Leadership for Transformation (LIFT)	*		
	Sheridan, CO New Principal Induction Program		*	
	Wake, NC Principal Induction Program	*		
State	Arkansas Beginning Administrator Induction Program	*	*	*
	Indiana Principal Leadership Academy (IPLA)	*	*	
	Mississippi Beginning Principal Mentorship Program and the Beginning Principals Network	*		
	Ohio Entry Year Program for Principals		*	
	Tennessee Academy for School Leaders (TASL)		*	
Professional Association	National Association of Elementary School Principals (NAESP) Principals Advisory Leadership Services (PALS) Massachusetts Elementary School Principals' Association (MESPA) The Consulting Mentor Program	*		
	New Jersey Principals and Supervisors Association (NJPSA) New Jersey Leaders to Leaders	*	*	*
	Texas Elementary School Principals and Supervisors Association (TEPSA)		*	
	National Association of Secondary School Principals (NASSP) Selecting and Developing the 21st Century Principal	*	*	
	Association of Washington School Principals (AWSP) Assessing and Developing the 21st Century Principal	*		
University	New Teacher Center, University of California, Santa Cruz, Coaching Leaders to Attain School Success (CLASS)	*	*	
	University of North Carolina Leadership Program for New Principals	*		
Collaborative	Arkansas Leadership Academy Master Principal Program	*	*	*
	San Diego, CA Educational Leadership Development Academy		*	
	Independence, Missouri, and University of Missouri			*
	New York City Leadership Academy's Principal Mentoring Program in Collaboration with New Visions for Public Schools	*	*	
	Principals' Leadership Academy Nashville, TN	*		

Resource C4   Mentor–New Principal Mentoring Ratio

Context	Model	1:1	1:2	1:3	1:4	No Mentoring
District and Regional	Albuquerque, NM Extra Support for Principals (ESP)	*				
	Bridgeport, CT New Administrator Induction Program	* The program facilitator individually mentors the new principals				
	Cooperative Educational Services (CES), CT New Administrator Induction Program	*				
	Chicago LIFT	* Mentor may work individually with several new principals				
	Sheridan, CO New Principal Induction Program	*				
	Wake, NC					*
State	Arkansas Beginning Administrator Induction Program	*				
	Indiana Principal Leadership Academy (IPLA)	*	*	*	*	
	Mississippi Beginning Principal Mentorship Program and the Beginning Principals Network	*				
	Ohio Entry Year Program for Principals	*				
	Tennessee Academy for School Leaders (TASL)	*				

Resource C4   (Continued)

Context	Model	1:1	1:2	1:3	1:4	No Mentoring
Professional Association	National Association of Elementary School Principals (NAESP) Principals Advisory Leadership Services (PALS) Massachusetts Elementary School Principals' Association (MESPA) The Consulting Mentor Program	* *				
	New Jersey Principals and Supervisors Association (NJPSA) New Jersey Leaders to Leaders	*				
	Texas Elementary School Principals and Supervisors Association (TEPSA)	*				
	National Association of Secondary School Principals (NASSP) Selecting and Developing the 21st Century Principal Association of Washington School Principals (AWSP) Assessing and Developing the 21st Century Principal	* *				
University	New Teacher Center, University of California, Santa Cruz Coaching Leaders to Attain School Success (CLASS)	*				
	University of North Carolina Leadership Program for New Principals					*
Collaborative	Arkansas Leadership Academy Master Principal Program					*
	San Diego, CA Educational Leadership Development Academy	*				
	Independence, Missouri, and University of Missouri	*				

Resource C4   (Continued)

Context	Model	1:1	1:2	1:3	1:4	No Mentoring
	New York City Leadership Academy's Principal Mentoring Program in Collaboration with New Visions for Public Schools	*				
	Principals' Leadership Academy of Nashville				*	

Resource C5   Cost of Programs

Context	Model	Cost	Mentor Remuneration
District	Albuquerque, NM Extra Support for Principals (ESP)	$30,000	$1,000/year
	Bridgeport, CT New Administrator Induction Program	$4,000 + cost of part-time facilitator and mentor of new principals	District mentors are not remunerated; outside consultants are
	Cooperative Educational Services (CES), CT New Administrator Induction Program	$550 per new principal	District mentors are not remunerated; outside consultants are
	Chicago Public Schools Leadership for Transformation (LIFT)	$262,500 + LIFT staff salaries	$1,500 per protégé
	Sheridan, CO New Principal Induction Program	$10,000	None
	Wake, NC Principal Induction Program	$10,000	Not applicable
State	Arkansas Beginning Administrator Induction Program	$200,000	$400/year
	Indiana Principal Leadership Academy (IPLA)	$487,000	$600/year
	Mississippi Beginning Principal Mentorship Program and the Beginning Principals Network	$131,000 the first year	Varies in each program
	Ohio Entry Year Program for Principals	$800,000 for the state	$750 for two years
	Tennessee Academy for School Leaders (TASL)	$199,000	None
Professional Associations	National Association of Elementary School Principals (NAESP) Principals Advisory Leadership Services (PALS)	Participants pay $750 for Immersion Institute	None, unless individual districts offer payment

Resource C5

Context	Model	Cost	Mentor Remuneration
	Massachusetts Elementary School Principals' Association (MESPA) The Consulting Mentor Program	$27,000 for 15 participants	$1,000/year
	New Jersey Principals and Supervisors Association (NJPSA) New Jersey Leaders to Leaders	Participants pay $1,800 for Year 1; $1,300 for Year 2; $800 for Year 3	$1,500 per first-year principal; $1,000 per second-year principal; $500 per third-year principal
	Texas Elementary School Principals and Supervisors Association (TEPSA)	Varies by district and region	Local decision
	National Association of Secondary School Principals (NASSP) Selecting and Developing the 21st Century Principal	It depends on the number of people trained	Choice of the sponsoring organization
	Association of Washington School Principals (AWSP) Assessing and Developing the 21st Century Principal	$650,000	$1,500
University	New Teacher Center, University of California, Santa Cruz Coaching Leaders to Attain School Success (CLASS)	$3,500 per coachee	$3,000 per coachee
	University of North Carolina Leadership Program for New Principals	$1,000 per participant	Mentoring is not a component
Collaborative	Arkansas Leadership Academy Master Principal Program	$500,000	Performance coaches earn $1,000
	San Diego, CA Educational Leadership Development Academy	$702,500	$3,000/semester $6,000 per year
	Independence, Missouri, and University of Missouri	$45,000	No additional compensation to district administrators for their mentoring work
	New York City Leadership Academy's Principal Mentoring Program in Collaboration with New Visions for Public Schools	$1.7 million	$2,500–$3,000 per semester
	Principals' Leadership Academy of Nashville	$176,500	Coaches earn $5,000/year

Resource C6 Unique Features of Programs

	Program	Unique Feature
District	Albuquerque, NM Extra Support for Principals (ESP)	New principals have a strong voice in the selection of their mentors
	Bridgeport, CT New Administrator Induction Program	New administrators participate in a regional network of collegial support; includes all positions in administration; includes expanded definition of "new"
	Cooperative Educational Services (CES), CT New Administrator Induction Program	New administrators participate in a regional network of collegial support; includes all positions in administration; includes expanded definition of "new" Program is part of a group of academies to support principals
	Chicago Public Schools Leadership for Transformation (LIFT)	
	Sheridan, CO New Principal Induction Program	Mentoring is provided for new principals in a very small district that is both rural and urban
	Wake, NC Principal Induction Program	Half day of media training for new administrators and monthly topical presentations on topics of need
State	Arkansas Beginning Administrator Induction Program	Mentoring is mandated and funded by the state
	Indiana Principal Leadership Academy (IPLA)	There is a voluntary Leadership Academy, ongoing course work for licensure, and optional coaching
	Mississippi Beginning Principal Mentorship Program and the Beginning Principals Network	Training for mentors and new principals; 90 contact hours between mentors and new principals
	Ohio Entry Year Program for Principals	Performance-based professional development
	Tennessee Academy for School Leaders (TASL)	New principals pick their mentors
Professional Associations	National Association of Elementary School Principals (NAESP) Principals Advisory Leadership Services (PALS)	Nationwide principal-mentor training and NAESP certification
	Massachusetts Elementary School Principals' Association (MESPA) The Consulting Mentor Program	Multiple forms of contact, including joint training, on-site visits, and online communication

Resource C6 (Continued)

	Program	Unique Feature
	New Jersey Principals and Supervisors Association (NJPSA) New Jersey Leaders to Leaders	Combines intensive and sustained mentoring support with an intensive and sustained, standards-driven, job-embedded leadership development program
	Texas Elementary School Principals and Supervisors Association (TEPSA)	The academy is a model that is replicated throughout the state
	National Association of Secondary School Principals (NASSP) Selecting and Developing the 21st Century Principal	Program is based on diagnostic assessment. NASSP works with sponsoring organizations to build their capacity to develop and implement a mentoring program
	Association of Washington School Principals (AWSP) Assessing and Developing the 21st Century Principal	A two-day assessment of principal leadership skills
University	New Teacher Center, University of California, Santa Cruz	One-on-one coaching for two years
	Coaching Leaders to Attain School Success (CLASS)	
	University of North Carolina Leadership Program for New Principals	An 18-day program, ISLLC based
Collaborative	Arkansas Leadership Academy Master Principal Program	This program begins after the Arkansas Beginning Administrator Induction Program ends for administrators with at least three years of experience. Forty-four partners work together to support educational leadership without duplicating services they each provide
	San Diego, CA Educational Leadership Development Academy	New principals can earn the next level of certification in this program. Mentors meet with new principals three hours/week; extensive training at university and coordination with district
	Independence, Missouri, and University of Missouri	Administrators may earn a doctorate in educational leadership through the University of Missouri, and courses are all offered in Independence. The coursework is related to the district and school program improvement goals and is tied to student achievement
	New York City Leadership Academy's Principal Mentoring Program in Collaboration with New Visions for Public Schools	Consistent program for new principals across all of the NYC public schools
	Principals' Leadership Academy of Nashville	Learning pairs, with coach and business member, work together for a year on school-and district-based issues

251

Resource D

Administrative Tasks on Which Beginning Principals Had a Vital or Important Need for Assistance and Information

Task	
1	Plan and manage school budget
2	Understand "unwritten" rules, procedures, and expectations
3	Plan and direct improvements in curriculum and instruction
4	Understand district goals, philosophy, and expectations of principals
5	Orientation to and understanding of staff
6	Assess relevance of instruction, curriculum, and evaluate program outcomes
7	Understand and implement school board policies, district rules, and administrative procedures
8	Supervise accounting procedures for school monies
9	Understand curriculum content, objectives, and organization
10	Understand and work through district decision-making processes
11	Assess community needs, problems, and expectations
12	Develop master schedule
13	Set goals and develop long-range plans
14	Supervise and evaluate staff
15	Deal with staff concerns and resolve conflicts
16	Help staff improve and plan staff development activities
17	Select, assign, and orient staff
18	Supervise and direct custodial services, maintenance of facilities, and plant systems
19	Supervise special programs
20	Supervise purchasing procedures
21	Coordinate the opening and closing of each school year

SOURCE: M. E. Anderson (1991).

Resource E

Educational Leader
Self-Inventory (ELSI)

The following inventory was adapted by Larry Jacobson, with reference to the Connecticut Standards, and is reprinted with his permission.

EDUCATIONAL LEADERSHIP
SELF-INVENTORY (ELSI)

Instructions: This Self Inventory is designed to provide a personal profile of educational leadership. It consists of 69 statements that describe performances contained within the CSDE Standards for School Leaders. You are asked to respond to each question by reflecting on your leadership performance over the past 10–12 months.

Read each question carefully. Then circle the number that indicates the extent to which you feel you have demonstrated the performance during the past 10-12 months. In responding to each question:

1 represents **Seldom/Almost Never**

2 represents **Sometimes**

3 represents **Frequently**

4 represents **Almost Always**

If you find some statements difficult to rate, use your judgment in selecting the most appropriate rating (e.g., something you never do may be rated as **Seldom/Almost Never** or, something that you do "more than frequently" or that you do "continually" may be rated as **Almost Always**). You may also want to make comments, in the space provided to clarify the rating selected or to further reflect on your performance. Circle only one number per question and try to respond to every question.

The format for this questionnaire is based on the The Principal Instructional Management Scale, Philip Hallinger (1984). The rating scale and the content of the questionnaire are based on the Connecticut State Department of Education's (CSDE) Standards for School Leaders and was adapted by Larry Jacobson (CSDE) in 1999.

To what extent do I . . .?

I. The Educated Person

	Seldom	Sometimes	Freq.	Almost Always
1. Develop a vision of the educated person; share that vision with the school community and work with parents, community members, staff, and students to create a shared vision of the educated person	1	2	3	4
2. Work with staff, parents, and students to translate the school's vision of the educated person into school goals and student standards	1	2	3	4
3. Work with parents and staff to identify the connection between the school's image of the educated person and a knowledge of contemporary learning theory	1	2	3	4
4. Work with staff, parents, and students to translate the school's vision of the educated person into a strategic plan of school improvement and program revision	1	2	3	4
5. Ensure that the school's vision of the educated person informs staff development and is incorporated into the criteria for evaluating teacher performance and school programs	1	2	3	4
6. Demonstrate sensitivity to and respect for all cultural groups	1	2	3	4
7. Model the school's image of the educated person and insist staff to do the same	1	2	3	4

Comments/Reflections: I. _____

To what extent do I . . .?

II. The Learning Process

	Seldom	Sometimes	Freq.	Almost Always
1. Stay current with research and theory regarding learning and motivation	1	2	3	4
2. Work with teachers to create a variety of formal and informal opportunities for teachers to further develop their understanding of the learning process and to examine the implications of the learning process for teaching	1	2	3	4
3. Ensure that students are provided with opportunities for active engagement and testing of ideas	1	2	3	4
4. Encourage students to assume responsibility for their learning	1	2	3	4
5. Work with teachers to assess individual and group performance in order to design instruction that meets learners' current needs and that leads to higher levels of development	1	2	3	4

Comments/Reflections: II. _____

To what extent do I . . .?

III. The Teaching Process

	Seldom	Sometimes	Freq.	Almost Always
1. Use effective strategies to promote the continuous development of individual teacher abilities	1	2	3	4
2. Work with staff to design professional development activities that improve teaching and learning	1	2	3	4
3. Involve staff in the exploration of effective instructional strategies	1	2	3	4
4. Use the evaluation process to promote teacher reflection and growth	1	2	3	4
5. Establish a climate of collegiality and cooperation where staff accept collective responsibility for improved teaching and learning	1	2	3	4
6. Work with teachers to implement a variety of formal and informal assessment techniques to enhance teachers' knowledge of learners, evaluate student progress and performance, and modify teaching and learning strategies	1	2	3	4

Comments/Reflections: **III. _____**

To what extent do I . . .?

IV. Diverse Perspectives

	Seldom	Sometimes	Freq.	Almost Always
1. Provide professional development experiences that help staff understand diverse cultures in our world, community, and school	1	2	3	4
2. Involve the staff in developing activities and curricula representative of diverse cultural groups	1	2	3	4
3. Work with staff to incorporate multiple perspectives into the school curricula	1	2	3	4
4. Involve the staff in creating, implementing, and assessing relevant programs for diverse groups	1	2	3	4
5. Work with staff, students, parents, and the community to provide experiences that promote sensitivity toward diverse perspectives	1	2	3	4
6. Work with staff to ensure that all groups of students achieve at high levels	1	2	3	4

Comments/Reflections: IV._____

To what extent do I . . .?

V. School Goals	Seldom	Sometimes	Freq.	Almost Always
1. Engage members of the school community in establishing goals that support the school's vision of the educated person	1	2	3	4
2. Involve the school community in the exploration of instructional and programmatic alternatives that have the potential to enhance goal attainment	1	2	3	4
3. Employ multiple strategies to promote individual commitment to school goals	1	2	3	4
4. Employ multiple assessment strategies to monitor progress toward school goals	1	2	3	4
5. Incorporate school goals into teacher appraisal objectives	1	2	3	4
6. Incorporate school goals in the planning of professional development activities	1	2	3	4

Comments/Reflections: V. _____

To what extent do I . . . ?

VI. School Culture

	Seldom	Sometimes	Freq.	Almost Always
1. Use current understandings of teaching and learning as a basis for establishing an ongoing dialogue regarding the school mission and goals	1	2	3	4
2. Engage members of different interest groups in the school to promote school goals and establish a common, underlying school purpose	1	2	3	4
3. Work with school constituents to enhance aspects of the school culture that promote student learning	1	2	3	4
4. Help the staff develop shared values that create a positive school climate of openness, mutual respect, support, and inquiry	1	2	3	4

Comments/Reflections: **VI. _____**

To what extent do I . . .?

VII. School Standards and Assessment	Seldom	Sometimes	Freq.	Almost Always
1. Work with the school community to develop rigorous academic standards for student performance	1	2	3	4
2. Work with teachers to assess student, individual, and group performance	1	2	3	4
3. Work with staff to implement multiple assessment strategies to monitor individual and group progress	1	2	3	4
4. Promote practices and programs that contribute to the achievement of academic standards by all students	1	2	3	4
5. Ensure that all students make continuous progress toward academic standards	1	2	3	4

Comments/Reflections: VII. _____

To what extent do I . . .?

VIII. School Improvement

	Seldom	Sometimes	Freq.	Almost Always
1. Ensure that all students make continuous progress toward academic standards	1	2	3	4
2. Ensure that all groups of students, regardless of ethnicity or gender, achieve at high levels	1	2	3	4
3. Work with staff to develop programs and incorporate practices that help all children reach high achievement standards	1	2	3	4
4. Actively involve staff in the exploration of promising instructional and programmatic alternatives	1	2	3	4
5. Works with staff to design policies that contribute to the use of sound assessments at all levels, and use assessment results for student, teacher, program, and building-level improvement	1	2	3	4
6. Use student outcomes to inform decisions regarding the quality of programs for students and the appropriateness of professional development for staff	1	2	3	4
7. Use a wide range of sources of information as the basis for evaluating school improvement (e.g., parent/teacher involvement, attendance, classroom observations)	1	2	3	4
8. Work with staff to establish a school culture that values and promotes individual and collective reflection and learning	1	2	3	4

Comments/Reflections: VIII. _____

To what extent do I . . .?

IX. Professional Development

	Seldom	Sometimes	Freq.	Almost Always
1. Work with staff to create a plan for professional development activities that promote staff growth and the achievement of school goals	1	2	3	4
2. Encourage staff to take responsibility for their own growth	1	2	3	4
3. Create ongoing opportunities for staff to engage in discussion about teaching practice and school goals	1	2	3	4
4. Provide a variety of opportunities for staff development	1	2	3	4
5. Use student learning as the basis for evaluating the success of the professional development program	1	2	3	4

Comments/Reflections: IX. _____

To what extent do I . . .?

X. Integration of Staff Evaluation, Professional Development, and School Improvement	Seldom	Sometimes	Freq.	Almost Always
1. Work with staff to improve teaching and learning for all students by linking staff selection, teacher evaluation, professional development, and school improvement to student standards and school goals	1	2	3	4
2. Tie teacher evaluation objectives to school improvement needs, and support school improvement and teacher development needs with appropriate professional development activities	1	2	3	4
3. Provide ongoing opportunities for staff to reflect on their roles and practices in light of student standards and school goals	1	2	3	4
4. Promote and reinforce a culture of staff collaboration and collegiality by sharing decision-making authority and delegating responsibility as staff pursue improved teaching and learning for all students	1	2	3	4
5. Hold teachers accountable for performance that supports the achievement of student academic standards	1	2	3	4

Comments/Reflections: X._____

To what extent do I . . .?

XI. Organization, Resources, and School Policies	Seldom	Sometimes	Freq	Almost Always
1. Engage the school community in developing organizational structures, resource allocation, policies, and procedures that promote the achievement of all subgroups of students	1	2	3	4
2. Shape policies inherited from larger systems to maximize the attainment of school goals	1	2	3	4
3. Engage in strategic planning to revise organizational structures and resource allocation to promote the attainment of school improvement goals	1	2	3	4
4. Seek the input of staff, parents, and community members in determining appropriate organizational structures and resource allocation	1	2	3	4
5. Articulate the value premises and ethical principles that guide decisions in the policy arena	1	2	3	4
6. Work to influence district, state, and federal policy	1	2	3	4
7. Work within the parameters of regulatory requirements, district policies, and contractual obligations to promote the achievement of all students	1	2	3	4

Comments/Reflections: **XI. _____**

To what extent do I . . .?

XII. School Improvement

	Seldom	Sometimes	Freq.	Almost Always
1. Work with staff and community to create and sustain a variety of opportunities for parent and community participation in the school	1	2	3	4
2. Apply problem solving and mediation skills to sustain parental and community participation in the life of the school	1	2	3	4
3. Access community resources for the benefit of the students	1	2	3	4
4. Work with staff to develop means for parents to support students' learning	1	2	3	4
5. Involve the community in evaluating the success of the school	1	2	3	4

Comments/Reflections: **XII. _____**

DEVELOPING YOUR EDUCATIONAL LEADERSHIP PROFILE

Purpose:

To provide participants with the opportunity to compare their own patterns of educational leadership performances with those contained in the Connecticut Standards for Educational Leaders.

Directions:

1. Complete the Educational Leadership Self Evaluation (ELSI) rating scale.

2. After completion, go back and add each rating by Standard I though XII. Simply add the scores within each standard (e.g., I. The Educated Person), and divide by the number of items. Fill in the mean rating in the space located on the right hand side of the page at the end of each standard.

3. Transfer your scores to the graph on the next page. This graph will display your areas of relative strength with respect to each of the 12 Standards.

4. Note: Your scores need not be shared with anyone else. A candid self-assessment will serve you best.

5. The completed graph on the last page has been provided to allow you to compare your ratings to the importance ratings of 251 Connecticut Principals who participated in the "Successful Principal Study" (Iwanicki, Carmelich, Fusco, Nocera, Russo and Wolters, 1995). Although you are being asked to consider the extent to which you perform in certain areas, remember that the ratings on the last page are based on **how important** the performances were to principals' effectiveness.

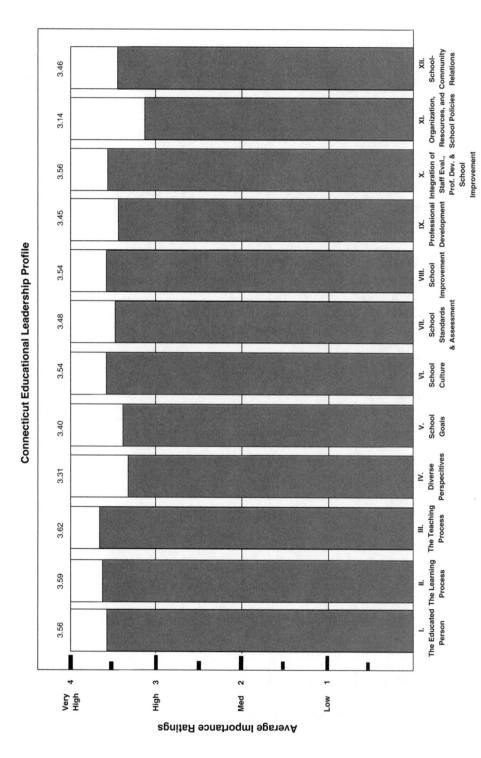

Connecticut Educational Leadership Profile

The shaded area represents the average importance ratings by principals participating in the University of Connecticut's Successful Principal study. Participants responded to the question: "How important is this to my success in my current position?" for each of the 69 Standards Performance Statements. n = 251

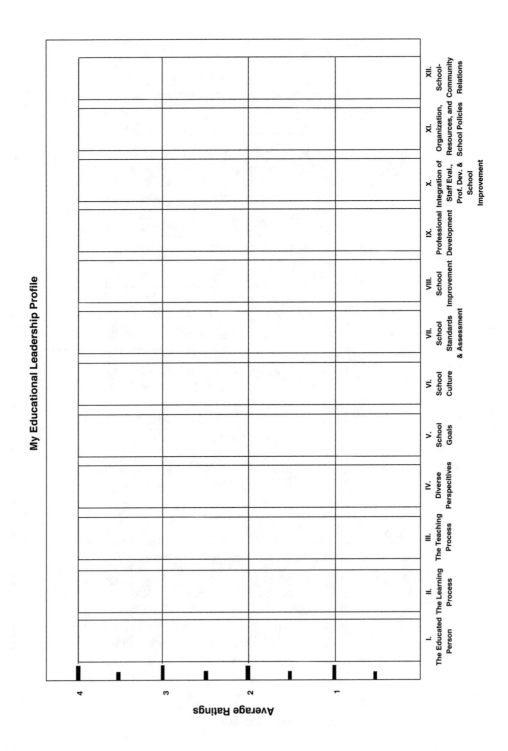

My Educational Leadership Profile

Average Ratings

4
3
2
1

I.
The Educated
Person

II.
The Learning
Process

III.
The Teaching
Process

IV.
Diverse
Perspecitives

V.
School
Goals

VI.
School
Culture

VII.
School
Standards
& Assessment

VIII.
School
Improvement

IX.
Professional
Development

X.
Integration of
Staff Eval.,
Prof. Dev. &
School
Improvement

XI.
Organization,
Resources, and
School Policies

XII.
School-
Community
Relations

Resource F

Expectations
of Key Players

The New York City Leadership Academy in collaboration with New Visions for Public Schools

NEW PRINCIPAL

Mentoring Program

Expectations of the Key Players in Principal Mentoring:

- The New Principal Mentee
- The Principal Mentor
- The Local Instructional Superintendent
- The Regional Liaison
- The Leadership Academy
- New Visions for Public Schools

Expectations of the Key Players in Principal Mentoring

The New York City Leadership Academy, in collaboration with New Visions for Public Schools, provides first year principals with mentors who are experienced and successful school leaders. Mentors are selected from the pool of currently active principals as well as recently retired principals. The success of the Principal Mentoring Program depends on the interrelationship of a number of key players involved in mentoring including the principal mentee, the principal mentor, the Local Instructional Superintendent (LIS), the Regional Liaison, the Leadership Academy, and New Visions. Since each play a pivotal role in the success of mentoring, it is important that each understand what is expected of them.

Expectations of the New Principal Mentee

The new principal mentee:

- Works with the mentor to develop a trusting relationship.
- Introduces the mentor to the staff and may use it as an opportunity to model the importance of lifelong learning.
- Shares with the mentor information about him/herself and the school including self-assessment, Principal Performance Review (voluntary), the Annual School Report, the Comprehensive Education Plan (CEP), recent student achievement data.
- Keeps the mentor informed about current expectations of the region, the LIS and the offsite training of the New Principal On Boarding Program.
- Involves the mentor in instructional leadership issues through learning walks, collegial review of students' work, observations of the instructional program and faculty meetings.
- Arranges and participates in a three-way discussion with the mentor and the LIS to insure that there is alignment in the assessment of the current status, the goals of the principal and the work ahead.
- Creates with the mentor a plan for professional growth as the school leader which establishes goals, builds on strengths and addresses areas in need of development to prepare for the Principal Performance Review (PPR) with the LIS.
- Welcomes face-to-face contact with the mentor several times a month. If the mentor is an active principal of a school, the mentor makes two visits each month for not less than 2½ hours in addition to an afterschool meeting each month. Retired principal mentor visits can be for either a full or half day with the frequency determined by the Regional Liaison.
- Visits the mentor's school once a month to observe school practices, special events and, most importantly, the mentor actively engaged in leading a school.
- Arranges for the mentor to join him/her at regional and network principals' meetings.
- Collaborates with the mentor in the development of nonevaluative descriptions of the work done and to be done with the mentor in the form of periodic Mentoring Reports prepared by the mentor and approved by both before it is forwarded to the Leadership Academy and Region.
- Extends the communication with the mentor beyond face-to-face through telephone and e-mail.
- Contacts the Leadership Academy early on if the match with the mentor seems not to be working.
- For program development purposes only, anonymously assesses the value added by the mentoring program.

Expectations of the Mentor

The mentor:

- Works with the mentee to develop a trusting relationship.
- Gathers and analyzes information about the mentee and the school including the principal's self-assessment, conversations with the mentee, Principal Performance Review (voluntary),

the Annual School Report, the Comprehensive Education Plan (CEP), recent student achievement data.

- Accompanies the principal through periodic learning walks, collegial review of students' work, informal and formal observations and faculty and parent meetings.
- Employs techniques such as questioning, active listening, scripting observations, role play, shared resources, joint problem solving, shadowing, research study, modeling and, when appropriate, direct instruction to develop the leadership capacities of the principal.
- Participates in a three-way discussion with the mentee and the LIS to insure that there is alignment in the assessment of the current status, the goals of the principal and the work ahead yet protects the confidentiality and trust of the mentor/mentee relationship.
- Creates with the mentee a plan for professional growth as school leader, most likely in the form of the PPR which establishes goals and defines actions that build on strengths and addresses areas in need of development.
- Makes face-to-face contact with the mentor several times a month. If the mentor is an active principal of a school, the mentor makes two visits each month for not less than 2½ hours in addition to an afterschool meeting each month. Retired principal mentor visits can be for either a full or half day with the frequency determined by the Regional Liaison.
- Invites the mentee to their school once a month to observe school practices, special event and, most importantly, the mentor actively engaged in leading a school.
- Joins the mentee at regional and network principals' meetings.
- Collaborates with the mentee in the development of non-evaluative descriptions of the mentoring work done and to be done with the mentee in the form of periodic Mentoring Reports prepared by the mentor and approved by both before it's forwarded to the Leadership Academy and Region.
- Extends the communication with the mentee beyond face-to-face through telephone and e-mail.
- Contacts the Leadership Academy early on if the match with the mentor seems not to be working.
- Participates in all mentor development sessions provided by the Leadership Academy and New Visions.
- Completes the administrative responsibilities of the mentoring program in a timely fashion.
- For program development purposes only, completes anonymous pre and postassessments of program quality and the mentee's professional growth.

Expectations of the Local Instructional Superintendent

The Local Instructional Superintendent:

- Assists the Regional Liaison in the match recommendation of mentor to mentee.
- Participates in several three-way discussions with the mentee and the mentor to insure that there is alignment in the assessment of the current status, the goals of the principal and the mentoring work ahead in a manner that protects the confidentiality and trust of the mentor/mentee relationship. These discussions should occur prior to the start of school and after the Mentoring Reports in the Fall and Spring.
- Periodically invites the mentor to accompany him/her on walk-throughs with the principal and to participate in follow-up discussions.
- Invites the mentor to regional and network principals' meetings.
- In preparation for the three-way meetings described above, reviews the periodic Mentoring Reports prepared by the mentor which describe in non-evaluative terms the mentoring work done and planned to be done.

- Communicates concerns to the mentor with the understanding that the mentor appreciates the input but can not compromise the confidentiality and trust of the mentor/mentee relationship.
- Contacts the Regional Liaison early on if the match with the mentor seems not to be working.

Expectations of the Regional Liaison

The Regional Liaison:

- Serves as the primary contact person in all aspects of professional development provided by the Leadership Academy.
- Attends Regional Liaison meetings every other month at the Leadership Academy with counterparts from other regions.
- Keeps the Academy informed regarding anticipated and actual principal retirements, recommendations of retirees as mentor candidates, the selection of active principals as mentors, the removal of current principals and the identity of new principals.
- Collaborates with the LISs to review mentor profiles and new principal needs and then matches mentors to mentees.
- Welcomes the mentor at regional principals' meetings.
- Contacts the Leadership Academy if a L.I.S. reports that the match of the mentee with the mentor seems not to be working.

Expectations of the Leadership Academy

The Leadership Academy:

- Oversees and administers new principal mentoring as part of its New Principal On Boarding Program.
- Continues to develop a systemic principal mentoring program with the goal of creating cross-regional equity and quality.
- Communicates regularly with Regional Liaisons to ensure that they are kept informed and that the mentoring program is addressing regional priorities and needs.
- Recruits, with regional assistance, mentors who are active principals and, with the assistance of New Visions, mentors who are retired principals.
- Makes final assignments of mentors to mentees guided by the recommendations of the Regional Liaisons and assisted by New Visions.
- Regularly seeks feedback from mentors and new principals regarding the effectiveness of the mentor relationship and the quality of the program.
- Conducts regular site visits to assess the needs of mentees, the quality of the service provided, and the professional development needs of mentees and mentors.
- Provides professional development with New Visions to all mentors, sitting and retired.

Expectations of New Visions for Public Schools

New Visions:

- Advises and assists the Leadership Academy in the development of a systemic principal mentoring program with the goal of creating cross regional equity and quality.
- Provides programmatic and administrative staff services for the development and operation of the Leadership Academy's Principal Mentoring Program.

- Assists in the recruitment of recently retired principals who demonstrate successful school leadership and the ability to transfer expertise.
- Assists in the administration of mentoring provided by retired principals.
- Assists in the planning and implementation of all mentor training and development.
- Coordinates with the Leadership Academy regular site visits to assess the needs of the mentees, the quality of the service provided, and the professional development need of mentors and mentees.
- Assists in the development of programmatic resource materials.
- Develops tools for principals and mentors to be shared with the Leadership Academy.

Resource G

Retired Principal Mentor Profile

NYC Leadership Academy

In Collaboration with
New Visions for Public Schools

Retired Principal
MENTOR PROFILE

Please submit this profile to New Visions for Public Schools, 320 West 13th Street, 6th floor, New York 10014; attention: Marcel Assenza. Your profile will be shared with the Regional Superintendents for the purpose of matching mentors with protégés.

Name _____ Date _____

School from which you retired _____ Region _____ Grades _____

School Address _____

Served as principal from _____ to _____ Date of retirement: _____ to: _____

Have you served as a Principal Mentor before? If so, from: _____

_____

(Continued)

List any training and/or experience that you may have had as a mentor.

Describe "Lessons Learned" from your mentoring experience.

Indicate whether you have received training in the following (Include when and by whom):

_____ Balanced Literacy _____

_____ Ramp Up _____

_____ Everyday Math _____

_____ Impact Math _____

_____ Math A _____

(Continued)

Describe the unique characteristics of your school/s where you have mentored principals. Include principal name, school, region/district and year.

Describe the strategic planning process used in your school.

Describe your leadership style.

(Continued)

How did you address the needs of the following cohorts of students in your school?

Not Meeting the Standard (levels 1 and 2)

Meeting the Standard (levels 3 and 4)

English Language Learners

Students with Special Education Needs

Resource H

Craft Wisdom

In addition to formal training, there are strategies you can use to support new principals. Roland S. Barth (1980), founder of the Principals Center at Harvard University, often refers to the importance of "craft wisdom." Carl Weingartner (2002) offers the following principles, based on his experience directing the Albuquerque, New Mexico, program and collaborating with other school districts across the nation.

PRINCIPLES FOR MENTORING PRINCIPALS

- *Celebrate the appointment.* Being appointed a principal for the first time is a big honor. Most new principals will be pleased and proud of their appointment. During your first contact with your protégé, let him or her know how happy you are about the appointment. Some little congratulatory gesture, such as a card of congratulations or a rose, might be a good way to start off your first meeting. This can go a long way in setting the tone of your mentorship.

- *Always be positive and supportive.* The ability of the protégé to grow is dependent on self-esteem, which is not at risk when ASKING for advice. Almost always, your desire to "suggest" meets your needs more than the protégé's. If you really question a practice, ask questions to reveal the thinking behind the decision.

- *Be willing to back off.* You'll make mistakes of timing or approach when your ideas may be very good. Be open about asking for feedback when that happens and learn from it. Don't create an impression of pushiness, because that won't be perceived as meeting a need of the new principal.

- *Be there for them.* Assure them that your main objective is to be there to support them, not to help them run their school.

- *Offer to support administrative efforts with the protégé.* In so doing, be careful not to assume the responsibilities that belong to the evaluator. The mentor program should not be part of any evaluation process. Mentors support! Supervisors evaluate!

- *Plan ahead so you are available during busy times.* Busy times for your protégé will come at just the time you are busiest, too. So get that work done ahead of time so you can say yes and collaborate when the opportunity arises.

- *Continually reinforce the confidential nature of the relationship.* Thank your protégé for the confidence and personal sharing. These are signs of a deepening relationship and trust, which a mentor must earn.

- *Collaborate with other mentoring teams.* Often mentoring teams may be working in the same feeder group or school cluster. This would be an excellent opportunity for two or more mentoring teams to meet on occasion to share ideas about cluster goals and objectives, issues, and successes.

- *Be careful about discussing the protégé with administrators.* Even the perception that this has happened can close doors with protégés. Just let the administrator know that the discussion makes you uncomfortable and ask to conduct it with the protégé present.

- *Recognize the need for time outside of school.* Plan some social times and allow for the protégé's other areas of life. Don't overdose on help.

PROFESSIONAL ASSOCIATIONS

Another way to access craft wisdom, as well current research and best practices, is through professional organizations. New principals often find support from local, state, and national professional organizations, which include those listed below. The state affiliates of the first three organizations are often more easily accessible to new principals.

- The National Association of Elementary School Principals and its state affiliates (www.naesp.org)
- The National Association of Secondary School Principals and its state affiliates (www.nassp.org)
- The National Staff Development Council (www.nsdc.org)
- The Association for Supervision and Curriculum Development and its state affiliates (www.ascd.org)
- The Principals Center at Harvard University (www.gse.harvard.edu/~principals/)

Resource I

Caveats for Mentor Program Leaders

1. Be watchful that cultural differences, including gender, race, and ethnicity, are celebrated and are not a source of misunderstanding. Mentors need to value the diversity new principals bring to their schools, districts, state and professional organizations.

2. Make sure that mentors' goals are to promote the reflection and growth of the new principals, not to create clones of their own leadership style and priorities.

3. Caution mentors about expecting too much from the new principals they mentor.

4. Be watchful that mentors don't hold new principals back because they are jealous as the new principals are recognized for their skills and accomplishments.

5. Encourage mentors to be careful that the new principals do not become too dependent on them.

6. Train and assist mentors in recognizing that their role changes as the new principals move through different developmental stages.

7. Provide time for new principals to participate in induction activities by lessening their districtwide responsibilities.

8. Provide mentors with enough time to support the new principals. Sometimes the administrators who offer to be mentors are also the ones who are involved in numerous other school, system, and state activities. Mentoring takes a lot of time. If this is the case, perhaps the administrator shouldn't mentor that year. Or maybe two people could share the mentoring role: one for issues specific to the district and the other for issues generic to a principalship.

9. Support mentors as they continue to grow, both as mentors and as educational leaders. When matching mentors and new principals, think about the developmental stage of the mentor, and help the mentors grow toward professional actualization as they are supporting new principals.

10. Promote your mentoring/induction program to perspective and current principals, school district staff, colleges, universities, area businesses, and the community at large.

References

Abeille, A., Hurley, N., & Nesbitt, J. (2001). *Leadership challenges: Supply and demand in Massachusetts schools.* A study conducted for the Massachusetts Education Reform Review Commission (MERRC).

Anderson, M. E. (1991). *Principals: How to train, recruit, select, induct, and evaluate leaders for America's schools.* Eugene, OR: ERIC Clearinghouse on Educational Management. (ERIC Document Reproduction Service No. ED 337 843)

Balch, B. V., Frampton, P., & Didelot, M. J. (2002). *Educational leadership for the 21st century: A keystone for quality Indiana schools.* Indianapolis, IN: Indiana Promise Consortium.

Barth, R. (1980). *Run school run.* Cambridge, MA: Harvard University Press.

Barth, R. (2003). *Lessons learned: Shaping relationships and the culture of the workplace.* Thousand Oaks, CA: Corwin.

Blackman, M. C., & Fenwick, L. T. (2000, March 29). The principalship. *Education Week on the Web.*

Blaydes, J. (2004). *Survival skills for the principalship: A treasure chest of time-savers, short-cuts, and strategies to help you keep a balance in your life.* Thousand Oaks, CA: Corwin.

Bloom, G. (1999). Sink or swim no more. *Educational Leadership, 29,* 14–17.

Bolman, L. G., & Deal, T. (2002). *Reframing the path to school leadership.* Thousand Oaks, CA: Corwin.

Bouchard, E. D., Cervone, L., Hayden, H., Riggins-Newby, C. G., & Zarlengo, P. (2002). *Chronicles: A history of the development of the principals' leadership network.* Providence, RI: Brown University.

Brackett, A., & Hurley, N. (2004). "Collaborative evaluation led by local educators: A practical, print- and web-based guide." Retrieved from www.neirtec.org/evaluation

Brock, B. L., & Grady, M. L. (2004). *Launching your first principalship.* Thousand Oaks, CA: Corwin.

California School Leadership Academy (CSLA) Ventures Web site: www.csla.org/ CSLA/ventures.html

Committee on the Future of School Leadership in Connecticut. (2000). *The future of school leadership in Connecticut.* Hartford, CT: Author.

Costa, A., & Garmston, R. (2002). *Cognitive coaching: A foundation for renaissance schools* (2nd ed.). Norwood, MA: Christopher-Gordon.

Crow, G. M., & Matthews, L. J. (1998). *Finding one's way: How mentoring can lead to dynamic leadership.* Thousand Oaks, CA: Corwin.

Crow, G. M., & Pounders, M. L. (1995, April). *Organizational socialization of new urban principals: Variations of race and gender.* Paper presented at the annual meeting of the American Educational Research Association, San Francisco.

Crowther, F., Kaagan, S. S., Ferguson, M., & Hann, L. (2002). *Developing teacher leaders: How teacher leadership enhances school success.* Thousand Oaks, CA: Corwin.

Daresh, J. (2001). *Beginning the principalship: A practical guide for new school leaders* (2nd ed.). Thousand Oaks, CA: Corwin.

Daresh, J. (2001). *Leaders helping leaders: A practical guide to administrative mentoring.* Thousand Oaks, CA: Corwin.

Denver, Board of Education. (2002, March 7). Minutes of the Regular Meeting of the Board of Education of School District No. 1.

Donaldson, G. A., Jr. (2001, October). The lose–lose leadership hunt. *Education Week.*

Dunne, K., & Villani, S. (in press). *Mentoring: A resource and training guide for educators.* Woburn, MA: Learning Innovations at WestEd.

Educational Research Service (ERS), National Association of Elementary School Principals (NAESP), & National Association of Secondary School Principals (NASSP). (2000a). *Is there a shortage of qualified candidates for the openings in the principalship? An exploratory study.* Alexandria, VA: Author.

Educational Research Service (ERS), National Association of Elementary School Principals (NAESP), & National Association of Secondary School Principals (NASSP). (2000b). *The principal, keystone of a high-achieving school: Attracting and keeping leaders we need.* Alexandria, VA: Author.

Educational Testing Service. (1998). *Promoting learning through effective school principals.* Princeton, NJ: Author.

Elmore, R. F. (1999). Leadership of large-scale improvement in American education. Draft for discussion and comment.

Elmore, R. F. (2000). *Building a new structure for school leadership.* Washington, DC: Albert Shanker Institute.

Elsberry, C. C., & Bishop, H. L. (1996). A new deal for new principals. *Principal,* January, 32–34.

Fenwick, L. T., & Pierce, M. C.. (2001) The principalship in crisis. *Principal, 80*(4), 24–32.

Ferrandino, V. L. (2003). *Reflections on the principalship.* Providence, RI: Education Alliance at Brown University.

Ferrandino, V. L., & Tirozzi, G. N. (2000, October 18). Principals' perspective: The shortage of principals continues. *Education Week.*

Georgia Department of Education Web site: www.doe.k12.ga.us/leadershipacademy/ id.asp

Goodman, R. H., & Zimmerman, W. G., Jr. (2000). *Thinking differently: Recommendations for 21st century school board/superintendent leadership, governance, and teamwork for high student achievement.* Arlington, VA: Educational Research Service and New England School Development Council.

Gupton, S. L., & Slick, G. A. (1996). *Highly successful women administrators: The inside stories of how they got there.* Thousand Oaks, CA: Corwin.

Guskey, T. (1999). *Evaluating professional development.* Thousand Oaks, CA: Corwin.

Hartzer, L., & Galvin, T. (2003). *Administrator induction programs: Summary of research and promising practices.* Hartford, CT: Connecticut State Department of Education.

Heifitz, R. (2002). *Leadership on the line: Staying alive through the dangers of leading.* Cambridge, MA: Harvard Business School Press.

Hurley, J. C. (2001, May). The principalship: Less may be more. *Education Week.*

Illinois State Board of Education. (2001). *Educator supply and demand in Illinois, 2001 annual report.* Springfield, IL: Author.

Institute of Educational Leadership. (2000). *Leadership for student learning: Reinventing the principalship, school leadership for the 21st century initiative.* Washington, DC: Task Force on the Principalship.

Jentz, B., & Wolford, J. (1981). *Entry.* New York: McGraw-Hill.

Johnston, R. C. (2001, March). Central office is critical bridge to help schools. *Education Week.* Retrieved from www.edweek.org/ew/ewstory.cfm?slug=25central.h20

Jones, E. (1983). *Black school administrators: A review of their early history, trends in recruitment, problems, and needs.* Arlington, VA: American Association of School Administrators.

Kennedy, C. (Ed.). (2000, July 24–26). *Summary of responses to NAESP/NASSP/ NMSA survey questions.* Principals' Leadership Summit, Washington, DC.

Kentucky Association of School Administrators and Appalachia Educational Laboratory. (1987). *A statewide program of support for beginning administrators: The Kentucky Institute for Beginning*

Principals. Charleston, WV: Appalachia Educational Laboratory. (ERIC Document Reproduction Service No. ED296454)

Lambert, L. (1998). *Building leadership capacity in schools.* Alexandria, VA: Association for Supervision and Curriculum Instruction.

Lambert, L. (2003). *Leadership capacity for lasting school improvement.* Alexandria, VA: Association for Supervision and Curriculum Instruction.

Lindley, F. (2003). *The portable mentor.* Thousand Oaks, CA: Corwin.

Lindsey, R. B., Roberts, L. M., & CampbellJones, F. (2005). *The culturally proficient school: An implementation guide for school leaders.* Thousand Oaks, CA: Corwin.

Lindstrom, P. H., & Speck, M. (2004.) *The principal as professional development leader: Building capacity for improving student achievement.* Thousand Oaks, CA: Corwin.

Malone, R. J. (2001, July). *Principal mentoring.* (ERIC Digest No. 149). Eugene, OR: ERIC Clearinghouse on Educational Management. (ERIC Document Reproduction Service No. ED457535)

Maryland Department of Education Web site: www.msde.state.md.us

Maryland Task Force on the Principalship. (2000). *Recommendations for redefining the role of the principal: Recruiting, retaining, and rewarding principals; and improving their preparation and development.* Baltimore, MD: Maryland State Board of Education.

McCarthy, M. (2002). Policy considerations based on the findings in literature and existing policy related to Indiana principals, superintendents and school board presidents. Recruitment, retention & professional development needs. Indianapolis, IN: Indiana Promise Consortium.

McCown, C., Arnold, M., Miles, D., & Hargadine, K. (2000). Why principals succeed: Comparing principal performance to national professional standards. *ERS Spectrum,* Spring, 15.

McEwan, E. (2003). *Ten traits of highly effective principals: From good to great performance.* Thousand Oaks, CA: Corwin.

Mehta, S. N. (2001). Why mentoring works: Everyone can use help in navigating corporate culture—especially minorities. Brief article in *Fortune,* July 9, 2001, p. 119; full text (2001) *Time.*

National Association of Elementary School Principals. (2001). *Leading learning communities: Standards for what principals should know and be able to do.* Alexandria, VA: Author.

National Association of Elementary School Principals & National School Public Relations Association. (2000). *Principals in the public. Engaging community support. Practical resources for public engagement, public relations, and marketing.* Alexandria, VA: Author.

National Elementary School Principals Association. (2004). *Fact sheet on the principal shortage.* Retrieved from www.naesp.org/ContentLoad.do?contentId=1097

Ortiz, F. I. (1982). *Career patterns in education: Women, men and minorities in public school administration.* New York: Praeger.

Parkay, F. W., Currie, G. D., Gaylon, D., & Rhodes, J. W. (1992). Professional socialization: A longitudinal study of first-time high school principals. *Educational Administration Quarterly, 28*(1), 43–75.

Pellicer, L. O. (2003). *Caring enough to lead: How reflective thought leads to moral leadership.* (2nd ed.). Thousand Oaks, CA: Corwin.

Playko, M. (1995). Mentor for educational leaders: A practitioner's perspective. *Journal of Educational Administration, 33*(5).

Public Agenda. (2001). *Trying to start ahead of the game: Superintendents and principals talk about school leadership.* New York: Author.

Richard, A. (2001, May 23). Growth of academies highlights new thinking about leadership. *Education Week.* Retrieved from www.edweek.org/ew/ewstory.cfm?slug= 371eadership.h20

Robbins, P., & Alvy, H. B. (1998). *The principal's companion: Strategies and hints to make the job easier.* Thousand Oaks, CA: Corwin.

Samier, E. (2000). Public administration mentorship: Conceptual and pragmatic consideration. *Journal of Educational Administration 38*(1), 83–101.

Sciarappa, K. (2004). Principal induction: Lessons from and for leaders in New Hampshire schools. Unpublished manuscript.

Sergiovanni, T. J. (1991). *The principalship: A reflective practice perspective* (2nd ed.). Needham Heights, MA: Allyn & Bacon.

Southern Regional Education Board. (2004). *SREB's leadership training modules engage leaders in solving real school problems.* Atlanta, GA: Author.

Sparks, D. (2000). Make principals' development a priority. *Results.* Retrieved from www.nsdc.org/library/publications/results/res4-00sparks.cfm

Van Maanen, J., & Schein, E. H. (1979). Toward a theory of organizational socialization. *Research in Organizational Behavior, 1,* 209–264.

Villani, S. (1983). Mentoring and sponsoring as ways to heighten career aspirations and achievement. Unpublished doctoral dissertation, Northeastern University.

Villani, S. (1999). *Are you sure you're the principal? On being an authentic leader.* Thousand Oaks, CA: Corwin.

Walker, A., & Stott, K. (1994, January). Mentoring programs for aspiring principals: Getting a solid start. *NASSP Bulletin.*

Weingartner, C. (2002). *Principles for mentoring principals.* Retrieved from http://glef.org/php/article.php?id=Art_1003&key-228

Wilmore, E. L. (2004). *Principal induction: A standards-based model for administrator development.* Thousand Oaks, CA: Corwin.

Young, P., & Sheets, J. (2003). *Mastering the art of mentoring principals.* Arlington, VA: KGE Press.

Zachary, L. J. (2000). *The mentor's guide.* San Francisco: Jossey-Bass.

Index

**CORWIN
PRESS**

The Corwin Press logo—a raven striding across an open book—represents the union of courage and learning. Corwin Press is committed to improving education for all learners by publishing books and other professional development resources for those serving the field of PreK–12 education. By providing practical, hands-on materials, Corwin Press continues to carry out the promise of its motto: **"Helping Educators Do Their Work Better."**